MICHAEL PUPIN

FROM
IMMIGRANT TO INVENTOR

BY

MICHAEL PUPIN

PROFESSOR OF ELECTRO-MECHANICS, COLUMBIA UNIVERSITY, NEW YORK

ILLUSTRATED

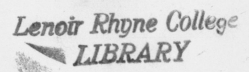
CHARLES SCRIBNER'S SONS

NEW YORK · LONDON

1924

TO THE MEMORY OF

MY MOTHER

PREFACE

Looking back over the development of this volume throughout the year or more during which I have been writing it, it seems to me that I cannot better express the end I have had in view than to repeat here what I wrote at the beginning of Chapter XI:

"The main object of my narrative was, and still is, to describe the rise of idealism in American science, and particularly in physical sciences and the related industries. I was a witness to this gradual development; everything that I have described so far was an attempt to qualify as a witness whose testimony has competence and weight. But there are many other American scientists whose opinions in this matter have more competence and weight than my opinion has. Why, then, should a scientist who started his career as a Serbian immigrant speak of the idealism in American science when there are so many native-born American scientists who know more about this subject than I do? Those who have read my narrative so far can answer this question. I shall only point out now that there are certain psychological elements in the question which justify me in the belief that occasionally an immigrant can see things which escape the attention of the native. Seeing is believing; let him speak who has the faith, provided that he has a message to deliver."

MICHAEL PUPIN.

CONTENTS

CONTENTS

ILLUSTRATIONS

FROM IMMIGRANT TO INVENTOR

I

WHAT I BROUGHT TO AMERICA

WHEN I landed at Castle Garden, forty-eight years ago, I had only five cents in my pocket. Had I brought five hundred dollars, instead of five cents, my immediate career in the new, and to me a perfectly strange, land would have been the same. A young immigrant such as I was then does not begin his career until he has spent all the money which he has brought with him. I brought five cents, and immediately spent it upon a piece of prune pie, which turned out to be a bogus prune pie. It contained nothing but pits of prunes. If I had brought five hundred dollars, it would have taken me a little longer to spend it, mostly upon bogus things, but the struggle which awaited me would have been the same in each case. It is no handicap to a boy immigrant to land here penniless; it is not a handicap to any boy to be penniless when he strikes out for an independent career, provided that he has the stamina to stand the hardships that may be in store for him.

A thorough training in the arts and crafts and a sturdy physique capable of standing the hardships of strenuous labor do entitle the immigrant to special considerations. But what has a young and penniless immigrant to offer who has had no training in any of the arts or crafts and does not know the language of the land? Apparently nothing, and if the present standards had prevailed forty-eight years ago I should have been deported. There are, however, certain things which a young immigrant may bring to this country that are far more precious than any of the things which the present immigration laws pre-scribe. Did I bring any of these things with me when I landed at Castle Garden in 1874? I shall try to answer this question in the following brief story of my life prior to my landing in this country.

Idvor is my native town; but the disclosure of this fact discloses very little, because Idvor cannot be found on any map. It is a little village off the highway in the prov-ince of Banat, formerly belonging to Austria-Hungary, but now an important part of the kingdom of the Serbs, Croats, and Slovenes. At the Paris peace conference, in 1919, the Rumanians claimed this province; they claimed it in vain. They could not overcome the fact that the population of Banat is Serb, and particularly of that part of Banat where Idvor is located. President Wilson and Mr. Lansing knew me personally, and when they were in-formed by the Yugoslav delegates in Paris that I was a native of Banat, the Rumanian arguments lost much of their plausibility. No other nationality except the Serb has ever lived in Idvor. The inhabitants of Idvor were always peasants; most of them were illiterate in my boy-hood days. My father and mother could neither read nor write. The question arises now: What could a penniless boy of fifteen, born and bred under such conditions, bring to America, which under any conceivable immigration laws would entitle him to land? But I was confident that I was so desirable an acquisition to America that I should be allowed to land, and I was somewhat surprised that people made no fuss over me when I landed.

The Serbs of Idvor from time immemorial always con-sidered themselves the brothers of the Serbs of Serbia, who are only a few gunshots away from Idvor on the south side of the Danube. The Avala Mountain, near Belgrade in Serbia, can easily be seen from Idvor on every clear day. This blue and, to me at that time, mysterious-looking peak seemed always like a reminder to the Serbs of Banat that the Serbs of Serbia were keeping an eye of affectionate watchfulness upon them.

When I was a boy Idvor belonged to the so-called military frontier of Austria. A bit of interesting history is attached to this name. Up to the beginning of the eighteenth century the Austrian Empire was harassed by Turkish invasions. At periodically recurring intervals Turkish armies would cross her southern frontier, formed by the Rivers Danube and Sava, and penetrate into the interior provinces. Toward the end of the seventeenth century they advanced as far as Vienna, and would have become a serious menace to the whole of Europe if the Polish king Sobiesky had not come to the rescue of Vienna. It was at that time that Emperor Leopold I, of Austria, invited Charnoyevich, the Serb Patriarch of Pech, in old Serbia, to move with thirty-five thousand picked families of old Serbia into the Austrian territory north of the Danube and the Sava Rivers, to become its guardians. For three hundred years these Serbs had been fighting the Turks and had acquired great skill in this kind of warfare. In 1690 the Patriarch with these picked families moved into Austria and settled in a narrow strip of territory on the northern banks of these two rivers. They organized what was known later as the military frontier of Austria. 1690 is, according to tradition, the date when my native village Idvor was founded, but not quite on its present site. The original site is a very small plateau a little to the north of the present site.

Banat is a perfectly level plain, but near the village of Idvor the River Tamish has dug out a miniature canyon, and on the plateau of one of the promontories of this canyon was the old site of Idvor. It is connected to the new site by a narrow neck. The old site was selected because it offered many strategical advantages of defense against the invading Turk. The first settlers of the old village lived in subterranean houses which could not be seen at a distance by the approaching enemy. Remnants of these subterranean houses were still in existence when I was a schoolboy in the village of Idvor, over fifty years ago. The location of the original church was marked by a little column built of bricks and bearing a cross. In a recess on the side of the column was the image of St. Mary with the Christ Child, illuminated by a burning wick immersed in oil. The legend was that this flame was never allowed to go out, and that a religious procession by the good people of Idvor to the old monument was sure to avert any calamity, like pestilence or drought, that might be threatening the village. I took part in many of these processions to the old deserted village, and felt every time that I was standing upon sacred ground; sacred because of the Christian blood shed there during the struggles of the Christian Serbs of Idvor against the Turkish invaders. Every visit to the old village site refreshed the memories of the heroic traditions of which the village people were extremely proud. They were poor in worldly goods, those simple peasant folk of Idvor, but they were rich in memories of their ancient traditions.

As I look back upon my childhood days in the village of Idvor, I feel that the cultivation of old traditions was the principal element in the spiritual life of the village people. The knowledge of these traditions was necessary and sufficient to them, in order to understand their position in the world and in the Austrian Empire. When my people moved into Austria under Patriarch Charnoyevich and settled in the military frontier, they had a definite agreement with Emperor Leopold I. It was recorded in an Austrian state document called Privilegia. According to

IN THE HOUSE ON THE LEFT WITH THREE WINDOWS, A TYPICAL
PEASANT HOUSE OF IDVOR, PUPIN WAS BORN

On the right is the spire of the church on the village green

THE OLD MONUMENT ON STARO SELO, THE OLD VILLAGE, WHERE
THE ORIGINAL SETTLERS OF IDVOR LIVED IN
SUBTERRANEAN DWELLINGS

this ancient document the Serbs of the military frontier were to enjoy a spiritual, economic, and political autonomy. Lands granted to them were their own property. In our village we maintained our own schools and our own churches, and each village elected its own local administration. Its head was the Knez, or chief, usually a sturdy peasant. My father was a Knez several times. The bishops and the people elected their own spiritual and political heads, that is, the Patriarch and the Voyvoda (governor). We were free and independent peasant landlords. In return for these privileges, the people obligated themselves to render military service for the defense of the southern frontiers of the empire against the invading Turks. They had helped to drive the Turks across the Danube, under the supreme command of Prince Eugene of Savoy, in the beginning of the eighteenth century. After the emperor had discovered the splendid fighting qualities of the Serbs of the military frontier, he managed to extend the original terms of the Privilegia so as to make it obligatory upon the military frontiersmen to defend the empire against any and every enemy. Subsequently the Serbs of the military frontier of Austria defended Empress Maria Theresa against Frederick the Great; they defended Emperor Francis against Napoleon; they defended Emperor Ferdinand against the rebellious Hungarians in 1848 and 1849; and in 1859 and 1866 they defended Austria against Italy. The military exploits of the men of Idvor during these wars supplied material for the traditions of Idvor, which were recorded in many tales and stirring songs. Reading and writing did not flourish in Idvor in those days, but poetry did.

Faithful to the old customs of the Serb race, the people of Idvor held during the long winter evenings their neighborhood gatherings, and as a boy I attended many of them at my father's house. The older men would sit around the warm stove on a bench which was a part of the stove and made of the same material, usually soft brick plastered over and whitewashed. They smoked and talked and looked like old senators, self-appointed guardians of all the wisdom of Idvor. At the feet of the old men were middle-aged men, seated upon low stools, each with a basket in front of him, into which he peeled the yellow kernels from the seasoned ears of corn, and this kept him busy during the evening. The older women were seated on little stools along the wall; they would be spinning wool, flax, or hemp. The young women would be sewing or knitting. I, a favorite child of my mother, was allowed to sit alongside of her and listen to the words of wisdom and words of fiction dropping from the mouths of the old men and sometimes also from the mouths of the middle-aged and younger men, when the old men gave them permission to speak. At intervals the young women would sing a song having some relation to the last tale. For instance, when one of the old men had finished a tale about Karageorge and his historic struggles against the Turks, the women would follow with a song describing a brave Voyvoda of Karageorge, named Hayduk Velyko, who with a small band of Serbians defended Negotin against a great Turkish army under Moula Pasha. This gallant band, as the song describes them, reminds one of the little band of Greeks at Thermoplyæ.

Some of the old men present at these gatherings had taken part in the Napoleonic wars, and they remembered well also the stories which they had heard from their fathers relating to the wars of Austria against Frederick the Great during the eighteenth century. The middle-aged men had participated in the fighting during the Hungarian revolution, and the younger men had just gone through the campaigns in Italy in 1859 and 1866. One of the old men had taken part in the battle of Aspern,

when Austria defeated Napoleon. He had received a
high imperial decoration for bravery, and was very proud
of it. He also had gone to Russia with an Austrian division during Napoleon's campaign of 1812. His name
was Baba Batikin, and in the estimation of the village
people he was a seer and a prophet, because of his wonderful memory and his extraordinary power of description. His diction was that of a guslar (Serbian minstrel). He not only described vividly what went on in
Austria and in Russia during the Napoleonic wars in
which he himself participated, but he would also thrill
his hearers by tales relating to the Austrian campaigns
against Frederick the Great, which his father upon his
return from the battle-fields of Silesia had related to him.
I remember quite well his stories relating to Karageorge
of Serbia, whom he had known personally. He called
him the great Vozhd, or leader of the Serbian peasants, and
never grew weary of describing his heroic struggles
against the Turks in the beginning of the nineteenth century. These tales about Karageorge were always received at the neighborhood gatherings with more enthusiasm than any other of his stirring narratives. Toward
the end of the evening Baba Batikin would recite some
of the old Serbian ballads, many of which he knew by
heart. During these recitations his thin and wrinkled
face would light up; it was the face of a seer, as I remember it, and I can see now his bald head with a wonderful
brow, towering over bushy eyebrows through which the
light of his deep-set eyes would shine like the light of the
moon through the needles of an aged pine. It was from
him that the good people of Idvor learned the history of
the Serb race from the battle of the field of Kossovo in
1389 down to Karageorge. He kept alive the old Serb
traditions in the village of Idvor. He was my first and
my best teacher in history.

The younger men told tales relating to Austrian campaigns in Italy, glorifying the deeds of valor of the men of Idvor in these campaigns. The battle of Custozza in 1866, in which the military frontiersmen nearly annihilated the Italian armies, received a great deal of attention, because the men who described it had participated in it, and had just returned from Italy. But I remember that every one of those men was full of praise of Garibaldi, the leader of the Italian people in their struggles for freedom. They called him the Karageorge of Italy. I remember also that in my father's house, in which these winter-evening gatherings took place, there was a colored picture of Garibaldi with his red shirt and a plumed hat. The picture was hung up alongside of the Ikona, the picture of our patron saint; on the other side of the Ikona was the picture of the Czar of Russia, who only a few years before had emancipated the Russian serfs. In the same room and hanging in a very conspicuous place all by itself was a picture of Karageorge, the leader of the Serbian revolution. The picture of the Austrian emperor was not there after 1869!

The Serb ballads recited by Baba Batikin glorified the great national hero, Prince Marko, whose combats were the combats of a strong man in defense of the weak and of the oppressed. Marko, although a prince of royal blood, never fought for conquest of territory. According to the guslar, Prince Marko was a true champion of right and justice. At that time the Civil War in America had just come to a close, and the name of Lincoln, whenever mentioned by Baba Batikin, suggested an American Prince Marko. The impressions which I carried away from these neighborhood gatherings were a spiritual food which nourished in my young mind the sentiment that the noblest thing in this world is the struggle for right, justice, and freedom. It was the love of freedom and of right and justice which made the Serbs of the military frontier desert their ancestral homes in old Serbia and move into Austria, where they gladly consented to live in subterranean houses and crawl like woodchucks under the ground as long as they could enjoy the blessings of political freedom.

The military frontiersmen had their freedom guaranteed to them by the Privilegia, and, in exchange for their freedom, they were always ready to fight for the Emperor of Austria on any battle-field. Loyalty to the emperor was the cardinal virtue of the military frontiersmen. It was that loyalty which overcame their admiration for Garibaldi in 1866; hence the Austrian victory at Custozza. The Emperor of Austria as a guardian of their freedom received a place of honor in the selected class of men like Prince Marko, Karageorge, Czar Alexander the Liberator, Lincoln, and Garibaldi. These were the names recorded in the Hall of Fame of Idvor. When, however, the emperor, in 1869, dissolved the military frontier and delivered its people to the Hungarians, the military frontiersmen felt that they were betrayed by the emperor, who had broken his faith to them recorded in the Privilegia. I remember my father saying to me one day: "Thou shalt never be a soldier in the emperor's army. The emperor has broken his word; the emperor is a traitor in the eyes of the military frontiersmen. We despise the man who is not true to his word." This is the reason why the picture of the Emperor of Austria was not allowed a place in my father's house after 1869.

As I look back upon those days I feel, as I always felt, that this treacherous act of the Austrian emperor in 1869 was the beginning of the end of the Austrian Empire. It was the beginning of nationalism in the realm of Emperor Francis Joseph of Hapsburg. The love of the people for the country in which they lived began to languish and finally died. When that love dies, the country also must die.   This was the lesson which I learned from the illiterate peasants of Idvor.

My teacher in the village school never succeeded in making upon my mind that profound impression which was made upon it by the men at the neighborhood gatherings.   They were men who had gone out into the world and taken an active part in the struggles of the world. Reading, writing, and arithmetic appeared to me like instruments of torture which the teacher, who, in my opinion at that time, knew nothing of the world, had invented in order to interfere as much as possible with my freedom, particularly when I had an important engagement with my chums and playmates.   But my mother soon convinced me that I was wrong.   She could neither read nor write, and she told me that she always felt that she was blind, in spite of the clear vision of her eyes.   So blind, indeed, that, as she expressed it, she did not dare venture into the world much beyond the confines of my native village.   This was as far as I remember now the mode of reasoning which she would address to me: "My boy, if you wish to go out into the world about which you hear so much at the neighborhood gatherings, you must provide yourself with another pair of eyes; the eyes of reading and writing.   There is so much wonderful knowledge and learning in the world which you cannot get unless you can read and write.   Knowledge is the golden ladder over which we climb to heaven; knowledge is the light which illuminates our path through this life and leads to a future life of everlasting glory."   She was a very pious woman, and had a rare knowledge of both the Old and the New Testaments.   The Psalms were her favorite recitations.   She knew also the lives of saints. St. Sava was her favorite saint.   She was the first to make me understand the story of the life of this wonderful Serb.   This, briefly stated, was the story which she told me: Sava was the youngest son of the Serb Zhupan

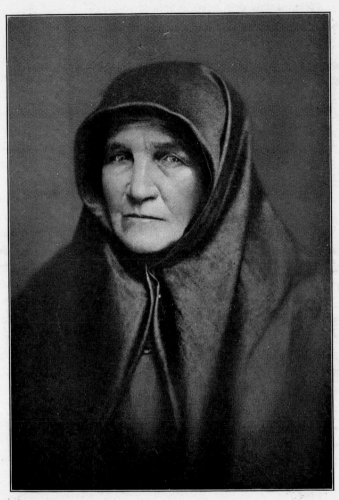

OLYMPIADA PUPIN, MOTHER OF MICHAEL PUPIN
From a photograph taken in 1880

Nemanya. At an early age he renounced his royal titles and retired to a monastery on Mount Athos and devoted many years to study and meditation. He then returned to his native land, in the beginning of the thirteenth century, and became the first Serbian archbishop and founded an autonomous Serbian church. He also organized public schools in his father's realm, where Serbian boys and girls had an opportunity to learn how to read and write. Thus he opened the eyes of the Serbian people, and the people in grateful recognition of these great services called him St. Sava the Educator, and praised forever his saintly name and memory. Seven hundred years had passed since St. Sava's time, but not one of them had passed without a memorial celebration dedicated to him in every town and in every home where a Serb lived.

This was a revelation to me. Like every schoolboy, I attended, of course, every year in January, the celebrations of St. Sava's day. On these occasions we unruly boys made fun of the big boy who in a trembling and awkward voice was reciting something about St. Sava, which the teacher had written out for him. After this recitation, the teacher, with a funny nasal twang, would do his best to supplement in a badly articulated speech what he had written out for the big boy, and finally the drowsy-looking priest would wind up with a sermon bristling with archaic Slavonic church expressions, which to us unruly boys sounded like awkward attempts of a Slovak mouse-trap dealer to speak Serbian. Our giggling merriment then reached a climax, and so my mischievous chums never gave me a chance to catch the real meaning of the ceremonies on St. Sava's day. My mother's story of St. Sava and the way in which she told it made the image of St. Sava appear before me for the first time in the light of a saint who glorified the value of books and of the art of writing. I understood then why mother placed such value upon reading and writing. I vowed to devote myself to both, even if that should make it necessary to neglect my chums and playmates, and soon I convinced my mother that in reading and writing I could do at least as well as any boy. The teacher observed the change; he was astonished, and actually believed that a miracle had occurred. My mother believed in miracles, and told the teacher that the spirit of St. Sava was guiding me. One day she told him in my presence that in a dream she saw St. Sava lay his hands upon my head, and then turning to her say: "Daughter Piada, your boy will soon outgrow the village school of Idvor. Let him then go out into the world, where he can find more brain food for his hungry head." Next year the teacher selected me to make the recitation on St. Sava's day, and he wrote out the speech for me. My mother amended and amplified it and made me rehearse it for her over and over again. On St. Sava's day the first public speech of my life was delivered by me. The success was overwhelming. My chums, the unruly boys, did not giggle; on the contrary, they looked interested, and that encouraged me much. The people said to each other that even old Baba Batikin could not have done much better. My mother cried for joy; my teacher shook his head, and the priest looked puzzled, and they both admitted that I had outgrown the village school of Idvor.

At the end of that year my mother prevailed upon my father to send me to a higher school in the town of Panchevo, on the Tamish River, about fifteen miles south of Idvor, quite near the point where the Tamish flows into the Danube. There I found teachers whose learning made a deep impression upon me, particularly their learning in natural science, a subject entirely unknown in Idvor. There I heard for the first time that an American named Franklin, operating with a kite and a key, had discovered that lightning was a passage of an electrical spark between clouds, and that thunder was due to the sudden expansion of the atmosphere heated by the passage of the electrical spark. The story was illustrated by an actual frictional electrical machine. This information thrilled me; it was so novel and so simple, I thought, and so contrary to all my previous notions. During my visit home I eagerly took the first opportunity to describe this new knowledge to my father and his peasant friends, who were seated in front of our house and were enjoying their Sunday-afternoon talks. I suddenly observed that my father and his friends looked at each other in utter astonishment. They seemed to ask each other the question: "What heresy may this be which this impudent brat is disclosing to us?" And then my father, glaring at me, asked whether I had forgotten that he had told me on so many occasions that thunder was due to the rumbling of St. Elijah's car as he drove across the heavens, and whether I thought that this American Franklin, who played with kites like an idle boy, knew more than the wisest men of Idvor. I always had a great respect for my father's opinions, but on that occasion I could not help smiling with a smile of ill-concealed irony which angered him. When I saw the flame of anger in his big black eyes I jumped and ran for safety. During supper my father, whose anger had cooled considerably, described to my mother the heresy which I was preaching on that afternoon. My mother observed that nowhere in the Holy Scriptures could he find support of the St. Elijah legend, and that it was quite possible that the American Franklin was right and that the St. Elijah legend was wrong. In matters of correct interpretation of ancient authorities my father was always ready to abide by the decisions of my mother, and so father and I became reconciled again. My mother's admission of the possibility that the American Franklin might, after all, be wiser than all the wise men of Idvor, and my father's silent consent, aroused in me a keen interest in America. Lincoln and Franklin were two names with which my early ideas of America were associated.

During those school-days in Panchevo I passed my summer vacation in my native village. Idvor, just like the rest of Banat, lives principally from agriculture, and during harvest-time it is as busy as a beehive. Old and young, man and beast, concentrate all their efforts upon the harvest operations. But nobody is busier than the Serbian ox. He is the most loyal and effective servant of the Serb peasant everywhere, and particularly in Banat. He does all the ploughing in the spring, and he hauls the seasoned grain from the distant fertile fields to the thresh-ing-grounds in the village when the harvesting season is on. The commencement of the threshing operations marks the end of the strenuous efforts of the good old ox; his summer vacation begins, and he is sent to pasture-lands to feed and to rest and to prepare himself for autumn hauling of the yellow corn and for the autumn ploughing of the fields. The village boys who are not big enough to render much help on the threshing-grounds are assigned to the task of watching over the grazing oxen during their summer vacation. The school vacation of the boys co-incided with the vacation of the good old ox. Several sum-mers I passed in that interesting occupation. These were my only summer schools, and they were the most inter-esting schools that I ever attended.

The oxen of the village were divided into herds of about fifty head, and each herd was guarded by a squad of some twelve boys from families owning the oxen in the herd. Each squad was under the command of a young man who was an experienced herdsman. To watch a herd of fifty oxen was not an easy task. In daytime the job was easy, because the heat of the summer sun and the torments of the ever-busy fly made the oxen hug the shade of the trees, where they rested awaiting the cooler hours of the day. At night, however, the task was much more difficult. Being forced to hug the shade of the trees during daytime, the oxen would get but little enjoyment of the pasture, and so when the night arrived they were quite hungry and eagerly searched for the best of feed.

I must mention now that the pasture-lands of my native village lay alongside of territory of a score of square miles which in some years were all planted in corn. During the months of August and September these vast corn-fields were like deep forests. Not far from Idvor and to the east of the corn-fields was a Rumanian settlement which was notorious for its cattle-thieves. The trick of these thieves was to hide in the corn-fields at night and to wait until some cattle strayed into these fields, when they would drive them away and hide them somewhere in their own corn-fields on the other side of their own village. To prevent the herd from straying into the corn-fields at night was a great task, for the performance of which the boys had to be trained in daytime by their experienced leader. It goes without saying that each day we boys first worked off our superfluous energy in wrestling, swimming, hockey, and other strenuous games, and then settled down to the training in the arts of a herdsman which we had to practise at night. One of these arts was signalling through the ground. Each boy had a knife with a long wooden handle. This knife was stuck deep into the ground. A sound was made by striking against the wooden handle, and the boys, lying down and pressing their ears close to the ground, had to estimate the direction and the distance of the origin of sound. Practice made us quite expert in this form of signalling. We knew at that time that the sound travelled through the ground far better than through the air, and that a hard and solid ground transmitted sound much better than the ploughed-up ground. We knew, therefore, that the sound produced this way near the edge of the pasture-land could not be heard in the soft ground of the corn-fields stretching along the edge. A Rumanian cattle-thief, hidden at night in the corn-fields, could not hear our ground signals and could not locate us. Kos, the Slovenian, my teacher and interpreter of physical phenomena, could not explain this, and I doubt very much whether the average physicist of Europe at that time could have explained it. It is the basis of a discovery which I made about twenty-five years after my novel experiences in that herdsmen's summer school in Idvor.

On perfectly clear and quiescent summer nights on the plains of my native Banat, the stars are intensely bright and the sky looks black by contrast. "Thy hair is as black as the sky of a summer midnight" is a favorite saying of a Serbian lover to his lady-love. On such nights we could not see our grazing oxen when they were more than a few score of feet from us, but we could hear them if we pressed our ears close to the ground and listened. On such nights we boys had our work cut out for us. We were placed along a definite line at distances of some twenty yards apart. This was the dead-line, which separated the pasture-lands from the corn-field territory. The motto of the French at Verdun was: "They shall not pass!" This was our motto, too, and it referred equally to our friends, the oxen, and to our enemies, the Rumanian cattle-thieves. Our knife-blades were deep in the ground and our ears were pressed against the handles. We could hear every step of the roaming oxen and even their grazing operations when they were sufficiently near to the dead-line. We knew that these grazing operations were regulated by the time of the night, and this we estimated by the position of certain constellations like Orion and the Pleiades. The positions of the evening star and of the morning star also were closely observed. Venus was our white star and Mars was called the red star. The Dipper, the north star, and the milky way were our compass. We knew also that when in the dead of the night we could hear the faint sound of the church-bell of the Rumanian settlement about four miles to the east of us, then there was a breeze from the corn-fields to the pasture-lands, and that it carried the sweet perfume of the young corn to the hungry oxen, inviting them to the rich banquet-table of the corn-fields. On such nights our vigilance was redoubled. We were then all eyes and ears. Our ears were closely pressed to the ground and our eyes were riveted upon the stars above.

The light of the stars, the sound of the grazing oxen, and the faint strokes of the distant church-bell were messages of caution which on those dark summer nights guided our vigilance over the precious herd. These messages appealed to us like the loving words of a friendly power, without whose aid we were helpless. They were the only signs of the world's existence which dominated our consciousness as, enveloped in the darkness of night and surrounded by countless burning stars, we guarded the safety of our oxen. The rest of the world had gone out of existence; it began to reappear in our consciousness when the early dawn announced what we boys felt to be the divine command, "Let there be light," and the sun heralded by long white streamers began to approach the eastern sky, and the earth gradually appeared as if by an act of creation. Every one of those mornings of fifty years ago appeared to us herdsmen to be witnessing the creation of the world—a world at first of friendly sound and light messages which made us boys feel that a divine power was protecting us and our herd, and then a real terrestrial world, when the rising sun had separated the hostile mysteries of night from the friendly realities of the day.

Sound and light became thus associated in my early modes of thought with the divine method of speech and communication, and this belief was strengthened by my mother, who quoted the words of St. John: "In the beginning was the word, and the word was with God, and the word was God."

I believed also that David, some of whose Psalms, under the instruction of my mother, I knew by heart, and who in his youth was a shepherd, expressed my thoughts in his nineteenth Psalm:

"The heavens declare the glory of God. . . ."
.   .   .   .
"There is no speech nor language, where their voice is not heard."

Then, there is no Serb boy who has not heard that beautiful Russian song by Lyermontoff, the great Russian poet, which says:

"Lonely I wander over the country road,
And in the darkness the stony path is glimmering;
Night is silent and the plains are whispering
To God, and star speaketh to star."

Lyermontoff was a son of the Russian plains. He saw the same burning stars in the blackness of a summer midnight sky which I saw. He felt the same thrill which David felt and through his Psalms transmitted to me during those watchful nights of fifty years ago. I pity the city-bred boy who has never felt the mysterious force of that heavenly thrill.

Sound and light being associated in my young mind of fifty years ago with divine operations by means of which man communicates with man, beast with beast, stars with stars, and man with his Creator, it is obvious that I meditated much about the nature of sound and of light. I still believe that these modes of communication are the fundamental operations in the physical universe and I am still meditating about their nature. My teachers in Panchevo rendered some assistance in solving many of the puzzles which I met in the course of these meditations. Kos, my Slovenian teacher, who was the first to tell me the story of Franklin and his kite, was a great help. He soon convinced me that sound was a vibration of bodies. This explanation agreed with the Serbian figure of speech which says:

"My heart quivers like the melodious string under the guslar's bow."

I also felt the quivering air whenever during my term of service as guardian of the oxen I tried my skill at the Serbian flute. Few things excited my interest more than the operations of the Serbian bagpiper as he forced the air from his sheepskin bellows and made it sing by regulating its passage through the pipes. The operations which the bagpiper called adjustment and tuning of the bag-pipes commanded my closest attention. I never dreamed then that a score of years later I should do a similar operation with an electrical circuit. I called it "electrical tuning," a term which has been generally adopted in wireless telegraphy. But nobody knows that the operation as well as the name were first suggested to me by the Serbian bagpiper, some twenty years before I made the invention in 1892.

Skipping over several sections of my story, I will say now that twenty years after my invention of electrical tuning a pupil of mine, Major Armstrong, discovered the electrical vacuum-tube oscillator, which promises to revolutionize wireless telegraphy and telephony. A similar invention, but a little earlier, was made by another pupil of mine, Mr. Vreeland. Both these inventions in their mode of operation remind me much of the operation of Serbian bagpipes. Perhaps some of those thrills which the Serbian bagpiper stirred up in me in my early youth were transferred to my pupils, Armstrong and Vreeland.

I was less successful in solving my puzzles concerning the nature of light. Kos, the Slovenian, my first guide

and teacher in the study of physical phenomena, told me
the story that a wise man of Greece with the name of
Aristotle believed that light originates in the eye, which
throws out feelers to the surrounding objects, and that
through these feelers we see the objects, just as we feel
them by our sense of touch. This view did not agree
with the popular saying often heard in Idvor: "Pick
your grapes before sunrise, before the thirsty sunbeams
have drunk up their cooling dew." Nor did it agree with
Bishop Nyegosh, the greatest of Serbian poets, who says:

"The bright-eyed dewdrops glide along the sunbeams to the heavens
    above."

The verse from Nyegosh I obtained from a Serbian poet,
who was an arch-priest, a protoyeray, and who was my
religious teacher in Panchevo. His name, Vasa Zhivkovich,
I shall never forget, because it is sweet music to my ears
on account of the memories of affectionate friendship he
cherished for me.

According to this popular belief a beam of light has
an individual existence just like that of the melodious
string under the guslar's bow. But neither the poet, nor
the wise men of Idvor, nor Kos the Slovenian, ever
mentioned that a beam of light ever quivered, and if it
does not quiver like a vibrating body how can the sun,
the moon, and the stars proclaim the glory of God, and
how can, according to David, their voice be heard wherever there are speech and language? These questions
Kos would not answer. No wonder! Nobody to-day
can give a completely satisfactory answer to questions
relating to radiation of light. Kos was non-committal
and did not seem to attach much importance to the authorities which I quoted; namely, the Serbian poet Nyegosh, the wise sayings of Idvor, and the Psalms of David.
Nevertheless, he was greatly interested in my childlike
inquiries and always encouraged me to go on with my

puzzling questions. Once he invited me to his house, and there I found that several of his colleagues were present. One of them was my friend the poet-priest, and another was a Hungarian Lutheran preacher who spoke Serbian well and was famous in Panchevo because of his great eloquence. They both engaged me in conversation and showed a lively interest in my summer vacation experiences as herdsman's assistant. The puzzling questions about light which I addressed to Kos, and the fact that Kos would not answer, amused them. My knowledge of the Bible and of the Psalms impressed them much, and they asked me quite a number of questions concerning my mother. Then they suggested that I might be transferred from the school in Panchevo to the famous schools of Prague in Bohemia, if my father and mother did not object to my going so far away from home. When I suggested that my parents could not afford to support me in a great place like Prague, they assured me that this difficulty might be fixed up. I promised to consult my parents during the approaching Christmas vacation. I did, but found my father irresistibly opposed to it. Fate, however, decreed otherwise.

The history of Banat records a great event for the early spring of 1872, the spring succeeding the Christmas when my father and mother agreed to disagree upon the proposition that I go to Prague. Svetozar Miletich, the great nationalist leader of the Serbs in Austria-Hungary, visited Panchevo, and the people prepared a torchlight procession for him. This procession was to be a protest of Panchevo and of the whole of Banat against the emperor's treachery of 1869. My father had protested long before by excluding the emperor's picture from our house. That visit of Miletich marks the beginning of a new political era in Banat, the era of nationalism. The schoolboys of Panchevo turned out in great numbers, and I was one of them, proud to become one of the torch-bearers. We shouted ourselves hoarse whenever Miletich in his fiery speech denounced the emperor for his ingratitude to the military frontiersmen as well as to all the Serbs of Voy-vodina. Remembering my father's words on the occasion mentioned above, I did not hesitate to shout in the name of the schoolboys present in the procession: "We'll never serve in Francis Joseph's army!" My chums responded with: "Long live the Prince of Serbia!" The Hungarian officials took careful notes of the whole proceeding, and a few days later I was informed that Panchevo was not a proper place for an ill-mannered peasant boy like me, and that I should pack up and return to Idvor. Kos, the Slovenian, and protoyeray Zhivkovich interfered, and I was permitted to stay.

On the first of May, following, our school celebrated the May-day festival. The Serb youngsters in the school, who worshipped Miletich and his nationalism, prepared a Serbian flag for the festival march. The other boys, mostly Germans, Rumanians, and Hungarians, carried the Austrian yellow-black standard. The nationalist group among the youngsters stormed the bearer of the yellow-black standard, and I was caught in the scrimmage with the Austrian flag under my feet. Expulsion from school stared me in the face. Again protoyeray Zivkovich came to my defense and, thanks to his high official position and to my high standing in school, I was allowed to continue with my class until the end of the school year, after promising that I would not associate with revolutionary boys who showed an inclination to storm the Austrian flag. The matter did not end there, however. In response to an invitation from the pro-toyeray, father and mother came to Panchevo to a conference, which resulted in a triumph for my mother. It was decided that I bid good-by to Panchevo, a hotbed of nationalism, and go to Prague. The protoyeray and his congregation promised assistance if the financial burden attached to my schooling in Prague should prove too heavy for my parents.

When the day for the departure for Prague arrived, my mother had everything ready for my long journey, a journey of nearly two days on a Danube steamboat to Budapest, and one day by rail from Budapest to Prague. Two multicolored bags made of a beautifully colored web of wool contained my belongings: one my linen, the other my provisions, consisting of a whole roast goose and a big loaf of white bread. The only suit of clothes which I had I wore on my back, and my sisters told me that it was very stylish and made me look like a city-bred boy. To tone down somewhat this misleading appearance and to provide a warm covering during my journey for the cold autumn evenings and nights, I wore a long yellow overcoat of sheepskin trimmed with black wool and embroidered along the border with black and red arabesque figures. A black sheepskin cap gave the finishing touch and marked me as a real son of Idvor. When I said good-by to father and mother on the steamboat landing I expected, of course, that my mother would cry, and she did; but to my great surprise I noticed two big tears roll down my father's cheeks. He was a stern and unemotional person, a splendid type of the heroic age, and when for the first time in my life I saw a tear in his luminous eyes I broke down and sobbed, and felt embarrassed when I saw that the steamboat passengers were taking a sympathetic interest in my parting from father and mother. A group of big boys on the boat took me up and offered to help me to orient myself on the boat; they were theological students returning to the famous seminary at Karlovci, the seat of the Serb Patriarch. I confided to them that I was going to the schools of Prague, that I never had gone from home farther than Panchevo, that I had never seen a big steamboat or a railroad-train, and that my journey gave me some anxiety because I could not speak Hungarian and had some difficulty in handling the limited German vocabulary which I learned in Panchevo. Presently we saw a great church-tower in the distance, and they told me that it was the cathedral of Karlovci, and that near the cathedral was the palace of his holiness, the Patriarch. It was at this place that the Turks begged for peace in 1699, having been defeated with the aid of the military frontiersmen. Beyond Karlovci, they pointed out, was the mountain of Frushka Gora, famous in Serbian poetry. This was the first time I saw a mountain at close range. One historical scene crowded upon another, and I had some difficulty to take them all in even with the friendly assistance of my theological acquaintances. When Karlovci was reached and my theological friends left the boat, I felt quite lonesome. I returned to my multicolored bags, and as I looked upon them and remembered that mother had made them I felt that a part, at least, of my honey-hearted home was so near me, and that consoled me.

I noticed that lunch was being served to people who had ordered it, and I thought of the roast goose which mother had packed away in my multicolored bag. I reached for the bag, but, alas! the goose was gone. A fellow passenger, who sat near me, assured me that he saw one of the young theologians carry the goose away while the other theologians engaged me in conversation, and not knowing to whom the bags belonged, he thought nothing of the incident. Besides, how could any one suspect a student of theology? "Shades of St. Sava," said I, "what kind of orthodoxy will these future apostles of your faith preach to the Serbs of Banat?" "Ah, my boy," said an elderly lady who heard my exclamation, "do not curse them; they did it just out of innocent mischief. This experience will be worth many a roast goose to you; it will teach you that in a world of strangers you must always keep one eye on what you have and with the other eye look out for things that you do not have." She was a most sympathetic peasant woman, who probably had seen my dramatic parting with father and mother on the steamboat landing. I took her advice, and during the rest of my journey I never lost sight of my multicolored bags and of my yellow sheepskin coat.

The sight of Budapest, as the boat approached it on the following day, nearly took my breath away. At the neighborhood gatherings in Idvor I had heard many a story about the splendor of the emperor's palace on the top of the mountain at Buda, and about the wonders of a bridge suspended in air across the Danube and connecting Buda with Pest. Many legends were told in Idvor concerning these wonderful things. But what I saw with my own eyes from the deck of that steamboat surpassed all my expectations. I was overawed, and for a moment I should have been glad to turn back and retrace my journey to Idvor. The world outside of Idvor seemed too big and too complicated for me. But as soon as I landed my courage returned. With the yellow sheepskin coat on my back, the black sheepskin cap on my head, and the multicolored bags firmly grasped in my hands, I started out to find the railroad-station. A husky Serb passed by and, attracted by my sheepskin coat and cap and the multicolored bags, suddenly stopped and addressed me in Serbian. He lived in Budapest, he said, and his glad eye and hand assured me that a sincere friend was speaking to me. He helped me with the bags and stayed with me until he deposited me in the train that was to take me to Prague. He cautioned me that at about four o'clock in the morning my train would reach Gaenserndorf (Goosetown), and that there I should get out and get another train which would take me to Prague.

The name of this town brought back to memory my goose which had disappeared at Karlovci, and gloomy forebodings disturbed my mind and made me a little anxious.

This was the first railroad-train that I had ever seen. It disappointed me; the legendary speed of trains about which I had heard so much in Idvor was not there. When the whistle blew and the conductor shouted "Fertig!" (Ready!), I shut my eyes and waited anxiously, expecting to be shot forward at a tremendous speed. But the train started leisurely and, to my great disappointment, never reached the speeds which I expected. It was a cold October night; the third-class compartment had only one other passenger, a fat Hungarian whom I could not understand, although he tried his best to engage me in a conversation. My sheepskin coat and cap made me feel warm and comfortable; I fell asleep, and never woke up until the rough conductor pulled me off my seat and ordered me out.

"Vienna, last stop," he shouted.

"But I was going to Prague," I said.

"Then you should have changed at Gaenserndorf, you idiot!" answered the conductor, with the usual politeness of Austrian officials when they see a Serb before them. "But why didn't you wake me up at Gaenserndorf?" I protested. He flared up and made a gesture as if about to box my ears, but suddenly he changed his mind and substituted a verbal thrust at my pride. "You little fool of a Serbian swineherd, do you expect an imperial official to assist you in your lazy habits vou sleepy muttonhead?"

"Excuse me," I said with an air of wounded pride, "I am not a Serbian swineherd; I am a son of a brave military frontiersman, and I am going to the famous schools of Prague."

He softened, and told me that I should have to go back

to Gaenserndorf after paying my fare to that place and back. When I informed him that I had no money for extra travelling expenses, he beckoned to me to come along, and after a while we stood in the presence of what I thought to be a very great official. He had a lot of gold braid on his collar and sleeves and on his cap, and he looked as stern and as serious as if the cares of the whole empire rested upon his shoulders.

"Take off your cap, you ill-mannered peasant! Don't you know how to behave in the presence of your superiors?" he blurted out, addressing me. I dropped my multicolored bags, took off my yellow sheepskin coat in order to cover the bags, and then took off my black sheepskin cap, and saluted him in the regular fashion of a military frontiersman. I thought that he might be the emperor himself and, if so, I wondered if he had ever heard of my trampling upon his yellow-black flag at that May-day festival in Panchevo. Finally, I screwed up my courage and apologized by saying:

"Your gracious Majesty will pardon my apparent lack of respect to my superiors, but this is to me a world of strangers, and the anxiety about my belongings kept my hands busy with the bags and prevented me from taking off my cap when I approached your serene Highness." I noticed that several persons within hearing distance were somewhat amused by this interview, and particularly an elderly looking couple, a lady and a gentleman:

"Why should you feel anxious about your bags?" said the great official. "You are not in the savage Balkans, the home of thieves; you are in Vienna, the residence of his Majesty, the Emperor of Austria-Hungary."

"Yes," said I, "but two days ago my roast goose was stolen from one of these bags within his Majesty's realm, and my father told me that all the rights and privileges of the Voyvodina and of the military frontier were stolen right here in this very Vienna."

"Ah, you little rebel, do you expect that this sort of talk will get you a free transportation from Gaenserndorf to Vienna and back again? Restrain your rebellious tongue or I will give you a free transportation back to your military frontier, where rebels like you ought to be behind lock and key."

At this juncture the elderly looking couple engaged him in conversation, and after a while the gold-braided mogul informed me that my ticket from Vienna to Prague by the short route was paid for, and that I should proceed. The rude conductor, who had called me a Serbian swineherd a little while before, led me to the train and ushered me politely into a first-class compartment. Presently the elderly looking couple entered and greeted me in a most friendly, almost affectionate, manner. They encouraged me to take off my sheepskin coat and make myself comfortable, and assured me that my bags would be perfectly safe.

Their German speech had a strange accent, and their manner and appearance were entirely different from anything that I had ever seen before. But they inspired confidence. Feeling hungry, I took my loaf of snowy-white bread out of my bag, and with my herdsman's knife with a long wooden handle I cut off two slices and offered them to my new friends. "Please, take it," said I; "it was prepared by my mother's hands for my long journey." They accepted my hospitality and ate the bread and pronounced it excellent, the best bread they had ever tasted. I told them how it was made by mixing leaf-lard and milk with the finest wheat flour, and when I informed them that I knew a great deal about cooking and that I had learned it by watching my mother, the lady appeared greatly pleased. The gentleman, her husband, asked me questions about farming and taking care of animals, which I answered readily, quoting my father as my authority. "You had two splendid teachers, your father and your mother," they said; "do you expect to find better teachers in Prague?" I told them briefly what had sent me to Prague, mentioning particularly that some people thought that I had outgrown the schools not only of my native village but also of Panchevo, but that in reality the main reason was because the Hungarian officials did not want me in Panchevo on account of my showing a strong inclination to develop into a rebellious nationalist. My new friends gave each other a significant look and said something in a language which I did not understand. They told me that it was English, and added that they were from America.

"America!" said I, quivering with emotion. "Then you must know a lot about Benjamin Franklin and his kite, and about Lincoln, the American Prince Marko."

This exclamation of mine surprised them greatly and furnished the topic for a lively conversation of several hours, until the train had reached Prague. It was conducted in broken German, but we understood each other perfectly. I told them of my experience with Franklin's theory of lightning, and of its clash with my father's St. Elijah legend, and answered many of their questions relating to my calling Lincoln an American Prince Marko. I quoted from several Serbian ballads relating to Prince Marko which I had learned from Baba Batikin, and at their urgent request described with much detail the neighborhood gatherings in Idvor. They returned the compliment by telling me stories of Benjamin Franklin, of Lincoln, and of America, and urged me to read "Uncle Tom's Cabin," a translation of which I discovered some time afterward. When the train reached Prague they insisted that I be their guest at their Prague hotel, called the Blue Star, for a day, at least, until I found my friends in Prague. I gladly accepted, and spent a delightful evening with them. The sweetness of their dis-

six weeks each summer I had lived under the wide canopy
of heaven, watching the grazing oxen, gazing upon the
countless stars at night, and listening to the sweet strains
of the Serbian flute. The people I met on the streets
were puffed up with Teutonic pride or with official arrogance; they had none of the gentle manliness and friend-
liness of the military frontiersmen. The teachers looked
to me more like Austrian gendarmes than like sympathetic friends. They cared more for my sentiments toward the emperor and for my ideas about nationalism
than for my ideas relating to God and his beautiful world
of life and light. Not one of them reminded me of Kos,
the Slovenian, or of protoyeray Zhivkovich in Panchevo.
Race antagonism was at that time the ruling passion.
If it had not been for the affectionate regard which the
Czech boys and their parents had for me I should have
felt most lonesome; from Banat to Prague was too sudden a change for me.

Another circumstance I must mention now which
helped to brace me up. I delivered, after many months
of delay, my letters of introduction to Rieger and to Palacky. I saw their pictures, I read about them, and finally
I heard them address huge nationalist meetings. They
were great men, I thought, and I could not screw up sufficient courage to call on them, as the protoyeray wished
me to do, and waste their precious time on my account.
But when I received a letter from the protoyeray in Panchevo asking why I had not delivered the letters of introduction he had given me, I made the calls. Rieger
looked like my father: dark, stern, reserved, powerful
of physique, with a wonderful luminosity in his eyes.
He gave me coffee and cake, consuming a generous supply of them himself. When I kissed his hand, bidding
him good-by, he gave me a florin for pocket-money, patted
me on the cheek, and assured me that I could easily come

up to the protoyeray's expectations and surprise my teachers if I would only spend more time on my books and less on my nationalist chums. This suggestion and indirect advice made me very thoughtful. Palacky was a gentle, smooth-faced, old gentleman, who looked to me then as if he knew everything that men had ever known, and that much study had made him pale and delicate. He was much interested in my description of the life and customs of my native village, and when I mentioned St. Sava, he drew a parallel between this saint and Yan Huss, the great Czech patriot and divine, who was burned at the stake in 1415 at Constance because he demanded a national democratic church in Bohemia. He gave me a book in which I could read all about Huss and the Hussite wars and about the one-eyed Zhizhka, the great Hussite general. He gave me no coffee nor cake, probably because his health did not permit him to indulge in eatables between meals, but assured me of assistance if I should ever need it. I eagerly read the book about Yan Huss and the Hussite wars, and became a more enthusiastic nationalist than ever before. I felt that Rieger's influence pulled me in one direction, and that Palacky encouraged me to persist in the opposite direction which I had selected under the influence of the spirit of Czech nationalism.

In my letters to my elder sisters, which they read to father and mother, I described with much detail the beauties and wonders of Prague, my receptions and talks with Rieger and Palacky, and elaborated much the parallel between St. Sava and Yan Huss to which Palacky had drawn my attention, and which I expected would please my mother; but I never mentioned Rieger's advice that I stick to books and leave the nationalist propaganda of the boys alone. I never during my whole year's stay in Prague sent a report home on my school work, because I never did more than just enough to prevent my dropping

to the lower grade. My mother and the protoyeray in
Panchevo expected immeasurably more. Hence, I never
complained about the smallness of the allowance which
my parents could give me, and, therefore, they did not
appeal to my Panchevo friends for the additional help
which they had promised. I felt that I had no right to
make such an appeal, because I did not devote myself
entirely to the work for which I was sent to Prague.

While debating with myself whether to follow Rieger's
advice and leave nationalism in the hands of more experienced people and devote myself to my lessons only,
an event occurred which was the turning-point in my life.
I received a letter from my sister informing me that my
father had died suddenly after a very brief illness. She
told me also that my father had had a premonition that
he would die soon and never see me again when, a year
before, he bade me good-by on the steamboat landing.
I understood then the meaning of the tears which on that
day of parting I had seen roll down his cheeks for the
first time in my life. I immediately informed my mother
that I wanted to return to Idvor and help her take care
of my father's land. But she would not listen, and insisted that I stay in Prague, where I was seeing and learning so many wonderful things. I knew quite well what
a heavy burden my schooling would be to her, and my
school record did not entitle me to expect the protoyeray
to make his promise of assistance good. I decided to
find a way of relieving my mother of any further burdens
so far as I was concerned.

One day I saw on the last page of an illustrated paper
an advertisement of the Hamburg-American line, offering
steerage transportation from Hamburg to New York for
twenty-eight florins. I thought of my mellow-hearted
American friends of the year before who bought a first-

class railroad-ticket for me from Vienna to Prague, and decided on the spot to try my fortune in the land of Franklin and Lincoln as soon as I could save up and otherwise scrape up money enough to carry me from Prague to New York. My books, my watch, my clothes, including the yellow sheepskin coat and the black sheepskin cap, were all sold to make up the sum necessary for travelling expenses. I started out with just one suit of clothes on my back and a few changes of linen, and a red Turkish fez which nobody would buy. And why should anybody going to New York bother about warm clothes? Was not New York much farther south than Panchevo, and does not America suggest a hot climate when one thinks of the pictures of naked Indians so often seen? These thoughts consoled me when I parted with my sheepskin coat. At length I came to Hamburg, ready to embark but with no money to buy a mattress and a blanket for my bunk in the steerage. Several days later my ship, the *Westphalia*, sailed—on the twelfth day of March, 1874. My mother received several days later my letter, mailed in Hamburg, telling her in most affectionate terms that, in my opinion, I had outgrown the school, the teachers, and the educational methods of Prague, and was about to depart for the land of Franklin and Lincoln, where the wisdom of people was beyond anything that even St. Sava had ever known. I assured her that with her blessing and God's help I should certainly succeed, and promised that I would soon return rich in rare knowledge and in honors. The letter was dictated by the rosiest optimism that I could invent. Several months later I found to my great delight that my mother had accepted cheerfully this rosy view of my unexpected enterprise.

The ship sailed with a full complement of steerage passengers, mostly Germans. As we glided along the

River Elbe the emigrants were all on deck, watching the land as it gradually vanished from our sight. Presently the famous German emigrant song rang through the air, and with a heavy heart I took in the words of its refrain:

"Oh, how hard it would be to leave the homeland shores
If the hope did not live that soon we shall see them again.
Farewell, farewell, until we see you again."

I did not wait for the completion of the song, but turned in, and in my bare bunk I sought to drown my sadness in a flood of tears. Idvor, with its sunny fields, vine-yards, and orchards; with its grazing herds of cattle and flocks of sheep; with its beautiful church-spire and the solemn ringing of church-bells; with its merry boys and girls dancing to the tune of the Serbian bagpipes the Kolo on the village green—Idvor, with all the familiar scenes that I had ever seen there, appeared before my tearful eyes, and in the midst of them I saw my mother listening to my sister reading slowly the letter which I had sent to her from Hamburg. Every one of these scenes seemed to start a new shower of tears, which finally cleared the oppressiveness of my spiritual atmosphere. I thought that I could hear my mother say to my sister: "God bless him for his affectionate letter. May the spirit of St. Sava guide him in the land beyond the seas! I know that he will make good his promises." Sadness deserted me then and I felt strong again.

He who has never crossed the stormy Atlantic during the month of March in the crowded steerage of an im-migrant ship does not know what hardships are. I bless the stars that the immigration laws were different then than they are now, otherwise I should not be among the living. To stand the great hardships of a stormy sea when the rosy picture of the promised land is before your mind's eye is a severe test for any boy's nerve and physical stamina; but to face the same hardships as a deported and

THE VILLAGE CHURCH IN IDVOR

penniless immigrant with no cheering prospect in sight
is too much for any person, unless that person is entirely
devoid of every finer sensibility. Many a night I spent
on the deck of that immigrant ship hugging the warm
smoke-stack and adjusting my position so as to avoid
the force of the gale and the sharpness of its icy chilliness.
All I had was the light suit of clothes which I carried on
my back. Everything else I had converted into money
with which to cover my transportation expenses. There
was nothing left to pay for a blanket and mattress for
my steerage bunk. I could not rest there during the cold
nights of March without much shivering and unbearable
discomfort. If it had not been for the warm smoke-stack
I should have died of cold. At first I had to fight for my
place there in the daytime, but when the immigrants
understood that I had no warm clothing they did not
disturb me any longer. I often thought of my yellow
sheepskin coat and the black sheepskin cap, and understood more clearly than ever my mother's far-sightedness
when she provided that coat and cap for my long journeys.
A blast of the everlasting gales had carried away my hat,
and a Turkish fez such as the Serbs of Bosnia wear was
the only head-gear I had. It was providential that I
had not succeeded in selling it in Prague. Most of my
fellow emigrants thought that I was a Turk and cared
little about my discomforts. But, nevertheless, I felt
quite brave and strong in the daytime; at night, however, when, standing alone alongside of the smoke-stack, I
beheld through the howling darkness the white rims of
the mountain-high waves speeding on like maddened
dragons toward the tumbling ship, my heart sank low.
It was my implicit trust in God and in his regard for my
mother's prayers which enabled me to overcome my fear
and bravely face the horrors of the angry seas.

On the fourteenth day, early in the morning, the flat
coast-line of Long Island hove in sight. Nobody in the

motley crowd of excited immigrants was more happy to see the promised land than I was. It was a clear, mild, and sunny March morning, and as we approached New York Harbor the warm sun-rays seemed to thaw out the chilliness which I had accumulated in my body by continuous exposure to the wintry blasts of the North Atlantic. I felt like a new person, and saw in every new scene presented by the New World as the ship moved into it a new promise that I should be welcome. Life and activity kept blossoming out all along the ship's course, and seemed to reach full bloom as we entered New York Harbor. The scene which was then unfolded before my eyes was most novel and bewildering. The first impressions of Budapest and of Prague seemed like pale-faced images of the grand realities which New York Harbor disclosed before my eager eyes. A countless multitude of boats lined each shore of the vast river; all kinds of craft ploughed hurriedly in every direction through the waters of the bay; great masses of people crowded the numerous ferry-boats, and gave me the impression that one crowd was just about as anxious to reach one shore of the huge metropolis as the other was to reach the other shore; they all must have had some important thing to do, I thought. The city on each side of the shore seemed to throb with activity. I did not distinguish between New York and Jersey City. Hundreds of other spots like the one I beheld, I thought, must be scattered over the vast territories of the United States, and in these seething pots of human action there must be some one activity, I was certain, which needed me. This gave me courage. The talk which I had listened to during two weeks on the immigrant ship was rather discouraging, I thought. One immigrant was bragging about his long experience as a cabinetmaker, and informed his audience that cabinetmakers were in great demand in America; another one was telling long tales about his skill as a mechanician; a third one was spinning out long yarns about the fabulous agricultural successes of his relatives out West, who had invited him to come there and join them; a fourth confided to the gaping crowd that his brother, who was anxiously waiting for him, had a most prosperous bank in some rich mining-camp in Nevada where people never saw any money except silver and gold and hardly ever a coin smaller than a dollar; a fifth one, who had been in America before, told us in a rather top-lofty way that no matter who you were or what you knew or what you had you would be a greenhorn when you landed in the New World, and a greenhorn has to serve his apprenticeship before he can establish his claim to any recognition. He admitted, however, that immigrants with a previous practical training, or strong pull through relatives and friends, had a shorter apprenticeship. I had no practical training, and I had no relatives nor friends nor even acquaintances in the New World. I had nothing of any immediate value to offer to the land I was about to enter. That thought had discouraged me as I listened to the talks of the immigrants; but the activity which New York Harbor presented to my eager eyes on that sunny March day was most encouraging.

Presently the ship passed by Castle Garden, and I heard some one say: "There is the Gate to America." An hour or so later we all stood at the gate. The immigrant ship, *Westphalia*, landed at Hoboken and a tug took us to Castle Garden. We were carefully examined and cross-examined, and when my turn came the examining officials shook their heads and seemed to find me wanting. I confessed that I had only five cents in my pocket and had no relatives here, and that I knew of nobody in this country except Franklin, Lincoln, and Harriet Beecher Stowe, whose "Uncle Tom's Cabin" I had read in a translation. One of the officials, who had one leg only, and walked with a crutch, seemed much impressed by this remark, and looking very kindly into my eyes and with a merry twinkle in his eye he said in German: "You showed good taste when you picked your American acquaintances." I learned later that he was a Swiss who had served in the Union army during the Civil War. I confessed also to the examining officials that I had no training in the arts and crafts, but that I was anxious to learn, and that this desire had brought me to America. In answer to the question why I had not stayed at home or in Prague to learn instead of wandering across the sea with so little on my back and nothing in my pocket, I said that the Hungarian and Austrian authorities had formed a strong prejudice against me on account of my sympathies with people, and particularly with my father, who objected to being cheated out of their ancient rights and privileges which the emperor had guaranteed to them for services which they had been rendering to him loyally for nearly two hundred years. I spoke with feeling, and I felt that I made an impression upon the examiners, who did not look to me like officials such as I was accustomed to see in Austria-Hungary. They had no gold and silver braid and no superior airs but looked very much like ordinary civilian mortals. That gave me courage and confidence, and I spoke frankly and fearlessly, believing firmly that I was addressing human beings who had a heart which was not held in bondage by cast-iron rules invented by their superiors in authority. The Swiss veteran who walked on crutches, having lost one of his legs in the Civil War, was particularly attentive while I was being cross-examined, and nodded approvingly whenever I scored a point with my answers. He whispered something to the other officials, and they finally informed me that I could pass on, and I was conducted promptly to the Labor Bureau of Castle Garden. My Swiss friend looked me up a little later and

informed me that the examiners had made an exception
in my favor and admitted me, and that I must look sharp
and find a job as soon as possible.

As I sat in the Labor Bureau waiting for somebody
to come along and pick me out as a worthy candidate
for some job, I could not help surveying those of my fellow immigrants who, like myself, sat there waiting for a
job. I really believed that they were in a class below
me, and yet they had had no trouble in being admitted.
They had not needed favors on the part of the officials
in order to be admitted. I had, and therefore, I inferred,
they must have appeared to the officials to be more desirable. It was true, I said, arguing with myself, that
they had a definite trade; they undoubtedly had some
money; and they certainly looked more prosperous than
I did, judging by their clothes. But why should the possession of a trade, of money, or of clothes stand so much
higher in America than it did in Idvor, my native village?
We had a blacksmith, a wheelwright, and a barber in
Idvor; they were our craftsmen; and we had a Greek
storekeeper who had a lot of money and wore expensive
city-made clothes, but there was not one respectable
Serb peasant in Idvor, no matter how poor, who did not
think that he was superior to these people who had only
a transient existence in our historic village. The knowledge of our traditions and our implicit belief in them made
us feel superior to people who wandered about like gypsies
with no traditions, and with nothing to anchor them to
a definite place. A newcomer to our village was closely
scrutinized, and he was judged not so much by his skill
in a craft, nor by his money, nor by his clothes, but by
his personality, by the reputation of his family, and by
the traditions of the people to whom he belonged. The
examiners at Castle Garden seemed to attach no importance to these things, because they did not ask me a

single question concerning my family, the history of my village, or the history of the military frontier and of the Serb race. It was no wonder, said I, consoling myself, that I appeared to them less desirable than many of the other immigrants who would never have been allowed to settle in Idvor, and whose society on the immigrant ship had interested me so little, and, in fact, had often been repulsive to me, because I could not help considering many of them a sort of spiritual muckers. My admission by a special favor of the examiners was a puzzle and a disappointment to me, but it did not destroy the firmness of my belief that I brought to America something which the examiners were either unable or did not care to find out, but which, nevertheless, I valued very highly, and that was: a knowledge of and a profound respect and admiration for the best traditions of my race. My mother and the illiterate peasants at the neighborhood gatherings in Idvor had taught me that; no other lesson had ever made a deeper impression upon me.

II

THE HARDSHIPS OF A GREENHORN

My first night under the Stars and Stripes was spent in Castle Garden. It was a glorious night, I thought; no howling of the gales, no crashing of the waves, and no tumbling motion of the world beneath my feet, such as I had experienced on the immigrant ship. The feeling of being on *terra firma* sank deep into my consciousness and I slept the sound sleep of a healthy youth, although my bed was a bare floor. The very early morning saw me at my breakfast, enjoying a huge bowl of hot coffee and a big chunk of bread with some butter, supplied by the Castle Garden authorities at Uncle Sam's expense. Then I started out, eager to catch a glimpse of great New York, feeling, in the words of the psalmist, "as a strong man ready to run a race." An old lady sat near the gate of Castle Garden offering cakes and candies for sale. A piece of prune pie caught my eye, and no true Serb can resist the allurements of prunes. It is a national sweetmeat. I bought it, paying five cents for it, the only money I had, and then I made a bee-line across Battery Park, at the same time attending to my pie. My first bargain in America proved a failure. The prune pie was a deception; it was a prune pie filled with prune pits, and I thought of the words of my fellow passenger on the immigrant ship who had said: "No matter who you are or what you know or what you have you will be a greenhorn when you land in America." The prune-pie transaction whispered into my ear: "Michael, you are a greenhorn; this is the first experience in your life as a greenhorn. Cheer up! Get ready to serve your apprenticeship as a

43

greenhorn before you can establish your claim to any recognition," repeating the words of my prophetic fellow passenger who had served his apprenticeship in America. No prophet ever uttered a truer word.

The old Stevens House, a white building with green window-shutters, stood at the corner of Broadway and Bowling Green. When I reached this spot and saw the busy beehive called Broadway, with thousands of telegraph-wires stretching across it like a cobweb between huge buildings, I was overawed, and wondered what it meant. Neither Budapest, nor Prague, nor Hamburg had looked anything like it. My puzzled and panicky expression and the red fez on my head must have attracted considerable attention, because suddenly I saw myself surrounded by a small crowd of boys of all sizes, jeering and laughing and pointing at my fez. They were newsboys and bootblacks, who appeared to be anxious to have some fun at my expense. I was embarrassed and much provoked, but controlled my Serbian temper. Presently one of the bigger fellows walked up to me and knocked the fez off my head. I punched him on the nose and then we clinched. My wrestling experiences on the pasturelands of Idvor came to my rescue. The bully was down in a jiffy, and his chums gave a loud cheer of ringing laughter. I thought it was a signal for general attack, but they did not touch me nor interfere in any way. They acted like impartial spectators, anxious to see that the best man won. Suddenly I felt a powerful hand pulling me up by the collar, and when I looked up I saw a big official with a club in his hand and a fierce expression in his eye. He looked decidedly unfriendly, but after listening to the appeals of the newsboys and bootblacks who witnessed the fight he softened and handed me my fez. The boys who a little while before had jeered and tried to guy me, evidently appealed in my behalf when the policeman interfered. They had actually become my friends. When I walked away toward Castle Garden, with my red fez proudly cocked up on my head, the boys cheered. I thought to myself that the unpleasant incident was worth my while, because it taught me that I was in a country where even among the street urchins there was a strong sentiment in favor of fair play even to a Serbian greenhorn. America was different from Austria-Hungary. I never forgot the lesson and never had a single reason to change my opinion.

A gentleman who had witnessed the fight joined me on my return trip to Castle Garden, and when we reached the employment bureau he offered me a job. When I learned that one of my daily duties would be to milk a cow, I refused. According to Serb traditions, milking a cow is decidedly a feminine job. Another gentleman, a Swiss foreman on a Delaware farm, offered me another job, which was to drive a team of mules and help in the work of hauling things to the field preparatory for spring planting. I accepted gladly, feeling confident that I knew all about driving animals, although I had never even seen a mule in all my experiences in Idvor. We left for Philadelphia that forenoon and caught there the early afternoon boat for Delaware City, where we arrived late in the afternoon.

As we passed through Philadelphia I asked the Swiss foreman whether that was the place where a hundred years before famous Benjamin Franklin flew his kite, and he answered that he had never heard of the gentleman, and that I must have meant William Penn. "No," said I, "because I never heard of this gentleman." "You have still to learn a thing or two about American history," said the Swiss foreman, with a superior air. "Yes, indeed," I said, "and I intend to do it as soon as I have learned a thing or two about the English language"; and I wondered whether the Swiss foreman who had never heard of Benjamin Franklin and his kite had really learned a thing or two in American history, although he had lived some fifteen years in the United States.

There were quite a number of farmers on the Delaware boat, every one of them wearing a long goatee but no mustache; such was the fashion at that time. Every one of them had the brim of his slouch hat turned down, covering his eyes completely. As they conversed they looked like wooden images; they made no gestures and I could not catch the expression of their hidden eyes; without these powerful aids to the understanding of the spoken word I could not make out a single syllable in their speech. The English language sounded to me like an inarticulate mode of speech, just as inarticulate as the joints of those imperturbable Delaware farmers. I wondered whether I should ever succeed in learning a thing or two in this most peculiar tongue. I thought of the peasants at the neighborhood gatherings in Idvor, and of their winged words, each of which found its way straight into my soul. There also appeared before my mental vision the image of Baba Batikin, with fire in his eye and a vibratory movement of his hand accompanying his stirring tales of Prince Marko. How different and how superior those peasants of Idvor appeared to me when I compared them with the farmers on that Delaware boat! "Impossible," said I, "that a Serb peasant should be so much superior to the American peasant!" Something wrong with my judgment, thought I, and I charged it to my being a greenhorn and unable to size up an American farmer.

At the boat-landing in Delaware City a farm-wagon was awaiting us, and we reached the farm at supper-time. The farm-buildings were fully a mile from the town, standing all by themselves; there was no village and there were no neighbors, and the place looked to me like a camp. There was no village life among American farmers, I was told, and I understood then why those farmers on the

Delaware boat were so devoid of all animation. The farm-hands were all young fellows, but considerably older than myself, and when the foreman introduced me to them, by my Christian name, I found that most of them spoke German with a Swiss accent, the same which the foreman had who brought me from New York. One of them asked me how long I had been in the country, and when I told him that I was about twenty-four hours in the country, he smiled and said that he thought so, evidently on account of the unmistakable signs of a greenhorn which he saw all over me.

The first impression of an American farm was dismal. In the messroom, however, where supper was served, everything was neat and lovely, and the supper looked to me like a holiday feast. I became more reconciled to the American farm. The farm-hands ate much and spoke very little, and when they finished they left the dining-room without any ceremony. I was left alone, and moved my chair close to a warm stove and waited for somebody to tell me what to do next. Presently two women came in and proceeded to clear the supper-table; they spoke English and seemed to pay no attention to me. They probably thought that I was homesick and avoided disturbing me. Presently I saw a young girl, somewhat younger than myself. She pretended to be helping the women, but I soon discovered that she had another mission. Her appearance reminded me of a young Vila, a Serbian fairy, who in the old Serbian ballads plays a most wonderful part. No hero ever perished through misfortune who had the good fortune to win the friendship of a Vila. Supernatural both in intelligence and in physical skill, the Vilæ could always find a way out of every difficulty. I felt certain that if there ever was a Vila this young girl was one. Her luminous blue eyes, her finely chiselled features, and her graceful movements made a strange impression upon me. I imagined that she could hear the faintest sound, that she could see in the darkest night, and that, like a real Vila, she could feel not only the faintest breezes but even the thoughts of people near her. She certainly felt my thoughts. Pointing to a table in a corner of the dining-room, she directed my attention to writing-paper and ink, placed there for the convenience of farm-hands. I understood her meaning, although I did not understand her words. I spent the evening writing a letter to my mother. This was my wish, and the Vila must have read it in my face.

One of the farm-hands, a Swiss, came in after a while in order to remind me that it was bedtime and to inform me that early in the morning he would wake me up and take me to the barn, where my job would be assigned to me. He kept his word, and with lantern in hand he took me long before sunrise to the barn and introduced me to two mules which he put in my charge. I cleaned them and fed them while he watched and directed; after breakfast he showed me how to harness and hitch them up. I took my turn in the line of teams hauling manure to the fields. He warned me not to apply myself too zealously to the work of loading and unloading, until I had become gradually broken in, otherwise I should be laid up stiff as a rod. The next day I was laid up, stiffer than a rod. He was much provoked, and called me the worst "greenhorn" that he ever saw. But, thanks to the skilled and tender care of the ladies on the farm, I was at my job again two days later. My being a greenhorn appealed to their sympathy; they seemed to have the same kind of soul which I had first observed in my American friends who paid my fare from Vienna to Prague.

One of my mules gave me much trouble, and the more he worried me the more amusement he seemed to furnish to the other farm-hands, rough immigrants of foreign birth. He did not bite, nor did he kick, as some of the mules did, but he protested violently against my putting the bridle on his head. The other farm-hands had no advice to offer; they seemed to enjoy my perplexity. I soon discovered that the troublesome mule could not stand anybody touching his ears. That was his ticklish spot. I finally got around it; I never took his bridle off on working-days, but only removed the bit, so that he could eat. On Sunday mornings, however, when I had all the time I wanted, I took his bridle off, cleaned it, and put it on, and did not remove it again for another week. The foreman and the superintendent discovered my trick and approved of it, and so the farm-hands lost the amusement which they had had at my expense every morning at the harnessing hour. I noticed that they were impressed by my trick and did not address me by the name of greenhorn quite so often. They were also surprised to hear me make successful attempts to speak English. Nothing counts so much in the immigrant's bid for promotion to a grade above that of a greenhorn as the knowledge of the English language. In these efforts I received a most unexpected assistance, and for that I was much indebted to my red fez.

On every trip from the barnyard to the fields, my mules and I passed by the superintendent's quarters, and there behind the wall of neatly piled-up cord-wood I observed every now and then the golden curls of my American Vila. She cautiously watched there, just like a Serbian Vila at the edge of a forest. My red fez perched up on a high seat behind the mules obviously attracted and amused her. Whenever I caught her eye I saluted in regular Balkan fashion, and it was a salute such as she had never seen before in the State of Delaware. Her curiosity seemed to grow from day to day, and so did mine.

One evening I sat alone near the warm stove in the messroom and she came in and said: "Good evening!" I answered by repeating her greeting, but pronounced it badly. She corrected me, and, when I repeated her greeting the second time, I did much better, and she applauded my genuine effort. Then she proceeded to teach me English words for everything in the dining-room, and before that first lesson was over I knew some twenty English words and pronounced them to her satisfaction. The next day I repeated these words aloud over and over again during my trips to the fields, until I thought that even the mules knew them by heart. At the second lesson on the following evening I scored a high mark from my teacher and added twenty more words to my English vocabulary. As time went on, my vocabulary increased at a rapid rate, and my young teacher was most enthusiastic. She called me "smart," and I never forgot the word. One evening she brought in her mother, who two weeks previously had taken care of me when I was laid up from overzealous loading. At that time she could not make me understand a single word she said. This time, however, I had no difficulty, and she was greatly surprised and pleased. My first examination in English was a complete success.

At the end of the first month on the Delaware farm my confidence in the use of the English language had grown strong. During the second month I grew bold enough to join in lengthy conversations. The superintendent's wife invited me often to spend the evening with the family. My tales of Idvor, Panchevo, Budapest, Prague, Hamburg, and the immigrant ship interested them much, they said. My pronunciation and grammar amused them even more than they were willing to show. They were too polite to indulge in unrestrained laughter over my Serbian idioms. During these conversations the Vila sat still and seemed to be all attention. She was all eyes and ears, and I knew that she was making mental notes of every mistake in my grammar and pronunciation. At the next lesson she would correct every one of these mistakes, and then she watched at the next family gathering to see whether I should repeat them. But I did not; my highest ambition was to show myself worthy of the title "smart" which she had given me.

One evening I was relating to the superintendent's family how I had refused the first offer of a job at Castle Garden, because I did not care to accept the daily duty of milking a cow, which, according to my Serbian notions, was a purely feminine job. I admitted that Serbian and American notions were entirely different in this particular respect, because, although over a hundred cows were milked daily on the farm, I never saw a woman in any one of the many barns, nor in the huge creamery. I confessed also that both the Vila and her mother would be entirely out of place not only in the cow-barns but even in the scrupulously clean creamery, adding that if the Vila had been obliged to attend to the cows and to the creamery, she would not have found the time to teach me English, and, therefore, I preferred the American custom. Vila's mother was highly pleased with this remark and said: "Michael, my boy, you are beginning to understand our American ways, and the sooner you drop your Serbian notions the sooner you will become an American."

She explained to me the position of the American woman as that of the educator and spiritual guide of the coming generation, emphasizing the fact that the vast majority of teachers in American primary schools were women. This information astonished and pleased me, because I knew that my mother was a better teacher than my schoolmaster, an old man with a funny nasal twang. Her suggestion, however, that I should drop my Serbian notions and become an American as soon as possible disturbed me. But I said nothing; I was a greenhorn only and did not desire to express an opinion which might clash with hers. I thought it strange, however, that she took it for granted that I wished to become an American.

The next day was Sunday, and I walked to church, which was in Delaware City. The singing of hymns did not impress me much, and the sermon impressed me even less. Delaware City was much bigger than my native Idvor, and yet the religious service in Idvor was more elaborate. There was no choral singing in the church of Delaware City, and there were no ceremonies with a lot of burning candles and the sweet perfume of burning incense, and there was no ringing of harmonious church-bells. I was disappointed, and wondered why Vila's mother expected me to drop my Serbian notions and embrace America's ways, which, so far as public worship was concerned, appeared to me as less attractive than the Serbian ways. Vila's family met me in front of the church and asked me to ride home with them. A farm-hand riding in a fine carriage with his employer struck me as extraordinary, and I wished to be excused, but they insisted. No rich peasant in Idvor would have done that. In this respect Delaware farmers with their American ways appealed to me more. Another surprise was in store for me: Vila's mother insisted that I share with the family their Sunday dinner, just as I had shared with them the divine service. I saw in it an effort on her part to show an appreciation of my religious habit and to encourage it, thus proving in practice what she preached to me about the spiritual influence of the American woman. During the dinner I described the Sundays of Idvor, dwelling particularly upon the custom among the Serbian boys and girls of kolo dancing on the village green in front of the church on Sunday afternoons. Vila approved of the custom enthusiastically, but her mother thought that a walk through the peach-orchards, which were then in full bloom, was at least as good. Vila and I walked together that Sunday afternoon. My attendance at church gained for me this favor also.

He who has never seen the Delaware peach-orchards

of those days in full bloom, when in the month of May the ground is a deep velvety green, and when the Southern sky seen through the golden atmosphere of a sunny May day reminds one of those mysterious landscapes which form the background in some of Raphael's Madonna pictures—he who has never seen that glorious sight does not know the heavenly beauty of this little earth. No painter would dare attempt to put on canvas the cloth of flaming gold which on that balmy Sunday afternoon covered the ripples of the sun-kissed Delaware River. Vila asked me whether I had ever seen anything more beautiful in Idvor, and I said no, but added that nothing is as lovely and as sweet as one's native village. When I informed her that some day I expected to return to it, enriched by my experiences in America, she looked surprised and said:

"Then you do not intend to become an American?"

"No," said I; and after some hesitation I added: "I ran away from the military frontier because the rulers of the land wanted to transform me into a Hungarian; I ran away from Prague because I objected to Austrian Teutonism; I shall run away from Delaware City also if, as your good mother suggested, I am expected to drop my Serbian notions and become an American. My mother, my native village, my Serbian orthodox faith, and my Serbian language and the people who speak it are my Serbian notions, and one might as well expect me to give up the breath of my life as to give up my Serbian notions."

"You misunderstood my mother, Michael," said the Vila; "she only referred to your notions about woman's work, and you know that European women are expected to do the hard work for which only men are strong enough."

"Very true," said I; "the strongest and ablest men in Europe spend the best part of their lives on battle-fields,

of the Delaware River was very little in her mind, and even Philadelphia was mentioned only on account of the Liberty Bell and the Declaration of Independence.

One evening, Vila's mother asked me about my mother and her hopes for my future. Remembering her remarks concerning the spiritual influence of the American women upon the coming generation, I gave her a glowing account of my mother, and wound up by saying that she did not expect me to become an American farmer, and that I came to America to learn what I could not learn in a peasant country like that of my native village. She was much touched, and then in simple and solemn language she revealed to me a new truth which I never forgot and which I found confirmed by all my experiences in this great land, the truth, namely, that this is a country of opportunities which are open equally to all; that each individual must seek these opportunities and must be prepared to make good use of them when he finds them. She commended me warmly for making good use of all the opportunities which I had found on the farm, and advised me strongly to go in search of new opportunities. Vila agreed with her, and I prepared to leave the hospitable shores of Delaware.

I made my return trip to Philadelphia on the same boat which had brought me to Delaware City. Things looked different from what they had on my first trip. The farmers of Delaware, my fellow passengers on the boat, did not look like wooden images, and their speech was not inarticulate. I understood their language, and its meaning found a sympathetic response in me. The trip reminded me much of the trip on the Danube some eighteen months prior to that time. One of my fellow passengers, a youngster of about my age, pointed out a place to me which he called Trenton, and assured me that the boat was passing over the spot where Washington crossed the Delaware. His geography was faulty as

I found out much later. But it was swallowed by a green-horn like me and it thrilled me, and I remembered then the first view of the Cathedral of Karlovci, the seat of the Serbian Patriarch, which was pointed out to me from the Danube boat by the theological students. I felt the same thrill in each case, and I knew that America was getting a hold upon my Serbian heart-strings. My appearance attracted no attention, either on the boat or at Philadel-phia after we landed. My hat and clothes were Ameri-can, but my heavy top-boots, so useful on the farm, were somewhat too heavy for the warm June days in Philadelphia.

The Swiss foreman had directed me to a Swiss acquaint-ance of his who had a small hotel in Philadelphia. He was very eager to have me take all my meals at the hotel, but my total capital of ten dollars made me cautious; be-sides, my days from early morning till late at night were spent in the heart of the city. No other human being ever saw so much of Philadelphia during a stay of five days as I did, hunting for a job, searching new oppor-tunities, as Vila's mother expressed it. But I searched in vain. I gained new information about William Penn and Benjamin Franklin and saw many buildings the his-tory of which is attached to these two great names, and I wondered why Benjamin Franklin ever deserted Boston to search new opportunities in a place like Philadelphia. But he did it, and succeeded. I was sure that neither he nor any other human being could walk more or chase after a job more diligently than I did, but then he was an American boy and he had a trade, and I was a Serbian greenhorn who did not know anything in particular, except how to drive a pair of mules. Besides, thought I, Phila-delphia might have lost its wealth of opportunities since Franklin's days. Such was my consolation while resting on a bench in Fairmount Park, near the grounds which were being prepared for the Centennial Exposition of

kins; I would not exchange that for any other honor," said I, returning jest for jest and watching the merry twinkle in the cardinal's fluorescent eyes. Some months later President Butler, of Columbia University, and I happened to be descending in the same lift at the Shoreham Hotel in Washington. Presently Cardinal Gibbons entered, and President Butler introduced me to his Eminence, who, recalling our former meeting in Baltimore, said, "I know Professor Pupin, and it is a great honor, indeed, to ride in the same lift with two eminent men who carry so many distinguished academic honors," and, as he looked at me with a genial smile which was brimful of Irish humor, I knew that he wished to remind me in a good-natured way of my high rating of an honorary Johns Hopkins degree in comparison with the honors attached to the titles of archbishop and cardinal.

The Pennsylvania train from Baltimore to New York delivered me to a ferry-boat, which landed me on West Street, where I found a small hotel kept by a German, a native of Friesland. He was a rugged old fellow who loved his low-German dialect, which I did not understand. He spoke in English to me, which, according to his son Christian, was much worse than mine, although he had been in America some twenty years. Christian was a yellow-haired and freckle-faced lad, of about my age, and we hit it off very well, forming a cross-matched team. He would have given anything, he said, to have my black hair and dark-red complexion. His almost white eyebrows and eyelashes and mischievous gray eyes and yellow freckles fascinated me. He was born in Hoboken and understood his father's low-German dialect, but whenever addressed in it, by his father or by the Friesland sailors who frequented his father's inn, he always answered in English, or, as he called it, "United States."

Christian managed somehow to get away every now and then from the little hotel and to accompany me on

my many long errands in search of a job. His familiarity
with the town helped me much to master the geography
of New York, and to find out what's what and who's
who in the great metropolis. He seemed to be the only
opportunity which New York offered to me, and it was
a great one. Every other opportunity which appeared
in newspaper advertisements had hundreds of applicants,
and they were lined up at the place of the promised opportunity, no matter how early Christian and I reached the
place. I was quite sure that those opportunity-chasers
lined up soon after the first issue of the morning papers.
I was told that the year before (in 1873) occurred the
Black Friday panic, and that New York had not yet
recovered from it. There were thousands of unemployed,
although it was summer. One morning Christian told
me that he had found a fine job for me, and he took me
to a tug anchored quite near his father's hotel. There
were quite a number of husky laborers on the tug, which
took us to the German docks in Hoboken. We were to
stay there and help in the loading of ships, replacing the
longshoremen who were on strike. The job assigned to
me was to assist the sailors who were painting the ship
and things on the ship. We never left the docks until
the strike was over, which lasted about three weeks. At
its termination I was paid and the tug delivered me to
the little hotel on West Street, where Christian received
me with open arms. I had thirty dollars in my pocket,
and Christian told me that I looked as rich as Commo-
dore Vanderbilt, whom Christian considered to be the
richest man in New York. Christian took me to Chatham
Square to buy a new suit of clothes and other wearing
apparel, and I thought that the Jewish clothing dealers
would cause a riot fighting for my patronage. The next
day when I appeared at the breakfast-table in my new
togs, Christian's father could hardly recognize me, but
when he did he slapped me on the back and exclaimed:

was quite expert in wood and metal turning, although he never served apprenticeship, as they do in Europe, in order to learn these things. When I told Christian that, according to my information on the immigrant ship, I was doomed to serve in America my apprenticeship as a greenhorn, he said that a European greenhorn must have told me that, and added, in an offhand manner, that I would be a greenhorn as long only as I thought that I was one. My description of a European apprenticeship amused him much, and he called it worse than the slavery which was abolished here by the Civil War only a few years prior to that date. When I asked him where he got all those strange notions, he told me that these notions were not strange but genuine American notions, and that he first got them from his mother, who was a native American. His father and his father's German friends, he admitted, had the same notions as that greenhorn on the immigrant ship. Christian certainly looked like a Friesland German, but his thoughts, his words, and his manner of doing things were entirely different from anything I ever saw in Europe. He was my first glimpse of an American boy, just as the Vila on the Delaware farm was my first vision of an American girl, and her mother my first ideal of a noble American woman. They were the first to raise that mysterious curtain which prevents the foreign-born from seeing the soul of America, and when I caught a glimpse of it I loved it. It reminded me of the soul of my good people in Idvor, and I felt much more at home. The idea of being a greenhorn lost many of its horrifying features.

Christian left New York during that autumn to go into a shop in Cleveland. Without him, West Street had no attractions for me. I moved to the East Side of New York, so as to be near Cooper Union and its hospitable library. I spent many hours in it after my days of labor, or after my numerous unsuccessful daily trips in search of employment. It was my spiritual refuge when things looked black and hopeless. As winter approached, jobs grew alarmingly scarce, and my money was rapidly approaching the zero level. My hall-room in Norfolk Street was cheerless and cold, worse even than my little attic in Prague. Neither the room nor its neighborhood attracted me in daytime; I preferred to walk along the endless avenues. This exercise kept me warm and gave me a chance to make frequent inquiries for a job at painters' and paper-hangers' shops. When the prospects for work of this kind appeared hopeless, I struck a new idea. Instead of walking more or less aimlessly, in order to keep myself warm and familiarize myself with the ways of the great city, I followed coal-carts, and when they dropped the coal on the sidewalk I rang the bell and offered my services to transfer the coal from sidewalk to cellar. I often got the job, which sometimes was a stepping-stone to other less humble and more remunerative employment. After placing the coal in the cellar and getting my pay, I would often suggest to the owner that his cellar and basement needed painting badly; most cellars and basements do. The owner on being informed that I was a painter out of work, a victim of the economic crisis, often yielded. The idea of a young and ambitious painter being compelled to carry coal from sidewalk to cellar at fifty cents a ton made a strong plea, stronger than any eloquence could make. The scheme worked well; it did not lead to affluence, but my room-rent was always paid on time, and I never starved. Often and often, however, I had to keep my appetite in check. I always had enough to buy my bowl of hot coffee and a brace of crullers for breakfast in a restaurant on wheels, stationed near Cooper Union, where Third Avenue car-drivers took their coffee on cold winter mornings.

During periods of financial stringency my lunches were a bowl of bean soup and a chunk of brown bread, which

preached. I thought of Vila and her mother on the banks of the golden Delaware, and of the glorious opportunities which they pointed out ahead of me, and I wondered whether farmer Brown was one of these opportunities; if so, then there were some opportunities in America from which I wished to run away.

One Sunday evening, after the church service, farmer Brown introduced me to some of his friends, informing them that I was a Serbian youth who had not enjoyed all the opportunities of American religious training, but that I was making wonderful progress, and that some day I might even become an active member of their congregation. The vision of my orthodox mother, of the little church in Idvor, of the Patriarch in Karlovci, and of St. Sava, shot before my eyes like a flash, and I vowed to furnish a speedy proof that farmer Brown was wrong. The next day I was up long before sunrise, having spent a restless night formulating a definite plan of deliverance from the intolerable boredom inflicted upon me by a hopeless religious crank. The eastern sky was like a veil of gold and it promised the arrival of a glorious April day. The fields, the birds, the distant woods, and the friendly country road all seemed to join in a melodious hymn of praise to the beauties of the wanderer's freedom. I bade good-by to the hospitable home of farmer Brown and made a bee-line for the distant woods. There the merry birds, the awakening buds on the blushing twigs, and the little wild flowers of the early spring seemed to long for the appearance of the glorious sun in the eastern sky. I did not, because I was anxious to put as much distance as possible between farmer Brown and myself before he knew that I had departed. When the sun was high in the heavens I made a halt and rested at the edge of woods on the side of a hill. A meadow was at my feet, and I, recalling the words of poet Nyegosh, watched for "the bright-eyed dewdrops to glide along the sunbeams

NASSAU HALL, PRINCETON UNIVERSITY

to the heavens above." The distant view as seen from the elevation of my resting-place disclosed, near the horizon, the silhouette of a town with towers and high roofs looking like roofs of churches. After some three additional hours of wandering, I crossed a bridge over a canal and found the distant town. There seemed to be one street only where business was done; the rest of the town appeared to me like so many beautiful convents. The tramp of many miles through woods and meadows without any breakfast had made me ravenously hungry and somewhat tired. The peaceful aspect of the monastic-looking town invited me to sit down and rest and enjoy some food. I bought a shining loaf of bread and, selecting a seat under an elm near a building which looked like the residence of the Archbishop of Prague, I started my breakfast. It consisted of bread only, and I enjoyed it as I had never enjoyed breakfast before. Many boys, looking like students, passed by on their way to the ecclesiastical-looking building; one of them watched my appetite as if he envied it, and inquired whether I should like some Italian cheese with my bread. He evidently thought that I was an Italian, being misled by my ruddy cheeks and dark-brown hair. I answered that Serbian cheese would suit me better. He laughed and said that Serbia and Serbian cheese were unknown at Princeton. I answered that some day perhaps Princeton might hear from Serbia. It is a curious fact that, in 1914, I was the first man who was invited to Princeton to give an address on the subject of the Austrian ultimatum to Serbia. The late Moses Taylor Pyne was my host, and I pointed out to him the elm in front of Nassau Hall where I had breakfasted some forty years prior to that time. The students received my address very enthusiastically; Dernburg addressed them two weeks later, and their heckling broke up the meeting.

After finishing the loaf, I basked in the warm rays of

III

THE END OF THE APPRENTICESHIP AS GREENHORN

The visions of Princeton persisted in my mind like after effects of strong light upon the retina. That gentle youth's suggestion that he might some day see me enrolled as a student at Princeton kept ringing in my ears, and sounded like mockery. A peasant boy from a Serb village who a little over two years previously was wearing a peasant's sheepskin coat and cap to become a fellow student of those youths who looked like young aristocrats seemed impossible. A European aristocrat would never have suggested such a thing, and that puzzled me. I saw an endless chain of difficult things between me and my enrolment as a student at Princeton, the home for gentle American youth. Social unpreparedness, I felt, was a much more serious difficulty than unpreparedness in things which one can learn from books. This difficulty could not be overcome by associating with people east of the Bowery, and I was heading that way. The nearer the train approached New York the less anxious I was to return to it. From Nassau Hall to the Bowery was too abrupt a change, and from the Bowery to Nassau Hall the change would have been even more abrupt. I compromised and looked up Christian's home on West Street.

Christian was still in Cleveland, but his father received me with open arms and promised to find me a job. In less than a week he found me one in a famous cracker factory on Cortlandt Street. An acquaintance of his with the name Eilers, a Frieslander and distant relative of a famous German writer of that name, was employed

72

there; he steered me during my first experiences in the factory. A place was given me in a squad of boys and girls who punched the firm's name upon a particular kind of biscuit. The job was easy from the point of view of physical strength, but it required much manual dexterity. In spite of my ambition to advance to a high place in the squad I progressed very slowly. I soon discovered that in manual dexterity the American boys and girls stood very high; my hands moved fairly rapidly after some practice, but theirs vibrated. I made up my mind that America was not a field in which I should gather many laurels by efforts requiring much manual dexterity. That idea had occurred to me before, when I first observed Christian handling his lathe. One day I was at the delivery desk of the Cooper Union Library, showing my library check to a youth behind the desk who countersigned it before a book was delivered to me. I noticed that he wrote rapidly, using sometimes his right hand and sometimes his left with equal ease and with much skill. "How can I ever compete with American boys," said I, "when they can write with either hand better than I can write with my right hand!"

There never was a doubt in my mind that American adaptability which I observed on every occasion was in a great measure due to manual training which young people used to get here. Christian's suggestion, mentioned above, that "a boy can learn anything quickly and well enough to earn a living if he will only try," I saw in a new light, when I watched the work of those boys and girls in the factory. Yes, American boys can, but not European, thought I. Lack of early manual training was a handicap which I felt on every step during my early progress in America. My whole experience confirmed me in the belief that manual training of the youth gives them a discipline which school-books alone can never give. I discovered later that three of the greatest characters in American history, Franklin, Jefferson, and Lincoln, excelled in practical arts requiring dexterity, and that the constructive genius of the American nation can, in part, be traced to the discipline which one gets from early manual training.

The great opportunities which, according to my good friends on the Delaware farm, awaited me in this country were certainly not in the direction of arts requiring great manual dexterity. The country of baseball offered, I thought, very few opportunities in this direction to a foreign-born boy. I was convinced of that every time I made a comparison between myself and the other boys who were doing the same manual work in the factory that I did. They were my superiors. In one thing, however, I thought I was their superior. They did not know much about the latest things described in the *Scientific American,* nor in the scientific supplements of the Sunday *Sun,* which I read assiduously with the aid of a pocket dictionary. The educational opportunities in the factory also escaped them. Jim, the boiler-room engineer and fireman of the factory, became interested in my scientific reading and encouraged me by paying several compliments to my interest in these things. He once suggested that some day, perhaps, I might become his scientific assistant in the boiler-room, if I did not mind shovelling coal and attending to the busy fires. He was joking, but I took him seriously. Every morning before the factory started I was with Jim, who was getting the steam up and preparing to blow the whistle and start the wheels going. I volunteered to assist him "shovelling coal and attending to the busy fires," and after a time I understood the manipulations in the boiler-room quite well, according to Jim. The steam-engine excited my liveliest interest. It was the first opportunity that I had ever had to study at close range the operations of a steam-engine, and I made the most of it, thanks to Jim's

Reproduced by permission of Cooper Union

AN EARLY VIEW OF COOPER UNION

patient interest in my thirst for new information. He was my first professor in engineering.

One exceptionally hot afternoon during that summer found Jim prostrated by heat and I volunteered to run the boiler-room until he got well. I did it during the rest of that afternoon, much to the surprise of everybody, but was not allowed to continue, because a fireman's license was required for that. When Jim returned I urged him to help me get a license, but he answered that an intelligent boy, eager to learn, should not cross the Atlantic for the purpose of becoming a fireman. "You must aim higher, my lad," said Jim, and he added that if I continued to make good use of my pocket dictionary and of my scientific reading I should soon outgrow the opportunities offered by the New England Cracker Factory in Cortlandt Street. He never missed a chance to encourage me and to promise new successes for new efforts. In that respect he reminded me much of my mother.

Jim was a humble fireman and boiler-room engineer; his early education was scanty, so that he was not much on books; but he stood in awe in the presence of books. Referring to my habit of carrying a pocket dictionary in my hip pocket and looking up in it the meaning and the pronunciation of every word which was new to me, he would exclaim, jokingly, "Look in the book," whenever some obscure points arose in our boiler-room discussions. His admiration for books was much increased when I related to him the story of James Watt and his experiments with the steam-engine, a story which I had dug out in an old encyclopædia in the Cooper Union Library. When I told him that James Watt had perfected his steam-engine and thus started the development of the modern steam-engine several years before the Declaration of Independence, he dropped a remark which I never forgot. He said: "The English made us write the Declaration of Independence, and they also gave us the steam-engine with which we made our independence good." Jim was not much on learning but he was brimful of native practical philosophy.

Jim had a relative attending classes at Cooper Union and encouraged me to join several of its evening classes, which I did. I reported to him regularly the new things which I learned there. This practice benefited me even more than it did Jim, because in trying to explain to him the laws of heat phenomena, which were explained to me in the evening lectures at Cooper Union, I got a very much better hold of them. The first ideas of sound and light I caught on the pasture-lands of my native village; the first ideas of the phenomena of heat I caught in the boiler-room in Cortlandt Street and at Cooper Union lectures. These lectures, supplemented by Jim's boiler-room demonstrations, proved much more effective than the instruction which I had received from my teacher Kos, in Panchevo. Kos was a Slovene, a native of that beautiful valley in Carniola, in the very bosom of the Dolomites; it is nearer to being an ideal dreamland than any other spot in Europe. To Kos, as to every true Slav, and particularly to the Slovenes of Carniola, the poetical side of physical phenomena appealed most strongly. Hence his patient listening to my enthusiastic professions of the belief that sound and light were different forms of the language of God. But as I watched the busy flames under Jim's boilers, and understood how they were sustaining the strenuous efforts of steam to supply every hustling wheel in the factory with driving power, I understood for the first time that there is also a prose in physics not a bit less impressive than its poetry. It is this prose which interested Jim, the fireman, just as it did the Cooper Union lecturer. Their chief concern was what heat can do and not what it is. My Slavonic craving for knowing what heat is was soon satisfied by reading a poem in prose concerning the nature of heat. But of that later.

During my very first visits to the Cooper Union Library I saw a great painting hung up in the northwest corner of its large reading-room. It was called "Men of Progress," and represented a group of very learned-looking men. I admired the painting, but took no pains to find out its meaning. One day, while reading in the Cooper Union Library, I saw quite near me an old gentleman standing and carefully scrutinizing what was going on. I imagined, at first, that he had stepped out of that painting. I looked again and found that the figure in the painting which I fancied had walked out was still there and that the old gentleman near me was undoubtedly the original from which the artist had painted that figure. The ambidextrous youth behind the library-desk told me afterward that the old gentleman was Peter Cooper, the founder of Cooper Union, and that he was one of the group of famous men represented in the great painting. He looked as I imagined the Patriarch of Karlovci must have looked. He was a striking resemblance to St. Sava, the Educator, as he is represented on an ikon in our church in Idvor. The same snowy locks and rosy complexion of saintly purity, and the same benevolent look from two luminous blue eyes. Peter Cooper was then eighty-five years of age, but he looked as lively as if he were going to live another eighty-five years. His personality as revealed by his appearance inspired me with awe, and I read everything I could lay my hands on concerning his life; then I read about the lives of the other great men who were associated with Peter Cooper in that historical painting. Some of these men were: Morse, the first promoter of the electric telegraph; Joseph Henry, the great physicist, head of the Smithsonian Institution, and founder of scientific bureaus in Washington; McCormick, the inventor of the reaper; Howe, the inventor of the sewing-machine; Ericsson, the engineer of the *Monitor*, and so forth. My study of their lives was a timely preparation for my visit to Philadelphia, to see the Centennial Exposition, the preparatory work for which I had seen two years prior to that time, when, returning from the Delaware farm, I stopped at Philadelphia to search for opportunities.

The work of those great captains of industry forming the group in the great painting, "Men of Progress," was in evidence in every nook and corner of the Centennial Exposition. This great show impressed me as a splendid glorification of all kinds of wonderful mechanisms, driven by steam and animal power, which helped to develop the great resources of the United States. All scientific efforts exhibited there concerned themselves with the question of what things can do, rather than what they are. The show was also a glorification of the great men who first formulated, clearly stated, and fought for the ideals of the United States. I saw that fact proclaimed in many of the historical features of the exposition, and I did not fail to understand clearly that the show took place in Philadelphia because the Liberty Bell and the Declaration of Independence were first heard in Philadelphia. When I left Philadelphia and its show I carried away in my head a good bit of American history. The Americanization process which was going on within me was very much speeded up by what I saw at the Centennial Exposition.

On my return to New York I told Jim, the fireman, that he was right when he said: "The English made us write the Declaration of Independence, and they also gave us the steam-engine with which we made our independence good." But, instructed by my study of the lives of men who were represented in the painting "Men of Progress," and by what I learned at the Philadelphia exposition of these men and of the leaders of the Amer-

From an engraving by John Sartain after a painting by J. Schussele, reproduced by the courtesy of Cooper Union

Dr. Morton   Colt   Saxton   Peter Cooper Professor Henry Ericsson   Bigelow

Bogardus   McCormick   Goodyear   Dr. Mott   Burden   Jennings

               Mott   Sickles   Morse   Hoe   Blanchard Howe

MEN OF PROGRESS—AMERICAN INVENTORS

ican Revolution, I suggested to Jim that the steam-engine without great men behind it would have been of little avail. "Yes," said Jim, "the Declaration of Independence without men of character and brains behind it would also have been of little avail; and the great aims of the Civil War without men like Lincoln and Grant behind them would have ended in a foolish fizzle. This country, my lad," exclaimed Jim with much warmth, "is a monument to the lives of the men of brains and character and action who made it." Jim threw out this chunk of wisdom with the same ease and in the same offhand manner which he displayed when he threw a few shovelfuls of coal upon the busy fires under his boilers. To him it was an obvious truth; to a lad like myself, who was accustomed to look upon countries as monuments to kings and princes and their victorious armies, it was a revelation; and I said so. This brought from Jim another epigrammatic remark to the effect that my trip to America would teach me nothing if it did not teach me first to squeeze out of my mind all foolish European notions and make room for new ideas which I might pick up here and there in this new world. Jim's sayings were always short and to the point and their record in my mind never faded.

Jim was very popular with everybody in the factory, and the fact that he thought well of me improved my standing much. A Mr. Paul, the youngest and most active member of the New England Cracker Factory in Cortlandt Street, paid frequent visits to the boiler-room. I had an idea that Jim's views of things interested him just as much as the operations of the boiler-room. One morning he made a very early visit before the steam-whistle had blown and the steam-engine had started on its daily routine, and he found me in the boiler-room, a busy volunteer fireman. Jim introduced me to him in a jocular way as a student who found his way from Princeton to Cortlandt Street, where in daytime I was rapidly learning every trick of the biscuit industry while in the evening I was absorbing all the wisdom of Cooper Union. A few days later Mr. Paul informed me that my fame as a painter of baker-wagons and of basements on Lexington Avenue, and also my record as a student in mechanical drawing in the evening classes of Cooper Union, had reached the board of directors of the New England Cracker Factory, and that they had resolved to offer me a new job. I was advanced to the position of assistant to the shipping clerk. It meant not only more pay but also social advancement. I was no longer a workman in the factory, who worked for wages; I was a clerk who received a salary. I felt as people in England probably feel when peerage is conferred upon them. My fellow workers in the factory, including Eilers, who first got me the job, showed no envy. They agreed with Jim, who told them that I was "smart." Jim used the same word which my Vila on the banks of the Delaware had used whenever I made a good recitation in English, and I saw in it a good omen. Jim and Vila and Christian of West Street were my authorities, who expressed what I considered a competent opinion upon my apprenticeship as greenhorn, and that opinion was favorable. I felt assured that the apprenticeship was soon coming to an end.

My duties as assistant to the shipping clerk were to superintend the packing of biscuits, to help address with brush and paint the boxes in which they were packed, and to see to it that they were shipped on time. A squad of some thirty girls did the packing and they seemed at first inclined to file objections whenever I found fault with their packing. They seemed to resent being bossed by an immigrant youth whose foreign accent would "stop a train," as they sometimes expressed it. I found out from Jim that the principal object of their resentment was to make me angry, because when my Serbian temper was up my accent became most atrocious and that furnished them a most hilarious amusement. I soon became convinced that my success as assistant to the shipping clerk demanded a perfect control of my temper and a speedy improvement of my accent, each of them a most difficult task.

My efforts to control my temper were frequently put to severe tests. Now and then a biscuit, well aimed, would hit me on the head, and my Serbian blood would rush to my cheeks and I would look daggers at the supposed offender. "Look at the bashibozouk," one of the girls would sing out on these occasions, and another would add: "Did you ever see such a Bulgarian atrocity?" These words were in everybody's mouth at that time and they referred to the incidents of the Balkan War of 1876–1878, which Serbia, Montenegro, and Russia were waging against the Turks. A third girl would stick her tongue out and make funny faces at me in response to my savage glare. She evidently tried to make me laugh, and I did laugh. Then a fourth girl would sing out: "Oh, look at the darling now; I just love him when he smiles." Then they all would sing:

> "Smile, Michael, smile,
> I love your sunny style."

I did smile, and every day I smiled more and more, after I had discovered that the girls did not really dislike me, but just loved to tease me whenever I showed any signs of a European greenhorn. I dropped the airs put on by European superiors in authority and gradually the girls became friendly and began to call me by my first name instead of mockingly addressing me as "Mister" as they addressed the old shipping clerk. "You are getting on swimmingly, my lad," said Jim one day, and he added something like this: "The girls are calling you Michael, just as they call me Jim. We are popular, my boy, but

life was a series of all kinds of controls difficult to manage, he answered that nothing is difficult when it becomes a habit. "Just examine my boiler-room," he said, "and you will find that everything is controlled. The centrifugal governor controls the speed of the engine; the safety-valve limits the pressure of steam; every fire has a regulator of its air draft, and every oven has a temperature indicator. I know them all and I watch their operations without knowing that I am doing it. Practice makes perfect, my lad, and perfection knows no difficulties even in a boiler-room as full of all kinds of tricks as human life is." Jim's sermons were always short and far ahead of anything I had ever heard in the churches in Delaware City, or in Dayton, New Jersey, or in the Bowery Mission, or in any other church which up to that time I had visited in this country; and, moreover, they were not accompanied by congregational singing, which bored me. I understood why so many blacksmiths and other people of small learning made a great success as preachers in this country, whereas in my native village the priest, who prided himself upon his learning, was obliged to read those sermons only which were sent to him by the bishop of the diocese. I suggested to Jim in a jocular way to quit the boiler-room and become a preacher, and he answered that the boys and girls of the New England Cracker Factory in Cortlandt Street furnished a sufficiently large field for his religious and educational mission. Jim's assistance helped me much to let the dream about Jane fade away gradually and make room in my imagination for the dreams which I first saw at Princeton under that elm-tree in front of Nassau Hall.

The factory in Cortlandt Street was in many respects a college in which Jim was the chaplain; and it had a professor who should be mentioned here. It also had a dormitory; several of the young fellows employed in the factory lived on the top floor of the building. I was one

of them, and I did not change my quarters when I was advanced to the position of assistant to the shipping clerk. Two great attractions kept me there. One was that the other fellows were out every evening visiting theatres and music-halls, so that I had the whole loft, and, in fact, the whole factory all to myself and to a chum of mine, who was much older than I in years but not in his position in the factory. His name was Bilharz, and he was the second attraction. He was the opposite to Jim and to every human being I had ever met. He knew nothing of nor did he care for the concrete or practical things of life, but always lived in dreams about things which happened centuries ago. He knew Latin and Greek and all kinds of literatures, but never made any attempts to make any use of his knowledge. Factory work of the humblest kind was good enough for him, and I believed that he would have been satisfied to work for his board only, if pay had been refused him. He informed me once by an accidental slip of the tongue that he had studied theology at the University of Freiburg, in southern Germany, and would have become a priest if an unfortunate love-affair had not put an end to his ecclesiastical aspirations. He had no other aims when he came to America, he said, than to work for a modest living and to lead a life of profound obscurity, until the Lord called him away from this valley of tears, as he expressed it. He used a German expression and called the earth a "Thraenenthal." Although a German he spoke English well, being a finished scholar and having lived in America for a number of years, and having a memory for sound which impressed me as most remarkable. He sang like a nightingale, but only on evenings when we were all alone. Ecclesiastical music was his favorite, and during many an evening the strains of "Gloria in Excelsis Deo," "Ave Maria," and "I Know That My Redeemer Liveth" rang forth from the spacious lofts of the

New England Cracker Factory and lost themselves in the silence of night among the deserted buildings of Cortlandt Street, which were alive in daytime only. I never tired listening to his recitations of Latin and Greek poetry, although I did not understand it, and of selected passages from Shakespeare and Goethe, which I did understand. He loved the art of articulate speech and of melody, and he thought of things only that happened three thousand years ago when Homer sang and the Olympian gods guided the destinies of men, but he cared for nothing else. The steam-engine and every other kind of mechanism were to him a deadly prose which, in his opinion, Satan had invented for the purpose of leading astray the spirit of man. "They are the weapons by which people like you are keeping in slavery people like me," he said once, jokingly, referring to my interest in the boiler-room operations and to my admiration of the great captains of industry whose lives I studied and whose work I had seen and admired at the Philadelphia exposition. I sometimes suspected that he felt alarmed by what he considered my worship of false gods, and that this impelled him to do everything he could for my redemption from heathenism. My admiration for his learning was great, but my sympathy for his misfortunes was even greater. His hands were once caught in a machine and most of his fingers had become stiff and crooked so that they looked like the talons of a falcon. His sharp features, a crooked nose and protruding eyes, supported this suggestion of a falcon, but his awkward, flat-footed walk suggested a falcon with broken wings; to say nothing of his other misfortunes which made him in spirit also a falcon with broken wings.

I felt that he knew a great deal more about the Jane incident than he cared to disclose to me. One day I referred to her as the Minnehaha of Cortlandt Street. "Minnehaha, laughing water," exclaimed Bilharz:

"where did you ever get that, you boiler-room bug?"
and he laughed as if he had never heard a funnier thing
in his life. "From Jim, the boiler-room hermit, to Longfellow, one of the greatest of American poets, is a tremendous jump, a *salto mortale*, as they call it in a circus,"
said Bilharz; and then, growing more serious and thoughtful, he added something like this: "It is really wonderful
what the eyes of a woman can do! They are just like the
stars in the heavens, encouraging us poor mortals to aim
at celestial heights. But many a sky-rocket seemed to
be sailing for the stars and suddenly it found itself buried
in mud. I am one of these sky-rockets," said Bilharz;
"you are not, thanks to the timely intervention of a kindly
divinity." He meant Jim. Then, continuing in his usual
dramatic manner, he recited in Latin an ode of Horace,
in which the poet speaks of a youth trusting to the beaming countenance of his lady-love as a mariner trusting
to the sunlit ripples of a calm sea who is suddenly upset
by a treacherous squall and, being rescued, gratefully
offers his wet garments in sacrifice to Neptune, the god
of the sea. After translating the ode and explaining its
meaning to me he urged me to hang my best clothes in
the boiler-room as a sacrifice to Jim, the divinity which
had rescued me from the treacherous waves of "Minnehaha, laughing water." "You are the luckiest of mortals, my boy," said Bilharz to me; "some day you will
provoke the envy of the gods and then look out for stern
Nemesis!" I did not understand the full meaning of these
classical allusions, but he assured me that some day I
should. I told Bilharz that my luck, of which he spoke
so often, was mostly due to my being so near to a man
of his learning, and that I thought he ought to be a professor in Nassau Hall at Princeton. He declined the
honor, but offered to prepare me for it, and I accepted.

Bilharz was very moody and for days and days he had
nothing to say to anybody, not even to me! Nobody

else cared, because nobody understood him, but I did care. When he discovered that I sincerely admired his learning and was interested in his puzzling personality he became more communicative, sometimes almost human. His English accent was excellent, and I asked his opinion about my accent and he assured me with child-like frankness that it was rotten, but that it could be fixed up if I submitted to a course of training prescribed for me by my Vila on the Delaware farm. "I could not be your Vila, deformed as I am," said he, referring to his crippled fingers and to his awkward walk, "but I will gladly be your satyr and teach you how to imitate not only the sounds of human language but also, if you wish it, the melodies of birds and the chirping of bugs. The satyrs are great in that." I knew that he could, because many an evening while I was on the dormitory loft of the factory reading the Mayflower Compact, the Declaration of Independence, the American Constitution, Patrick Henry's and Daniel Webster's speeches, and Lincoln's speech at Gettysburg, Bilharz, in another part of the building, would be imitating sounds of all kinds of birds and bugs, after he had grown tired reciting Greek and Latin poetry and singing ecclesiastical songs. That was his only amusement, and he enjoyed it when he was sure that nobody was listening; he made an exception in my case. We finally made the start in what he called my preparation for Nassau Hall. In the course of less than a month I finished reciting to Bilharz the Declaration of Independence, the American Constitution, and Lincoln's speech at Gettysburg, submitting to many corrections and making many efforts to give each word its proper pronunciation, and finally he accepted my performance as satisfactory. By that time I knew these documents by heart and so did Bilharz, and he, in spite of himself, liked them so well that he accused me of conspiring to make an American out of him. "You are sinking rapidly,

my boy, in the whirlpool of American democracy, and
you are dragging me down with you," said Bilharz one
evening, when I objected to some of the amendments
which he offered in order to harmonize the American
theory of freedom with the principles of German socialism.
He admitted that he, a loyal Roman Catholic, did not
care much for German social democracy, but that he often
wondered why the American enthusiasts for democracy
did not take German social democracy and save themselves the trouble of writing the Declaration of Independence. I called his attention to the fact that American
democracy is much older than German social democracy,
and he, somewhat irritated by that suggestion and by
my defense of American democracy, as I understood it,
suggested that he should resign his position as my teacher
and become my pupil. His flippant criticism of American
democracy and my stiff defense of it helped me much to
see things which otherwise I should have missed, but
these discussions threatened the entente cordiale between Bilharz and myself. Finally we compromised and
changed our course of reading, dropping things relating
to political theories and taking up poetry. Longfellow's
and Bryant's poetry were my favorites. "The Village
Blacksmith" and "Thanatopsis" I knew by heart and enjoyed reciting to Bilharz, who was greatly pleased whenever in these recitations I avoided making a single serious
break in my pronunciation. After reading some of Shakespeare's dramas which Booth and other famous actors
like Lawrence Barrett and John McCullough were playing at that time, I visited the theatre often, and from
my modest gallery seat I would analyze carefully the
articulation of every syllable which Booth and the other
actors were reciting. Booth did not have a big voice;
it was much smaller than the voice of Lawrence Barrett
or of powerful John McCullough, but I understood him
better. Bilharz explained it by saying that Booth had

a perfect articulation. "Articulation is an art which the Greeks invented; big voice is brute force common among the Russians," he used to say, protesting whenever he had an opportunity against mere physical strength, which was natural considering his scanty physical resources. He hated both the Russians and the Prussians, because, in his opinion, they both were big brutes. In those days the southern Germans had no love for the Prussians. He never missed a single chance to sing the praises of Greek drama and of the Greek theatre and of everything which flourished during the classical age. He called my attention to the enormous size of Greek theatres and to the necessity of perfect articulation on the part of Greek actors if they were to be heard. "They were great artists," said he; "our actors are duffers only. We are all duffers! Give me the Greeks, give me Homer, Pindar, Demosthenes, Plato, Praxiteles, Phidias, Sophocles, and hundreds of others who spoke the language of the gods and did things which only the divine spirit in man can do, and you can have your Morse, McCormick, Howe, Ericsson, and the rest of the materialistic crew who ran the show at Philadelphia." He certainly told many a fine story when he spoke of the great poets, orators, philosophers, and sculptors of Greece, and his stories impressed me much because they were great revelations to me; they were the first to arouse my interest in the great civilization of Greece. They would have impressed me even more if Bilharz had not displayed a glaring tendency to exaggerate, in order to create a strong contrast between what he called the idealism of classical Greece and what he called the realistic materialism of modern America. According to him the first had its seat among the gods on the ethereal top of Mount Olympus and the second one was sinking deeper and deeper through the shafts of coal and iron mines into the dark caverns of material earth. "No action," said Bilharz, "which needs the assistance of a

steam-engine or of any other mechanism can trace its
origin to idealism nor can it end in idealism." I suggested that every animal body is a mechanism and that
its continuous evolution seems to indicate that the world
is heading for a definite ideal. Bilharz flew up like a hornet
when he heard the word evolution.

A lively discussion was going on in those days between
the biological sciences and theology, Huxley and many
other scientists championing the claims of Darwin's evolution theory and the theologians defending the claims
of revealed religion. I was too young and too untutored
to understand much of those learned discussions, but
Bilharz followed them with feverish anxiety. His theological arguments did not appeal to me, and so far as I
was concerned they lost even the little force they had
when Bilharz turned them against what he called American mechanism and materialism, which he tried to make
responsible for the alleged materialism of the evolution
theory. His political and philosophical theories based
upon blind prejudice created a gap between him and me
which widened every day. Here are some illustrations
of it.

When I described to him the election day of 1876, telling
him that I and thousands of others had stood quietly and
patiently hours and hours in drenching rain in front of
the New York *Tribune* building waiting for the returns
which would tell us whether Hayes or Tilden was to be
the supreme executive head of the United States during
the coming four years; how the next day some of the newspapers had raised a howl of "fraud," accusing the Re-
publican party of tampering with the election returns in
one of the States, but that the people of New York City
and of the whole country had paid no attention, trusting
implicitly to the machinery of government to straighten
out crookedness if it existed, and how this dignity of
American democracy thrilled me when I compared it

with the rows and scandals accompanying elections in
the countries of the military frontier of Austria-Hungary,
he only laughed and ridiculed the whole procedure of
electing by ignorant voters the supreme executive head
of a nation. He told me a story of Aristides of Athens,
who, being requested by a voter to write upon a shell
the name of the man who was to be condemned for some
crime which was not quite clear to the Athenian voter,
wrote down his own name, and Aristides, the just, the
noblest character of Athens, was condemned. But the
condemnation of this just and noble and innocent man
was, according to Bilharz, a condemnation of the Athenian
democracy, whose shortcomings brought the downfall of
Greek civilization, and he added that the shortcomings
of American democracy would bring the downfall of the
old European civilization. The Aristides story interested
me much, but the inference he drew from it made me
think of Christian of West Street, and of his blunt remark: "A European greenhorn must have told you that."
Jim was present at this discussion. He was a strong Pres-
byterian and ridiculed on every occasion what he called
Bilharz's Roman Catholic views. This time he quoted
Lincoln by saying "that government of the people, by
the people, for the people, shall not perish from the earth."
Then he added for the edification of Bilharz that religion
in the Roman Catholic church is of the church, by the
church, for the church, and that this was the real reason
why Bilharz, trained in this kind of theology, would never
understand American democracy. This shocked me, because I expected a fist fight between my two best friends,
but . . . the fist fight did not take place.

I enjoyed taking long walks on Broadway whenever I
had free time, going up on one side and coming down on
the other, inspecting every window in bookstores and
art stores and looking at the latest things in pictorial art,
at the titles of the latest things in literature, and at the

photographs and engravings of prominent men of the day. This gave me quite an idea of what was going on in the American world of intellect. Bilharz never joined me because, he said, there was nothing worth seeing on these inspection tours of mine. Once during the noon recess I managed to take him around the corner of Cortlandt Street and Broadway trusting to luck to meet a certain great person whom I had seen several times before and recognized because I saw his photograph in the shop-windows of Broadway. I succeeded, for there in the midst of the Broadway crowd appeared before us William Cullen Bryant, the author of "Thanatopsis"! He was then the editor of *The Evening Post*, which was located on Broadway not far from Cortlandt Street. I pointed him out; Bilharz held his breath and, referring to the wonderful appearance of the great poet, he said: "There is the only man in this materialistic land of reapers and mowing-machines and chattering telephone disks who could take a seat among the gods on Mount Olympus and be welcomed there by the shades of the great idealists of Greece."——

At another time I managed to take him as far as City Hall; it was some holiday, and the papers had announced that President Hayes and his secretary of state, William Evarts, would be at City Hall at noon, and they were there. Bilharz and I stood in a huge crowd, but we had a good view of the President and of his secretary of state, and we heard every word of their short speeches. They were dressed just like everybody else, but their remarkable physiognomies and their scholarly words convinced me that they belonged to the exalted position into which the vote of the people had placed them. The New York *Sun* was a bitter opponent of President Hayes and published his picture on the editorial page of every one of its issues. In this picture the letters spelling "fraud" were represented as branded across the expansive brow

the peasants are apt to buy. A Kranyats was a familiar sight in my native village, and he was always welcome there, because he was a Slovene, a near kin to the Serb; and the Serb peasants of the Banat plains loved to hear a Kranyats describe the beauties of the mountainsides of little Slovenia on the eastern slope of the Dolomites. When I disclosed my name to Lukanitch he asked me for my father's name, and when I told him that it was Constantine and that he lived in Idvor, Banat, his eyes looked like two scintillating stars. He gave me a big hug and a a big tear threatened to roll down his cheek when he said: "Ko che ko Bog?" (Who can fathom the will of God?) After relating to me that my father had befriended him nearly thirty years prior to that time and that he had often stayed as guest at my father's house whenever his annual tours as Kranyats took him through Idvor, he begged me to come to his house on the following Sunday and dine with his family. I did, and there I met his good wife, a fine Slavonic type, and also his son and daughter, who were born in this country and who looked like young Slavs with Americanism grafted upon them. His son was about to graduate from a high school, and his daughter was preparing for Normal College. They were both American in manner and sentiment, but father and mother, although deeply devoted to the United States, the native country of their children, were still sincerely attached to the beautiful customs of the Slovene land. The children preferred to speak English, but they delighted in Slovene music, which they cultivated with much enthusiasm. That made their parents most happy. Their home was a beautiful combination of American and Slovene civilization. Once they invited me to an anniversary party and I found the whole family dressed in most picturesque Slovenian costumes; but everybody in the party, including even old Lukanitch and his wife and all the Slovenian guests, spoke English. Most of the guests were Americans, but they enjoyed the Slovenian dishes and the Slovenian music, singing, and dancing as much as anybody. To my great surprise the American girls, friends of Miss Lukanitch, played Slovenian music exceedingly well, and I thought to myself that a sufficiently frequent repetition of parties of that kind would soon transform the American population in the vicinity of Prince Street into Slovenians. This interaction between two very different civilizations gave me food for thought, which I am still digesting mentally.

Lukanitch and his family became my devoted friends, and they were just as interested in my plans and aspirations as if I had been a member of their family. The old lady had a tender heart, and she shed many a tear listening to bits of my history from the time when I bade good-by to father and mother at the steamboat landing on the Danube, five years before. The disappearance of my roast goose at Karlovci, my first railroad ride from Budapest to Vienna, my dialogues with the train conductor and the gaudy station-master at Vienna, and my free ride in a first-class compartment from Vienna to Prague in company with American friends amused her and her husband hugely. I had to repeat the story many a time for the benefit of her Slovenian friends. She begged me repeatedly to tell the story of my crossing of the Atlantic and of my hardships as greenhorn, being evidently anxious to have her children hear it. I did it several times, scoring much success on each occasion, and as a reward she loaded me with many little gifts and with many enjoyable feasts on Sundays and holidays. My interpretation of the American theory of freedom, which I had derived from reading the lives and the utterances of the great men who made this country and from my three years' struggles as greenhorn, found a most appreciative audience in the Lukanitch family. They applauded Jim's sentiment, that this country is a monument to the great men who made it, and not to a single family like the Hapsburgs of Austria-Hungary. Old Lukanitch offered to engage me as his teacher in American history, and young Lukanitch offered to get me an invitation from the principal of his high school to deliver an oration on the Declaration of Independence. The offers were not meant very seriously, but there was enough sincerity in them to make me believe that my training in America was recognized as having substantial value by people whose opinion deserved respect. I saw in it the first real recognition referred to in the prophecy of my fellow passenger on the immigrant ship who said: "No matter who you are or what you know or what you have, you will be a greenhorn when you land in the New World, and a greenhorn has to serve his apprenticeship as greenhorn before he can establish his claim to any recognition." I said to myself: "Here is my first recognition small as it may be, and I am certainly no longer a greenhorn."

No longer a greenhorn! Oh, what a confidence that gives to a foreign-born youth who has experienced the hardships of serving his apprenticeship as a greenhorn! Then there were other sources of confidence: I had a goodly deposit in the Union Dime Savings Bank and it was several thousand times as big as the nickel which I brought to Castle Garden when I landed. Besides, I had learned a thing or two in the evening classes at Cooper Union, and my English was considered good not only in vocabulary and grammar, but also in articulation, thanks to Bilharz. Young Lukanitch assured me that my knowledge of English, mathematics, and science would easily take me into college. He even prophesied a most successful college career, pointing at my big chest and broad shoulders and feeling my hard biceps. "You will make a splendid college oarsman," said he, "and they will do anything for you at Columbia if you are a good oarsman, even if you do not get from Bilharz so very much Greek or Latin." At that time Columbia stood very high in rowing. One of her crews won in the Henley Regatta, and its picture could be seen in every illustrated paper. I had seen it many a time and remembered the looks of every member of that famous crew. Young Lukanitch was so enthusiastic about it that he would have gone to Columbia himself if his father had not needed him so much in his steel-tool business. He did his best to turn my eyes from Nassau Hall to Columbia. He succeeded, but not so much on account of my prospects in rowing as on account of other things, and among them was the official name of that institution: "Columbia College in the City of New York." The fact that the college was located in the city of New York carried much weight, because New York appealed to my imagination more than any other place in the world. The impression which it made upon my mind as the immigrant ship moved into New York Harbor on that clear and sunny March day when I first passed through Castle Garden, the Gate of America, never faded. My first victory on American soil was won in New York when I fought for my right to wear the red fez.

IV

FROM GREENHORN TO CITIZENSHIP AND COLLEGE DEGREE

THE Columbia boat-race victory at Henley occurred in 1878. By that time I had already with the assistance of Bilharz finished a considerable portion of my Greek and Latin preparation for Princeton—or, as I called it, for "Nassau Hall." My change of allegiance from Princeton to Columbia was gradual.

Columbia College was located at that time on the block between Madison and Park Avenues and between Forty-ninth and Fiftieth Streets in New York City. One of its proposed new buildings was, according to report, to be called Hamilton Hall, in honor of Alexander Hamilton. When I learned this I looked up the history of Alexander Hamilton. One can imagine how thrilled I was when I found that Hamilton left the junior class at Columbia College and joined Washington's armies as captain when he was barely nineteen, and at twenty was lieutenant-colonel and Washington's aide-de-camp! What an appeal to a young imagination! Few things ever thrilled me as much as the life of Alexander Hamilton. Every American youth preparing for college should read the history of Hamilton's life.

One cannot look up the history of Hamilton's life without running across the name of another great Columbia man, John Jay, first Secretary of Foreign Affairs, appointed by Congress, and the first Chief Justice of the United States, appointed by Washington, and a stanch backer of brilliant Hamilton. Chancellor Livingston,

100

another great Columbia man, administered the first constitutional oath of office to Washington; he also completed the purchase of Louisiana from France. The more I studied the history of Hamilton's time the more I saw what tremendous influence Columbia's alumni exerted at that time. Cortlandt Street being near Trinity Church, I walked there to look at the Hamilton monument in the Trinity churchyard. This monument was the first suggestion to me of a bond of union between Trinity Church and Columbia College. Before long I found many other bonds of union between these two great institutions.

Every time I passed Columbia College in my long walks up-town and looked at the rising structure of Hamilton Hall, I thought of these three great Columbia men. What student of Hamilton's life could have looked at Hamilton Hall on Madison Avenue without being reminded of the magnificent intellectual efforts which two young patriots, Hamilton and Madison, made in the defense of the federalist form of the new American Republic? It happened thus that my memory of Nassau Hall at Princeton gradually faded, although it never vanished. The famous boat-race victory of a Columbia crew at Henley would not alone have produced this effect. It was produced by three great New York men of the Revolutionary period who were alumni of "Columbia College in the City of New York." Columbia had at that time a school of mines and engineering, separate from the college. I was much better prepared for it than for Columbia College, thanks to the evening lectures at Cooper Union, and to my natural inclination to scientific studies, but I imagined that the spirit of Hamilton, Jay, and Livingston hovered about the academic buildings of Columbia College only.

Bilharz rejoiced when I informed him of my decision to put on extra pressure in my classical studies preparatory for Columbia College, and congratulated himself, as I found out later, that he had succeeded in rescuing me

College, from Jim and Bilharz to patriarchal President Barnard and the famous professors at Columbia, appeared to me like a jump over Columbia's great and venerable traditions. Old Lukanitch and his family and their American friends helped me much to start building a bridge over this big gap, but the more I associated with these people, who lived around humble Prince Street, not far from the Bowery, the more I saw my shortcomings in what I called, for want of a better name, "social preparedness." "How shall I feel," I asked myself, "when I begin to associate with boys whose parents live on Madison and Fifth Avenues, and whose ancestors were friends of Hamilton and of Jay?" Their traditions, I was sure, gave them an equipment which I did not have, unless my Serbian traditions proved to be similar to their American traditions. My native village attached great importance to traditions, and I knew how much the peasants of Idvor would resent it if a stranger not in tune with their traditions attempted to settle in their historic village.

The examination of immigrants which I saw at Castle Garden, when I landed, had made me think that traditions did not count for much in Castle Garden. But my principal acquisition from my apprenticeship as greenhorn had been the recognition that there are great American traditions, and that the opportunities of this country are inaccessible to immigrants who, like Bilharz, do not understand their meaning and their vital importance in American life. Vila's mother on the Delaware farm, my experiences with Christian of West Street, and Jim's little sermons in the Cortlandt Street boiler-room had impressed this idea upon my mind very strongly. The mental attitude of a young Serb from the military frontier was naturally very receptive to impressions of that kind. My respect for the traditions of my own race had prepared me to respect the traditions of the country which

I expected to adopt, and hence I was afraid that my cultural equipment was not up to the standards of the college boys who were brought up in accordance with American traditions. My subsequent experience showed me that my anxiety was justifiable.

I have already mentioned that a short time before I ran away from Prague and headed for the United States I had read a translation of Harriet Beecher Stowe's "Uncle Tom's Cabin." It had been recommended to me by my American friends who gave me a free ride in a first-class compartment from Vienna to Prague. My mention of the name of this great woman, together with the names of Lincoln and of Franklin, as Americans that I knew something about, had won me the sympathy of the immigration officials at Castle Garden, who, otherwise, might have deported me. Her name was deeply engraved upon the tablets of my memory. The famous Beecher-Tilton trial was much discussed in those days in the New York press, and when I heard that Henry Ward Beecher was a brother of the author of "Uncle Tom's Cabin" my opinion of Tilton was formed, and no judge or jury could have changed it. Beecher's photographs, which I saw in my inspection tours on Broadway, confirmed me in my belief that he was a brother worthy of his great sister. Young Lukanitch and his sister knew of Beecher's fame and, although strict Roman Catholics, they consented to accompany me on my first pilgrimage to Beecher's Plymouth Church, and there I saw the great orator for the first time.

His face looked to me like that of a lion and his long gray locks, reaching almost to his shoulders, supported this illusion. The church provided a setting worthy of his striking appearance. The grand organ behind and above the pulpit supplied a harmonious musical background to the magnificent singing of the large choir. I felt that the thrilling music was tuning me up for the

One of those honey-hearted disciples was a Doctor Charles Shepard, of Columbia Heights, Brooklyn. He and his family were Unitarians, I think, but they often attended Plymouth Church on account of their great admiration for Beecher. Doctor Shepard's family was, in my opinion, a family of saints; generosity, refinement, and spiritual discipline filled the golden atmosphere of their home. When I disclosed my plans to the good doctor, he offered to help me carry them out. He was an ardent advocate of the curative powers of hydropathy in conjunction with proper diet and total abstinence from alcohol and tobacco. "Cleanliness is next to godliness" was his motto, and by cleanliness he meant freedom from unclean habits of every kind. His theory was successfully practised in his hydropathic establishment, and he flourished, and his institution was famous. His very old father, over eighty years of age, who managed the office of the establishment, needed assistance, and Doctor Shepard offered me the position and spoke of getting a friend of his to help me prepare for entrance to Columbia. His friend was Professor Webster, who taught Greek and Latin at the Adelphi Academy in Brooklyn. I jumped at Doctor Shepard's offer, although the prospect of deserting Jim and Bilharz made me hesitate. But Jim applauded my decision and he recalled his prophecy that I should soon outgrow the opportunities of the New England Cracker Factory. Bilharz expressed his gratification that he had contributed to my progress, and he certainly had, both by what he praised and by what he condemned. He was sincere in both, but his praise was founded upon a rare knowledge of classical literatures, while his condemnation was due to prejudice against science and against American democracy. The real secret of his grip upon my imagination I shall disclose later.

Professor Webster was an ideal pedagogue; his pupils were boys and girls from some of the best families of

Brooklyn. Their teacher was to them an apostle of classical culture, in which they were much interested, partly because of their admiration for their beloved teacher. After a few private lessons he invited me to join his classes in Greek and Latin, where I was received with many signs of cordiality from both the boys and the girls. Like myself, they were preparing for college. I attended these classes three times a week and entertained them much by my continental pronunciation of Greek and Latin, which I had learned from Bilharz, who had also taught me to recite the Greek and Latin hexameter with proper intonation. This delighted the heart of Professor Webster and of his pupils. Recitations of Greek and Latin verses with faultless rhythm were all which at first I could offer to the entertainment of my classmates. After a while I entertained some of them with Serbian poetry and also with Serbian kolo dancing. I made every effort to make them forget that I was a Balkan barbarian; but everybody, as if reading my thoughts, assured me that I was contributing more to the Adelphi Academy than I was getting in return. I knew better. I felt that the association with those splendid boys and girls and with Professor Webster contributed much more to my preparation for Columbia than all the book work which I had ever done anywhere.

Doctor Shepard and his family saw the rapid change in me, I thought, and many of their evidences of approval were very encouraging. When I first met Doctor Shepard he was strongly pro-Turkish whenever the Balkan war, which was raging at that time, was discussed. He had a notion that the Serbians were a rebellious and barbarous race. During the early part of 1879 he gradually shifted to the Serbian side, and I was bold enough to take all credit for it to myself. I considered his and his family's approval the best test of the success of my efforts to understand the American standards of conduct. This success

ginning of my college career; muscle and brawn are splendid things to take along when one enters college, and have while in college. Several incidents in my college career bear upon the interesting feature of athletics in American college life, and I shall describe them later even at the risk of appearing egotistical. This feature is characteristically American and is quite unknown on the continent of Europe.

Eight hours each day I devoted to study: three in the morning to Greek, three in the afternoon to Latin, and two in the evening to other studies. It was a most profitable summer outing of over three months, and it cost me only thirty dollars; the rest was paid in sawing and splitting of kindling-wood. Whenever I read now about the Kaiser's activities at Doorn, I think of my summer activities in 1879, and I wonder who in the world suggested my scheme to William Hohenzollern!

During the last week of September of that year I presented myself at Columbia for entrance examinations. They were oral, and were conducted by the professors themselves and not by junior instructors. The first two books of the Iliad, excepting the catalogue of ships, and four orations of Cicero, I knew by heart. My leisure time at my Passaic River "villa" had permitted me these pleasant mental gymnastics; I wanted to show off before Bilharz with my Greek and Latin quotations; to say nothing of the wonderful mental exhilaration which a young student gets from reading aloud and memorizing the words of Homer and of Cicero. The professors were greatly surprised and asked me why I had taken so much trouble. I told them that it was no trouble, because Serbs delight in memorizing beautiful lines. The Serbs of Montenegro, for instance, know by heart most of the lines which their great poet Nyegosh ever wrote, and particularly his great epic "The Mountain Glory." I told them also of illiterate Baba Batikin, the minstrel of my native village, who knew most of the old Serbian ballads by heart. Besides, I assured the professors, I wanted to do in Greek and Latin as well as I possibly could, so as to gain free tuition. For the other studies I was not afraid, I told them, and they assured me that my chances for free tuition were certainly good. The other examinations gave me no trouble, thanks to my training with Bilharz and with the lecturers in the evening classes at Cooper Union. A note from the Registrar's office informed me a few days later that I was enrolled as a student in Columbia College with freedom from all tuition fees. There was no person in the United States on that glorious day happier than I!

The college atmosphere which I found at Columbia at that time gave me a new sensation. I did not understand it at first and misinterpreted many things. The few days preceding the opening of the college sessions I spent chasing around for a boarding-house, while my classmates were hanging around the college buildings, making arrangements to join this or that fraternity, and also solidifying the line of defense of the freshmen against the hostile sophomores. There was a lively process of organization going on under the leadership of groups of boys who came from the same preparatory schools. These groups led and the others were expected to follow without a murmur. Insubordination or even indifference was condemned as lack of college spirit. This spirit was necessary among the freshmen particularly, because, as I was informed later, there was a great common danger—the sophomores! I saw some of this feverish activity going on, but did not understand its meaning and hence remained outside of it, as if I were a stranger and not a member of the freshman class, which I heard described, by the freshmen themselves, as the best freshman class in the history of Columbia. The sophomores denied this in a most provoking manner; hence the hostility. Notion. But how many immigrants to this land can be made to understand this?

Some little time after this incident I was approached by the captain of the freshman crew, who asked me to join his crew. I remembered young Lukanitch's opinion about oarsmanship at Columbia, and I was sorely tempted. But, unfortunately, I had only three hundred and eleven dollars when I started my college career, and I knew that if I was to retain my free tuition by high standing in scholarship and also earn further money for my living expenses I should have no time for other activities. "Study, work for a living, no participation in college activities outside of the recitation-room! Do you call that college training?" asked the captain of the freshman crew, looking perfectly surprised at my story, which, being the son of wealthy parents, he did not understand. I admitted that it was not, in the full sense of the word, but that I was not in a position to avail myself of all the opportunities which Columbia offered me, and that, in fact, I had already obtained a great deal more than an immigrant could reasonably have expected. I touched his sympathetic chord, and I felt that I had made a new friend. The result of this interview was that my classmates refrained from asking me to join any of the college activities for fear that my inability to comply with their request might make me feel badly. I had their sympathy, but I missed their fellowship, and therefore I missed in my freshman year much of that splendid training outside of the classroom which an American college offers to its students.

At the end of the freshman year I gained two prizes of one hundred dollars each, one in Greek and the other in mathematics. They were won in stiff competitive examinations and meant a considerable scholastic success, but, nevertheless, they excited little interest among my classmates. Results of examinations were considered a personal matter of the individual student himself and not of his fellow classmen. The prizes were practically the only money upon which I could rely to help carry me through my second year. The estimated budget for that year, however, was not fully provided for, and I looked for a job for the long summer vacation. I did not want a job in the city. My kindling-wood activity of the preceding summer suited me better, and after some consultation with my friend Christopher, the kindling-wood peddler of Rutherford Park, I decided to accept a job on a contract of his to mow hay during that summer in the various sections of the Hackensack lowlands. No Columbia athlete ever had a better opportunity to develop his back and biceps than I had during that summer. I made good use of it, and earned seventy-five dollars net.

When my sophomore year began I awaited the cane rush which, according to old Columbia custom, took place between the sophomores and the freshmen at the beginning of each academic year, and I was prepared for it; I knew also what it meant to "play the game." This time my class had to do the attacking and I helped with a vengeance. The muscles which had been hardened in the Hackensack meadows proved most effective and the result was that shortly I had the freshmen's cane on the ground, and was lying flat over it, covering it with my chest. The pressure of a score of freshmen and sophomores piled up on top of me threatened to squeeze the cane through my chest bone, which already, I imagined, was pressing against my lungs, my difficult breathing leading me to think that my last hour had come. Fortunately, the umpires cleared away the lively heap of struggling boys on top of me, and I breathed freely again. Some freshmen were found stretched alongside of me with their hands holding on to the stick. An equal number of sophomores held on, and, consequently, the umpires declared the rush a draw. Nobody was anxious to have another

man of the board of trustees of Columbia College. They thought that he paid too much attention to the fashion-plates of London, and dressed too fashionably. There were other Columbia boys at that time who, I thought, dressed just as fashionably, and yet they were very popular; but they were fine athletes, whereas my opponent was believed to rely too much upon the history of his long name and upon his splendid appearance. He certainly was a fine example of classical repose; his classmates, however, admired action. He was like a young Alcibiades in breeding, looks, and pose, but not in action.

Some of the old American colleges have been accused from time to time of encouraging snobbery and a spirit of aristocracy which is not in harmony with American ideas of democracy. My personal experience as student at Columbia gives competency to my opinion upon that subject. Snobs will be found in every country and clime, but there were fewer snobs at Columbia in those days than in many other much less exalted places, although Columbia at that time was accused of being a nest of dudes and snobs. This was one of the arguments advanced by those friends of mine at the Adelphi Academy who tried to persuade me to go to Princeton or Yale. The spirit of aristocracy was there, but it was an aristocracy of the same kind as existed in my native peasant village. It was a spirit of unconscious reverence for the best American traditions. I say "unconscious," and by that I mean absence of noisy chauvinism and of that racial intolerance by which the Teutonism of Austria and the Magyarism of Hungary had driven me away from Prague and from Panchevo. A name with a fine American tradition back of it attracted much attention, but it was only a letter of recommendation. He who was found wanting in his make-up and in his conduct when weighed by the best Columbia College traditions —and they were a part of American traditions—had a lonely time during his college career, in spite of his illustrious name or his family's great wealth. Foreign-born students, like Cubans and South Americans, met with a respectful indifference so long as they remained foreigners. Needless to say, many of them adopted rapidly the attractive ways of the Columbia boys. But nobody would have resented it, or even paid any attention to it, if they had retained their foreign ways. A hopeless fellow became a member of that very small class of students known at that time as "muckers." They complained bitterly of snobbery and of aristocracy. I do not believe that either the spirit of plutocracy, or of socialism and communism, or of any other un-American current of thought could ever start from an American college like Columbia of those days, and bore its way into American life. That type of aristocracy which made the American college immune from contagion by un-American influence existed; it was very exacting, and it was much encouraged. But when American college boys, accused of bowing to the spirit of aristocracy, have among them a Hamilton, a Livingston, a DeWitt, and several descendants of Jay, and yet elect for class president the penniless son of a Serbian peasant village, because they admire his mental and physical efforts to learn and to comply with Columbia's traditions, one can rest assured that the spirit of American democracy was very much alive in those college boys.

My success with the Octagon class established my reputation as a doctor for "lame ducks." This was the name of those students who failed in their college examinations, usually examinations in Greek, Latin, and mathematics. Lame ducks needed a special treatment, called *coaching*. I became quite an expert in it, and presently I saw a flock of lame ducks gathering around me, offering liberal rewards for a speedy cure. My summer vacations no longer called me to the Passaic River to cut kindling-

"Winthrop is very fond of you," said Rutherfurd, senior, before he sailed for Europe, "and if you fail to pull him through, that will be the end of his college career. Your job is a difficult one, almost hopeless, but if you should succeed you would place me under a very great obligation." I was already under great obligations to him, for he had disclosed a view of the world of intellect before my eyes such as nobody else ever had. New York never produced a finer type of gentleman and scholar than was Lewis Rutherfurd. His personality impressed me as Henry Ward Beecher's had, and I could easily have persuaded myself that he was the reincarnation of Benjamin Franklin. I vowed to spare no effort in my attempts to "place" him "under a very great obligation."

Winthrop co-operated at first. But Winthrop's friends at the Racquet Club, at the Rockaway Hunt Club, and at Newport were puzzled, and they inquired what strange influences kept Winthrop in monastic seclusion at the Rutherfurd Stuyvesant estate in the backwoods of New Jersey. Besides, a stableful of steeplechasers, which had won many prizes, stood idle and looked in vain for their master, Winthrop, to train them. Even the servants on the estate looked puzzled and could not decipher the mysterious change that had come over their young auto-crat. A foreign-born youngster, a namesake of Michael, the Irish gardener on the estate, seemed to be supreme in authority, and that puzzled the servants still more. Winthrop was making great scholastic efforts, in order to please his distinguished father, but he was a high-strung youth and after a while his behavior began to suggest the fretting of a thoroughbred protesting against the bit handled by the heavy touch of an unskilled trainer. I saw a crisis approaching, and it finally came. Winthrop suddenly refused to do another stroke of work unless the programme of work was greatly modified to permit him to make occasional trips to the Racquet Club, to the

Rockaway Hunt Club, and to Newport. I knew what that meant, and promptly refused; a hot discussion followed, and some harsh words were spoken, resulting in a challenge by Winthrop; I accepted and agreed that the best man was to have his way during the remainder of the summer. Winthrop, the great racquet player of America, the famous steeplechase rider of Long Island, and the young aristocrat, kept his word, and responded eagerly to my calls for additional scholastic efforts. He was a noble, handsome, and manly American youth whose friendship I was proud to possess.

In the autumn Winthrop got rid of most of his conditions, proceeded with his class, and eventually graduated from Columbia in 1884. My imaginative chum, Winthrop's cousin, composed a great tale describing this incident and called it: "A Serbian Peasant versus an American Aristocrat." Those who had the good fortune to enjoy the humor of this tale (and among them was F. Marion Crawford, the novelist and cousin of my chum) pronounced it a great literary accomplishment, and they all agreed that Winthrop was the real hero of the story; he had played the game like a thoroughbred. Mr. Rutherfurd, senior, enjoyed the tale as much as anybody, and he was delighted with the result of our summer work. Winthrop's behavior did not surprise him, because, he assured me, Winthrop played the game as every American gentleman's son would have played it. "Every one of your classmates," exclaimed this trustee of Columbia College, "would have done the same thing; or he would be unworthy of a Columbia degree." The first function of the American college, according to him, was to train its students in the principles of conduct becoming an American who is loyal to the best traditions of his country.

My senior year opened even more auspiciously than my sophomore or my junior year had. Lewis Ruther-

ship and scientific learning, he told me, had been acquired long after he had graduated from Williams College.

Many of my fellow students were, just like myself, very fond of athletics and of other activities outside of the college curriculum, and yet we were enthusiastic students of Greek literature, of history and economics, of constitutional history of the United States, and of English literature. But here was the secret: Professor Merriam was a wonderful expounder of the great achievements of Greek civilization; Professor Monroe Smith made every one of us feel that history was an indispensable part of our daily life; Professor Richmond Mayo-Smith made us believe that political economy was one of the most important subjects in the world; and Professor Burgess' lectures on the Constitutional History of the United States made us all imagine that we understood the spirit of 1776 just as well as Hamilton did. These professors were the great scholars of Columbia College when I was a student there, and they had most attractive personalities too. The personality of the professors, like that of the famous Van Amringe, and their learning, like that of the venerable President Barnard, were the best safeguards for students who showed a tendency to devote themselves too much to the worship of muscle and the fighting spirit, and of activities outside of the college curriculum. Fill your professorial chairs in colleges with men of broad learning, and of commanding personality, and do not worry about the alleged evil influences of athletics, and of other college activities outside of the recitation-room. That was the recommendation of trustee Rutherfurd forty years ago; to-day I add: the college needs great professors just as much as the various research departments of a university need them; perhaps even more.

Literary societies, college journalism, glee-club practice, and exercises in the dramatic art consumed, when I was a college student, just as much of the college student's time as athletics did. They and athletics constituted the outside college activities. The recitation-room brought the student into touch with the personalities of the professors; college activities outside of the recitation-room, whether they were athletics or anything else, brought the student into touch with the personalities of his fellow students. Each one of these influences had, according to the experiences of my college life, its own great value, and contributed its distinct share to what is usually called the character-forming of the college student, but what Rutherfurd, the Columbia College trustee, called training in the principles of conduct becoming an American who is loyal to the best traditions of his country. Neither one nor the other influence can be weakened without crippling seriously that great object which trustee Rutherfurd called "the historical mission of the American college."

There was another educational activity which should be mentioned here. My regular attendance at Plymouth Church I considered one of my most important college activities outside of the recitation-room. Beecher's sermons and Booth's interpretations of Shakespeare were sources of stirring inspiration. They occupied a very high place among my spiritual guides. Beecher, Booth, and several other men of genius who were active in New York in those days were, as far as my college training was concerned, members of the Columbia College faculty. This is what I probably meant when I said to my friends at the Adelphi Academy that "Columbia College in the City of New York" was the port for which I was sailing and that Beecher's church in Brooklyn was a component part of Columbia College. Taking college activities in this broader sense I always believed that the spiritual, intellectual, and artistic activities in the city of New York were component parts of Columbia College; they certainly contributed much to the fulness of my college life. I often wondered whether this was in the minds of

from the first day of my landing at Castle Garden was due to my feeding upon the spiritual food offered to me daily by a civilization in which I was living, and which I wished to understand but did not understand. My preparation for college lifted here and there the mist which prevented my vision from seeing the clear outline of American civilization. Columbia College brought me into touch with the college life of American boys and with men of great learning and wonderful personalities, and they helped me to dispel every particle of that mist, and there in the clear sunshine of their learning I saw the whole image of what I believed to be American civilization: a beautiful daughter of a beautiful mother, which is the Anglo-Saxon civilization. The memory of this vision always recalled to my mind the ode of Horace which opens with the line:

"O matre pulchra filia pulchrior!"

The study and the contemplation of these two civilizations, the ancient civilization of Greece and the new civilization of the Anglo-Saxons, which appealed to me as the two greatest civilizations of human history, made every other study in my college curriculum appear insignificant, although I gained several prizes in the exact sciences, and although I never gave up the idea that my future work would be in the field of science.

But there is another and perhaps the most potent reason why science figures so little in the preceding part of the story of my college career. Instruction in the exact sciences in those days was most elementary, not only at Columbia College but also in most American colleges. For instance, laboratory work in physics and in chemistry was not a part of the Columbia College curriculum, and the lecture-room told me less about physics than I had known from my studies of Tyndall's popular publications and from the Cooper Union instruction before I entered college. The question "What is Light?" I brought with me from the pasture-lands of my native village, and the professor of physics at Columbia College offered no answer to it except to refer to vibrations in an ether, the physical properties of which he admitted he could not satisfactorily describe. On this point he did not seem to be much wiser than my humble teacher Kos in Panchevo. My mentor, Rutherfurd, was always interested in this question, as in many other advanced questions in science, and he took much delight in discussing them with me. He was the first to inform me that the great question, "What is Light?" would probably be answered when we understood more clearly a new electrical theory advanced by a Scotch physicist, Maxwell by name, who was a pupil of the great Faraday.

One day toward the end of my senior year I told my mentor, Rutherfurd, of a lecture-room experiment performed by Rood, his friend, at that time professor of physics at Columbia College. This experiment was the first announcement to me that Faraday was one of the great discoverers in electrical science. The experiment was simplicity itself, and consisted of a loose coil of copper wire, held in the left hand of the lecturing professor, the terminals of the coil being connected to a galvanometer supported on the wall of the lecture-room, so that its needle could be seen by every student in the room. When Rood, like a magician manipulating a wand, moved with his right hand a small magnet toward the coil, the distant galvanometer needle, impelled by a force which up to that time was a mystery to me, swung violently in one direction, and when the magnet was moved away from the coil the galvanometer needle swung just as violently in the opposite direction. When one terminal, only, of the coil was connected to the galvanometer, and thus the electric circuit of the coil was broken, the motion of the magnet produced no effect. *"This is Faraday's*

in the naturalization office to witness the naturalization ceremony except myself and a plain little clerk. The graduation ceremonies in the Academy of Music were presided over by the venerable President Barnard; his luxuriant snowy-white locks and long beard, and his luminous intelligence beaming from every feature of his wonderful face, gave him the appearance of Moses, as Michael Angelo represents him; and the academy was crowded with a distinguished and brilliant audience. The little clerk in the office handed me my naturalization papers in an offhand manner, thinking, apparently, of nothing but the fee due from me. President Barnard, knowing of my high standing in the graduating class and of my many struggles to get there, beamed with joy when he handed me my diploma amidst the applause of my numerous friends in the audience. When I left the naturalization office, carrying my precious multicolored and very ornate naturalization papers, the crowd in City Hall Park was moving about as though nothing had happened; but when I stepped down from the academy stage, with my Columbia diploma in hand, my old friend Doctor Shepard handed me a basket of roses with the best wishes of his family and of Henry Ward Beecher; Mr. and Mrs. Lukanitch were there, and the old lady kissed me, shedding tears copiously and assuring me that if my mother were there to see how well I looked in my academic silk gown she also would have shed many a tear of joy; numerous other friends were there and made much fuss over me, but all those things served only to increase the painful contrast between the gay commencement ceremonies and the prosy procedure of my naturalization on the preceding day. One ceremony made me only a Bachelor of Arts. The other made me a citizen of the United States. Which of the two should have been more solemn?

There was a picture which I had conjured up in my

PHOTOGRAPH OF PUPIN TAKEN IN 1883 WHEN
HE GRADUATED AT COLUMBIA

imagination when first I walked one day from the Cortlandt Street factory to Wall Street to see the site of old
Federal Hall. The picture was that of Chancellor Livingston administering the constitutional oath of office to
President Washington. To me it was a picture of the
most solemn historical act which New York or any other
place in the world ever had witnessed. When the little
clerk in the naturalization office handed me my naturalization papers, and called upon me in a perfunctory way
to promise that I would always be loyal to the Constitution of the United States, the picture of that historical
scene in Federal Hall suddenly reappeared to me, and
a strange mental exaltation made my voice tremble as I
responded: "I will, so help me God!" The little clerk
noticed my emotion, but did not understand it, because
he did not know of my long-continued efforts throughout
a period of nine years to prepare myself for citizenship of
the United States.

As I sat on the deck of the ship which was taking me
to the universities of Europe, and watched its eagerness
to get away from the busy harbor of New York, I thought
of the day when, nine years before, I had arrived on the
immigrant ship. I said to myself: "Michael Pupin, the
most valuable asset which you carried into New York
harbor nine years ago was your knowledge of, and profound respect and admiration for, the best traditions
of your race . . . the most valuable asset which you are
now taking with you from New York harbor is your knowledge of, and profound respect and admiration for, the
best traditions of your adopted country."

V

FIRST JOURNEY TO IDVOR IN ELEVEN YEARS

It was a beautiful June afternoon when from the gay deck of the *State of Florida* I saw the low coast-line of Long Island disappear in the distance. With it disappeared the land the first glimpse of which I had caught so eagerly on that sunny March morning nine years before, when the immigrant ship *Westphalia* carried me into New York harbor. As I had approached this coast my busy imagination had suggested that it was the edge of the cover of a great and mysterious book which I had to read and decipher. I had read it for nine long years, and my belief that I had deciphered it made me confident that I was quite rich in learning. Besides, there were my Bachelor of Arts diploma and my naturalization papers; and, of course, I thought, they were the best evidence in the world that I was returning to see my mother again rich in learning and in academic honors, as I had promised her nine years before in that letter from Hamburg.

The sky was clear, the sea was smooth, and its sharp and even horizon line toward which the ship was heading promised a peaceful temper of the powers which controlled the motions of the air above and of the waters below our ship. The comforts of the ship and the fair prospects of a fine voyage were recorded in the smiling faces of my fellow passengers. A group of lively schoolgirls from Washington, making their first trip to Europe under the guidance of an old professor with long gray hair and shaggy beard, looked like so many nymphs playing around

a drowsy Neptune. They formed the central group of
the happy passengers. There were a number of college
boys on board. Some of them had friends among the
Washington nymphs; by clever manœuvring it was arranged that the college boys, including myself, should
sit at the same table with the playful nymphs. The gray-
locked professor, whom I called Father Neptune (and
the title stuck to him), was somewhat reluctant at first,
but finally he gave his consent to this "wonderful" proposition, as the girls called it, and he sat at the head of
the table, presiding with a dignity which fully demonstrated that he deserved the title "Father Neptune."
The jolly captain assured us that his good old ship never
carried a more exuberant company of youngsters across
the Atlantic. But this was not the fierce Atlantic which
I had seen nine years before. It was an Atlantic which
apparently studied to please and to amuse. All kinds of
pleasant things happened during the voyage, as if arranged purposely for our amusement. Many schools of
porpoises approached the merry ship, and I suggested
that they visited us in order to pay their respects to Father
Neptune and his beautiful nymphs. This suggestion was
accepted with vociferous acclamation, and it was agreed
that free play be granted to our imaginations. Let your
fancy take any course at your own risk, was our motto.
When the visiting porpoises hustled off like a squadron
of reconnoitring horsemen leaping gaily over the smooth
waves, as if in a merry steeplechase, it was suggested by
one of the girls with a lively imagination that they were
anxious to report to the chief of staff of a great host which,
hidden in the depths of the quiescent Atlantic, controlled
the ocean waves. She, the oracle, as we called her,
prophesied that when these heralds had delivered the
report that Father Neptune and his fair nymphs were
passing in triumphal procession through their watery
realm, then all things in the heavens above and in the

sea below would bow to the will of Neptune and his play-ful crew.

Two spouting whales appeared one day in the distance, and our busy imaginations suggested that they were two men-o'-war, sent by the friendly submarine host to pay their homage to Neptune and his nymphs, and to serve as escort to our speedy ship. Nothing happened which did not receive a fanciful interpretation by our playful imaginations. The wonderful phosphorescence of the waves, which were ploughed up in the smooth sea by the gliding ship, supported the illusion that our voy-age was a triumphal procession along an avenue illumi-nated by the mysterious phosphorescent glow. We were headed for Scotland, by a route which passed to the north of Ireland, and as our course approached the northern latitudes the luminous twilights of the North Atlantic made us almost forget that there ever was such a thing as a dark night. Good old Neptune had quite a job to round up his nymphs in the late hours of the evening and make them turn in and exchange the joys of the busy days for the blessings of the restful nights. His job was hopeless when the northern midnights displayed the awe-inspiring streamers of the northern lights, and that hap-pened quite frequently. Those wonderful sights in them-selves would have made it worth while crossing the At-lantic. On such evenings the exuberance of the college boys and of the schoolgirls from Washington was wide awake until after midnight, watching the luminous and continuously changing streamers of the polar regions, telling stories, and singing college songs. These evenings reminded me much of the neighborhood gatherings in Idvor. One of them was devoted to original stories; each member of the gay party had to spin out an original tale. My story was called "Franciscus of Freiburg," and it referred to Bilharz, the Greek guslar of Cortlandt Street. The disappointments of his youth, the calm resignation with which in his more mature years he passed his hermit days on a top loft in Cortlandt Street, and his search for consolation in the poetry of Rome and Greece made quite an impression; and to my great surprise there was not a single giggle on the part of the irrepressible nymphs. This was the first story that I ever composed, and it made a hit, but its success was completely ruined when, prompted by modesty, I suggested that any tale describing disappointments in love is sure to be taken very seriously and sympathetically by young girls. A violent protest was filed by the girls, and I pleaded guilty of the offense of disturbing public peace. A mock trial, with Father Neptune as the presiding judge, condemned me and imposed the fine that I tell at once, and without preparation, another original tale. I described the first speech of my life on St. Sava's day, some thirteen years earlier, and its unexpected effect upon my mischievous chums in Idvor, comparing it with the unexpected effect of my Franciscus story. I regretted it, because the fairies from Washington had an endless chain of questions about Idvor and my prospective visit to it. Never before had I had a better opportunity to observe the beautiful relationship between American boys and girls. Its foundation I recognized to be the idea of the big brother looking after the safety, comfort, and happiness of his sister, the same idea which is glorified in the Serbian national ballads.

One pleasant incident followed another in quick succession during our triumphant procession over the northern Atlantic, and all the powers which control the temper of the ocean were most kind and generous to us, just as our fair oracle had prophesied it. When the cliffs of Scotland hove in sight, reminding us that our voyage was approaching its end, there was no thrill of joy such as there was when the immigrant ship, which first took me into New York harbor, approached the Long Island coast.

Not even the countless sea-gulls which gracefully circled around the black cliffs, and with their shrill notes welcomed us to the hospitable shores of Scotland, were able to dispel the gloom which the sight of land produced among the members of Neptune's table. Nobody in our congenial company seemed to be anxious to say good-by to the good old ship and to the golden atmosphere of the sweet-tempered Atlantic. Most of them had never crossed the Atlantic before, and since the voyage was practically over I thought that there was no harm in describing to them some of the terrors of the Atlantic, which I had experienced when I crossed it nine years before. The pictures of those experiences were like the pictures from another world, and not from the same Atlantic which thrilled us with its sunshine, twilight, phosphorescent glows, and glorious streamers of the northern lights. The comparison between my wretched fellow passengers on the storm-tossed immigrant ship and the radiant company on the ship which brought us to Scotland afforded me a splendid opportunity to thank Father Neptune for permitting me to join his beautiful court. His favor, I said, was almost as great as the favor of the immigrant officials at Castle Garden, who had allowed me to land with only five cents in my pocket. The professor complimented me upon my word pictures which showed the glaring contrasts between the two voyages, and then he referred to two pictures which, he said, he had in his mind. They also showed, he said, in glaring contrasts, the difference between a certain youngster on the immigrant ship to which I referred, and a Columbia College graduate, who had contributed his share to the comfort and happiness of Neptune's court. When he suggested that he would give much to be with me when I met my mother, and that he wondered whether she would recognize me, my young friends suggested, quite seriously, that they would all go to Idvor if I joined them in their continental tour. I replied that their tour was along a meandering line through the great places of Europe, whereas mine was a straight line from Greenock to little Idvor, so little that it cannot be found on any map.

There was just one thing which delayed my straight-line journey to Idvor. A visit to Cambridge was necessary in order to arrange for my work at this university during the coming academic year, and I lost no time in reaching it. The sight of the Firth of Clyde, with its wonderfully green slopes, of Greenock, of Glasgow, and even of London made feeble impressions. My mind was centred upon one thought only: the speedy return to Idvor. This also explains why my first sight of Cambridge impressed me much less than my first sight of Princeton when, eight years before, I had enjoyed my loaf of bread under an elm-tree in front of Nassau Hall. F. Marion Crawford, the novelist, had given me a letter of introduction to Oscar Browning, a fellow of King's College; and George Rives, the late chairman of the Board of Trustees of Columbia University, had given me a letter to W. D. Niven, a fellow of Trinity College. Rives, after graduating at Columbia College, won a prize scholarship in classics at Trinity College, and gained there many scholastic honors.

The man at the ancient gate of King's College informed me that Mr. Oscar Browning was away on his summer vacation. At Trinity College I had better luck, and the man at the still more ancient gate of Trinity College took me to Mr. Niven, who reminded me much of Professor Merriam, the great Greek scholar of Columbia College; the same kindly expression of a most intelligent face, and the same gentle light from two thoughtful eyes. As I looked into his eyes I felt that I was catching a glimpse of a world full of those beautiful things which make life worth living. I informed Niven that I wished to come to Cambridge and study under Professor James Clerk Maxwell, the creator of the new electrical theory. Niven looked puzzled and asked me who had told me of this new theory, and when I mentioned Rutherfurd, he asked me what Rutherfurd had told me about it. "That it will probably give a satisfactory answer to the question: 'What is Light?'" I answered, and watched for his reaction. "Did not Mr. Rutherfurd tell you that Clerk Maxwell died four years ago?" asked Niven, and when I said no, he asked me whether I had not seen it in the preface to the second edition of Maxwell's great book which Niven himself had edited. This question embarrassed me, and I confessed frankly that Rutherfurd's son, my chum Winthrop, had presented me with this book on the day of the sailing of my ship; that it was packed away in my bags; and that I did not have any time to examine it during the voyage, because I was too busy helping to entertain twelve beautiful schoolgirls from Washington, who were making their first trip to Europe. Niven laughed heartily and admitted, jokingly, that twelve beautiful girls from Washington were certainly more attractive than any theory, not excepting even Maxwell's great electrical theory. He suggested then that I could study at Cambridge under Lord Rayleigh, who had succeeded Maxwell as professor of physics. I declined the suggestion on the ground that I had never heard of Lord Rayleigh before. Niven laughed again, even more heartily than before, and assured me that Lord Rayleigh was a great physicist in spite of the fact that his great fame had never reached my ears. An English lord a great physicist! The idea struck me as strange, but Niven looked so friendly and so sincere that I could not help believing that he really meant what he said. He invited me to lunch, and before we parted I assured him that I would come back to Cambridge in the following October and place myself under his guidance.

This conference with Niven sobered me up very considerably; it convinced me that my great aspiration and my small preparation in physics were far from being of the same order of magnitude. I confessed to Niven that my success in winning prizes in science at Columbia College had led to my belief that I knew more physics than I really did. "Confession is a splendid thing for the soul," said Niven, and added: "But do not permit that anything I have said dampen your courage. A physicist needs courage, and few mortals were braver than Maxwell. The world knows only a little of his great electrical theory, but it knows even less of his great moral courage." He gave me a copy of Campbell's life of Maxwell; I read it from cover to cover before I left London, and it contributed much to the learning which I had promised to bring to Idvor. It certainly convinced me that Maxwell had a vastly better knowledge of physics when he graduated at Cambridge than I had picked up at Columbia. That gave me much healthy food for serious thought.

A straight line from London to Idvor passes through Switzerland, and I proposed to follow that line in my journey as closely as practicable. My ticket took me from London to Lucerne directly; the journey from Lucerne to Idvor I left undetermined until I reached Lucerne. I had no time nor inclination to explore the wonders of London, Paris, or of any other great place in Europe before I had seen Idvor again. Mother, Idvor, and Maxwell's new electrical theory had brought me to Europe, and I wished to see them as soon as possible, and in the order named; everything else could wait. Besides, I sincerely believed that these places had little to offer to a fellow like me, who knew the great things of New York. I was much disposed to look down upon things in Europe, a mental attitude which is not uncommon among American immigrants when they go back to

pay a temporary visit to Europe. I had it quite strongly, but sobering experiences like the conference with Niven in Cambridge helped me to apply suitable correction factors to this mental attitude. The following brief description of one of these experiences bears upon this point.

The London-Lucerne train crossed the Franco-Swiss frontier very early in the morning, somewhere near Neuchâtel. The delay necessary for the rearrangement of the train gave the passengers ample time to enjoy their breakfast in the garden of the station restaurant. A look to the east caught a sight which made me almost forget my breakfast. The distant snow-covered Alps, bathed in the early sunshine and projected against the background of the luminous blue sky of a July morning, furnished a picture never to be forgotten. I had never seen the Alps before, and this first view of them was of overpowering beauty. An Englishman, a fellow traveller, sitting opposite me at the breakfast-table, noticed my mental exaltation, and asked: "You have never seen the Alps before, have you?" "No," said I. "Oh, what a lucky lad you are!" said the Englishman, adding that he would give much to be in my place. He confessed that he had to climb the peaks of the Alps in order to get those thrills which in former days, when he was of my age, he got by looking at them from the valleys below. At his suggestion we continued our journey to Lucerne in the same compartment, and the stories of his climbing exploits stirred up mightily my imagination, which was already throbbing under the inspiration of the Alpine view which had greeted me that morning. When I informed him that I was in a hurry to reach my native village of Idvor, otherwise I might try some climbing myself, he assured me that a ten days' delay in Lucerne would suffice to prepare me for climbing one of the lesser

peaks, and he mentioned Titlis, not far from Lucerne. He prescribed the training which would provide me with sufficiently steady Alpine legs. From the peak of the Titlis, he said, I could see old Switzerland where the famous legend was born which relates how Tell drove the fear of God into the hearts of the Austrians. I always loved that legend, perhaps because I did not love the Austrian tyrants. When the train had reached Lucerne I saw the wonderful Alpine panorama spread out like an amphitheatre of snow-covered Alpine peaks around its deep-blue lake, and I knew that in spite of my great haste to reach Idvor I would not leave this fairy-land before I had reached the snow-covered peak of Titlis.

I immediately hired a rowboat for a week, and, clad in a rowing shirt with blue and white Columbia stripes and thin tennis trousers, I spent that afternoon exploring the beauty spots of the meandering shore of the historic lake. The joy of rowing and the busy rays of the July sun made me yield to the invitation of the clear waters of the lake to plunge in and hug the waves, which once upon a time carried Tell to safety after he had sent his arrow through the heart of the Austrian tyrant, Gessler. As if imitating the example of Tell, I jumped in just as I was, trusting that subsequent rowing and the sun would dry my scanty attire, and they did. A glorious feeling of freedom from all earthly restraints came over me as, floating on my back, I beheld the blue sky above and the snow-covered peaks around me. It was the same sky and the same luminous peaks, I thought, which five hundred years before saw William Tell chase away the Austrian tyrants from the historic cantons surrounding the lake; from Uri, Schwyz, and Unterwalden. I felt that I was floating in the very cradle where real freedom first saw the light of day. No other spot on earth was more worthy of that immortal fame. My admiration for it never faded after that memorable July afternoon.

Europe rose in my estimation; I was much less inclined to look down upon things European.

The next day I was up very early, feeling "as a strong man ready to run a race," the same feeling which I had experienced at Castle Garden when, nine years before, I woke up early in the morning and hurried off to catch my first glimpse of the great American metropolis. I was just as anxious to hurry off and catch from some mountain-top my first glimpse of Switzerland. Mindful of the suggestions of my English acquaintance on the train, I started with the easiest climb, the Rigi Culm. It is a very easy effort, but I made it difficult by rowing first some ten miles to Weggis, going up to the Rigi and walking down, and then rowing back to Lucerne again on the same day, in the waning hours of the afternoon. An unexpected squall upset my boat, and I had quite a struggle to get back to Lucerne, very late in the evening. The hotel proprietor noticed my mussed-up appearance, but said nothing, seeing that I was not in a communicative mood.

The same strenuous method of preparatory training for the Titlis climb took me up to Mount Pilatus on the next day. But I was not allowed to return on the same day on account of a fierce thunder-storm raging in the valley below, which I watched from the top of the Pilatus. The innkeeper congratulated me upon my rare luck, not only because I had a chance to see the beautiful sight of a thunder-storm as viewed from a point above the thundering clouds, but principally because this thunder-storm prevented me from running the serious risk of descending and rowing back to Lucerne on the same day. Commenting upon the overconfidence of youth, the innkeeper said that every person has a guardian angel, but people intoxicated by wine or by exuberance of youth have two, one on each side. That was his explanation for the alleged fact, he said, that young people and intoxicated

people seldom meet with serious accidents in mountain climbing. Some Americans, he thought, should have several guardian angels. This sarcasm was aimed at me, and it did not miss its mark.

Nevertheless, when on my fifth day in Lucerne I started out very early for the Titlis, I adopted the same strenuous method: rowing to Stansstadt, walking to Engelberg, and climbing to the hospice where I arrived at 11 P. M. I reached at sunrise of the following morning the top of Titlis, and saw the glories of Uri, Schwyz, and Unterwalden as my English friend had promised. But I reached it much exhausted, and if it had not been for the skilled assistance of my trusty Swiss guide, the last four lines of Longfellow's "Excelsior" would have described my Titlis climb quite accurately. I quote the lines:

> "There in the twilight cold and gray,
> Lifeless, but beautiful, he lay,
> And from the sky, serene and far,
> A voice fell, like a falling star,
>   Excelsior!"

Returning from Titlis, I ran into my English friend, and he remarked that I looked a little overtrained. We dined together, and when I told him the story of my six days' Alpine experience, he begged me to hustle off to Idvor and see my mother first, and then return if I cared to pursue my own methods of exploring the beauties of Switzerland. "If you continue pursuing these methods now, I am afraid that your mother will never see you again, because there are not enough guardian angels in all the heavens to prevent you from breaking your neck." I agreed, but assured him that my overstrenuous method of climbing Titlis was worth the risk; it had humbled my vanity and false pride, and made me more respectful to some of the slow ways of old Europe. It convinced me that even after serving my apprenticeship as green-that they attracted my attention. One of them remarked that I could pass for a Serb, if it were not for my manner, my dress, and my very ruddy complexion. The voyage across the Atlantic and a week's tramping in Switzerland were responsible for my exaggerated ruddiness. A second one thought that young Serb peasants in Banat are just as ruddy, particularly during the harvest season, but he admitted that my appearance did not suggest that my occupation was that of a peasant. Another one suggested that I was probably a rich South American with very much red Indian blood in my veins. I laughed and, introducing myself, informed him, speaking Serb with some difficulty, that I was neither a South American nor an Indian, but just a Serb student who was a citizen of the United States. A Serb from the United States was a very rare bird in those days and, needless to say, I was invited most cordially to join the group, which I did. Not one of them reminded me of the alert, well-groomed, athletic, and playful American college boys. They all had long hair brushed back in a careless fashion, affecting the appearance of dreamy poets or disciples of radical doctrines. Most of them had slouch hats with wide brims, indicating radical tendencies. Their faces looked pale and suggested excessive indoor confinement in Vienna and Budapest cafés, playing chess or cards, or discussing radical doctrines. Most of them would have been hazed if they had matriculated in any American college without modifying much their appearance and manner. They certainly took themselves very seriously. They knew, I thought, many things which they had read in books, principally in books dealing with radical social-science theories. Tolstoy's name was mentioned quite often, and the latest apostles of socialistic doctrines also had their share of adulation. They must have observed that conversation about these things bored me, and they asked me, with some display of sarcasm, I thought, whether

American college students took any interest in modern advanced thought. "They do," said I, considerably irritated, "and if it were not for Maxwell's new electrical theory and for other advanced theories in modern physics I should not have come to your moribund old Europe." "Advanced thought in social and not in physical sciences," they said, explaining their original question, and I answered that the most popular American doctrine in social science still rested upon foundations laid a hundred years before that time, in a document called the Declaration of Independence. They knew very little about it, and I knew even less about their radical social-science theories, and we changed the subject of our conversation.

Late in the afternoon the boat approached Karlovci and the hills of Frushka Gora. I could not help reminiscing, and entertained my Serb acquaintances with a description of my experiences with the theological students eleven years before, including the disappearance of my roast goose. My Serbian vocabulary was quite shaky, but nevertheless I made quite a hit, and they begged me to go on with my reminiscences. Whenever I was at a loss for a word, they helped me out. Toward sunset Belgrade hove in sight, and its majestic appearance thrilled me and made my Serb vocabulary run as smoothly as ever. I saluted Belgrade as the acropolis of all the Serbs, and expressed the hope that it might soon become the metropolis of all the southern Slavs. "This is the kind of advanced thought in social and political science that American students are interested in," I said, reminding them of their former question, and I added a few sarcastic remarks about advanced thoughts in social and political science which are not born in the heart of a nation but imported from the dens of French, German, and Russian theorists. They quickly caught what I called the American point of view, but they did not oppose it, for fear, I

thought, of offending me. They saw the American chip on my shoulder, and did not care to knock it off.

I had not seen Belgrade since I was a little boy, and as the boat approached it I saw its high fort rising like a Gibraltar above the waters of the Danube and looking anxiously across the endless plains of Austria-Hungary, which, like wide-open jaws of a hungry dragon, seemed to threaten to swallow it up. Everything I saw in Austria-Hungary looked small and shrivelled up, but Belgrade looked to me as if its proud head would touch the stars. The history of the long-suffering Serb race was grouped around it, and that lifted it up in my imagination to sublime heights. I was much tempted to stop there and climb up to the top of Mount Avala, near Belgrade, and from there send my greetings to heroic Serbia, just as I had sent my greetings to heroic Switzerland from the top of snow-covered Titlis. But I was told to look sharp if I wished to catch the last local boat to Panchevo, and so I bade good-by and au revoir to white-towered Belgrade, as the Serbian guslars call it.

When the local boat arrived in Panchevo a delegation of young men, including one of the Serb students who had come with me from Budapest, transferred me to another boat, which was crowded with what looked like a gay wedding-party. The singing society of Panchevo had chartered this boat to take it and its friends to Karlovci, where a great national gathering of Serbs was to take place on the following day. The earthly remains of the great Serb poet Branko Radichevich were to arrive there from Vienna, where, when still a youth, he died and had been buried thirty years before. His body was to be transferred to and buried near Karlovci, on Strazhilovo hill, which was glorified by his immortal verses. His lyrics were messages to all Serbs, calling upon them to nurse their traditions and prepare for their national reunion. Representative Serbs from all parts of Serbdom

were to assemble in Karlovci to escort the earthly remains of the popular poet to his last resting-place. I was to represent America, hence the invitation to join the Panchevo delegation. Serb nationalism flamed up in my heart again.

Our boat arrived at Karlovci in the early hours of the following morning, and there we found many singing societies and delegates from Voyvodina, Serbia, Bosnia, Hercegovina, and Montenegro—a most picturesque gathering of splendid-looking young men and women, many of them in their national costumes of brilliant colors. The funeral procession started early in the afternoon. The singing societies from the principal centres of Serbdom, lined up in the march in proper succession, took up in turn the singing of the solemn and wonderfully harmonious funeral hymn: "Holy God, almighty God, immortal God, have mercy upon us."

The Orthodox church permits no instrumental music. Those who have had the good fortune to listen to Russian choirs know the power and the spiritual charm of their choral singing. Serb choirs are not their inferiors. No music appeals to our hearts so strongly as the music of the human voice. Every one of the singers in that procession at Karlovci felt that he was paying his last vocal tribute to the sacred memory of the national poet, and his voice rose up to the heavens above as if carried there by the wings of his inspired soul. The effect was irresistible, and there was not a single dry eye in the great national gathering. A dismembered nation united in tears was a most solemn and inspiring spectacle. One could not help feeling that these tears were welcome to the thirsty soil which nourished the roots of Serb nationalism. A nation which is united in song and in tears will never lose its unity. If the governments of Vienna and Budapest had foreseen the emotions which that solemn ceremony would arouse in the hearts of that vast

and representative gathering coming from every part of the dismembered Serbdom, they would never have permitted it. But that would have meant the exercise of the perceptions of subtle psychology, which these governments never had.

When the boat returned to Panchevo, Protoyeray Zhivkovich, the poet-priest, who had first suggested my transference from Panchevo to Prague, was watching for my arrival, and received me with tears of joy in his eyes. He was a protecting friend and adviser of my boyhood days, and he always considered himself indirectly responsible for my wandering away to the distant shores of America. When I thanked him for the choice feast which he had prepared for me, he assured me that his feast was only a feast of food, whereas the feast which I spread out before him when I answered his questions about America was a feast for his soul. I certainly did it, if I interpreted correctly the luminous flashes of his intelligent eyes. He was a man of about sixty, but his vigorous eye was still just as eloquent as the stirring verses of his younger days. "Tell your mother," he said, "that I am happy to bear the whole responsibility for your wandering away to distant America. It is no longer distant; it is now in my heart; you have brought America to us. It was a new world in my terrestrial geography; it is now a new world in my spiritual geography." His generous enthusiasm threatened to undo some of the sobering effects of Niven's conference at Cambridge. During my several visits at his house that summer I had to repeat again and again my description of Beecher and of his sermons. He called him the brother of Joan of Arc of the new spiritual world; her flaming sword, he said, was "Uncle Tom's Cabin."

My older sister and her husband drove to Panchevo and escorted me to Idvor. When Idvor's territory was reached I begged them to make a detour which would

take me through the pasturelands and vineyards of Idvor, where I had seen my happiest boyhood days. There, as if in a dream, I saw the boys of Idvor watching herds of oxen just as I used to do, and playing the same games which I used to play. The vineyards, the summer sky above them, and the river Tamish in the distance, where I had learned to swim and dive, looked the same as ever. Presently the familiar church-spire of Idvor hove in sight, and gradually the sweet sound of the church-bells, announcing vespers, awakened countless memories in my mind and I found it difficult to control my emotions. As we drove slowly through little Idvor everything looked exactly as it had looked eleven years before. There were no new houses, and the old ones looked as old as ever. The people were doing the same work which they always did during that season of the year, and they were doing it in the same way. When we reached the village green I saw the gate of my mother's yard wide open, a sign that she expected a welcome guest. She sat alone on the bench under a tree in front of her house, and waited, looking in the direction from which she expected me to come. When she saw my sister's team, I observed that suddenly she raised her white handkerchief to her eyes, and my sister whispered to me: "Mayka plache!" ("Mother is weeping!") I jumped out of the wagon and hastened to embrace her. Oh, how wonderful is the power of tears, and how clear is our spiritual vision when a shower of tears has purified the turbulent atmosphere of our emotions! Mother's love and love for mother are the sweetest messages of God to the living earth.

Everything in Idvor looked the same, but my mother had changed; she looked much older, and much more beautiful. There was a saintly light in her eyes which disclosed to me the serene firmament of the spiritual world in which she lived. Raphael and Titian, I thought, never painted a more beautiful saint. I gazed and worshipped and felt most humble. "Come," she said, "and walk with me; we shall be alone; I want to hear your voice and see the light of your face, undisturbed." We walked slowly, and my mother recalled many things, reminding me of the familiar objects of my boyhood days, as: "Here is the path on which you walked to school; there is the church where you read the epistles on Sundays and holidays; there is the mill with the funnel-shaped thatched roof from the top of which you once removed the shining new tin star, imagining that it was a star from heaven; there is the house where Baba Batikin, of blessed memory, lived and taught you so many ancient tales; there is the house where old Aunt Tina cured your whooping-cough with charms and with herbs steeped in honey; here lived old Lyubomir, of blessed memory, who was so fond of you, and made your sheepskin coats and caps; here is the field where every evening you brought our horses to the chikosh (the village herdsman) to take them to the pasturelands."

By that time we had reached the end of the little village, but my mother prolonged our leisurely walk and presently we stood at the gate of the village cemetery. Pointing to a cross of red marble my mother said that it marked the grave of my father. When we reached it I kissed the cross, and, kneeling upon the grave, I prayed. My mother, loyal to Serb traditions, addressed the grave, saying: "Kosta, my faithful husband, here is your boy whom you loved more dearly than your own life, and whose name was on your lips when you breathed your last. Accept his prayer and his tears as his affectionate tribute to your blessed memory, which he will cherish forever."

On the way back we stopped at the church and kissed the icons of our patron saint and of St. Sava, and lighted two wax candles which mother had brought with her. I confessed to her that I felt as if a sacred communion had reunited me with the spirit of Idvor. That was her wish, she said, because she did not want Idvor to think that I was like a proud stranger from a proud, strange land. "I did not recognize you," she said, "when I first saw you in your sister's wagon until you smiled with the smile of your boyhood days, and then I shed the sweetest tears of my life. You looked so learned and so far above us plain folks of Idvor that nobody will recognize the Misha they used to know, and whom they long to see, unless you show them the boy that they used to know." My promise to return to Idvor "rich in learning and academic honors" was evidently made good, according to my mother's opinion. But did not this learning and these academic honors carry with them an air which did not harmonize with the old-fashioned notions of Idvor? This, I believed, was in my mother's mind, and I made a careful note of it.

Idvor came to see me, and it assured me that there was no youngster in all the great plains of Voyvodina who was nearer to the heart of his native village than Misha. This affectionate regard was won by my strict observance of all the old customs of Idvor, as, for instance, kissing the hand of the old people of Idvor, and in return being kissed by them on the forehead. On the other hand, young peasant boys and girls of Idvor kissed my hand, and I kissed them on the cheek and petted them. My cousin, much older than I, was an ex-soldier and a stern *Knez* (chief) of the village. He was the oldest male member and, therefore, the head of the Pupins. I was expected to keep this in mind constantly, and I did it whenever I stood in his mighty presence. American citizenship eliminated my allegiance to the Emperor of Austria-Hungary but not to the autocratic *Knez* of Idvor. There was another great person in Idvor whose presence inspired awe. He was my *koum* (godfather). My mother had lost all her children that were born in her earlier years, and was left childless for many years. She then bore two daughters when she was over thirty. I was born when she was over forty, in answer to her fervent prayer, she firmly believed, that God grant her a son. A boy born late in life, if he is to live, must, according to a popular belief in Idvor, be handed out through the front window to the first person who comes along, and that person has to carry the baby to church quickly and have it baptized. In this manner a very poor and humble peasant of Idvor became my *koum*. A *koum's* authority over his godchild is, theoretically at least, unlimited, according to Serbian custom. In practice, a godchild must eat humble pie when the *koum* is present. Between my cousin, who, as *Knez*, was at the head of the village, and my *koum*, who was somewhere near the bottom of the village, I had some difficulty to steer the correct course of conduct. I succeeded, thanks to my efforts to please my mother; and the peasants of Idvor most cheerfully admitted that America must be a fine Christian country, since it had given me a training which harmonized so well with the Christian traditions of Idvor. My presidency in the junior year at Columbia College, my undisputed authority among some of the young aristocrats of New York, and the many scholastic successes in my academic career had sown some seeds of vanity and false pride in my heart. But these seeds were smothered by the inexorable rigors of Idvor's traditions. Humility is the cardinal virtue in a youth among the peasants of Idvor.

Needless to say, the story of my life since I had left Idvor was retold many a time, until my mother and my sisters knew it by heart. It was sweet music to their ears. I enjoyed it, too, because summer evenings in a Serbian garden are most conducive to the spinning out of reminiscent tales. The village worthies spent many Sunday afternoons in my mother's garden asking many,

many a question about America. Tales about things
like the Brooklyn Bridge, the elevated railroad, the tall
buildings in New York, and the agricultural operations
of the West were received with many expressions of wonder, but at times also, I thought, with some reserve. A
simple peasant mind could not accept without considerable reserve the statement that a machine can cut, bind,
and load the seasoned wheat, all at the same time, with
nothing but a few stupid horses to drag it along. After
a while my store of information became exhausted, and
I had much less to say, but the wise men of Idvor urged
me to go on. They met my apologies with the statement
that peasant Ghiga had never left Idvor in all his life
until one day he went to a neighboring village, about
ten miles away, and saw the county fair. He returned
to Idvor on the same day, and for six weeks he never
ceased talking about the great things which he had seen
at that county fair. "Just imagine," said the priest,
"how much he would have had to say if he had been
nine years in great America!"

I was overwhelmed with invitations to attend concerts
and festivals in many places of my native Banat, and
when I attended I was often called upon to say something
about America, and, of course, I spoke about my favorite
subject: "The American Doctrine of Freedom." People
talked and papers wrote about it. One day the Fehispan,
the governor of Torontal, where Idvor belonged under
the new division of Hungary, sent for me, and appointed
the hour for a conference. I went, carrying my American
citizenship papers and my Columbia diploma in my
pocket. When I entered his office I saw a handsome
young man of about thirty, quite athletic in appearance,
and looking like an English aristocrat in dress and in
manner. I was told beforehand that he was a young
Hungarian nobleman who prided himself upon his English university training. I wondered how he would act

when he saw before him a Serb youth from the peasant village of Idvor who prided himself upon his American college training. He looked puzzled when I entered and saluted him with a Serbian "Dobroytro gospodine!" ("Good morning, sir"), accompanying my salute with an Anglo-Saxon bow, that is a jerky motion of the head from the shoulders up. The bow of continental Europe is much more elaborate. After some hesitation he asked me to sit down, and then, as if by an afterthought, he brought a chair himself and offered it to me. We spoke in English, since I did not understand Hungarian, and he did not care to speak Serb. By way of introduction I showed him my American citizenship papers and my diploma, and he remarked that these documents agreed with my appearance and manner, adding quickly that he meant a compliment. He asked me how I liked Idvor and Hungary. Then I told him that I never had known much about Hungary, but that Budapest and even its famous bridge looked to me small and shrivelled up, probably because I compared things there with things in New York. "It is big enough, is it not, to be the metropolis of the southern Slavs in Hungary?" he asked. "It undoubtedly is," said I, "but somewhat inconvenient and unnatural." I volunteered this opinion, seeing from his somewhat inquisitorial manner that he knew much about my doings, and that he had heard of my salute to Belgrade when my boat from Budapest approached it a month earlier.

"This, I suppose, is the doctrine which you preached at Karlovci, at the national gathering there?" asked the handsome and genial inquisitor, and I answered: "No; I had no time; I was too busy carrying the body of the great poet to Strazhilovo. Besides, the Karlovci ceremony itself was really a grand sermon which glorified that doctrine, and some day it may prevail, when the slow mind of the southern Slav wakes up and does the

natural thing." "The quick mind of the Hungarian
crown may wake up sooner and do the natural thing,"
said the young Fehispan, and added: "What you say
now confirms my information that in your public utterances you deny the divine right of the crown and proclaim the divine right of the people." "That is one of
the messages of our American Declaration of Independence," said I, "and I delivered that message to people
here who were anxious to hear something about America."
Then I added that Kossuth, while in America, was glorifying the divine right of the Hungarian people and denying the divine right of the Hapsburg crown in Hungary.
I had heard this and many other Hungarian democratic
doctrines from Henry Ward Beecher, who was a great
friend and admirer of Kossuth, and I told him that. He
saw that my trigger was ready if he attempted any further moves in this direction. "You are certainly frank
and honest, like all real Americans that I know; that
makes them most attractive. But why don't you naturalized Americans mind your own business when you
visit us?" He was much less stern and serious when he
said this, and I was only too glad to play a more cheerful
tune, and said: "Our most important business here is
our mission to make you, our poor relations here, happy
and prosperous by having you adopt the American point
of view."

He was a wealthy Hungarian magnate who owned
several villages, each of them bigger than Idvor, and
this answer coming from a son of poor Idvor amused
him much. From that moment on our conference was
much less formal, and became even cordial when he offered me coffee and cigarettes. I jokingly told him that
Magyarism and Teutonism had driven me away from
Panchevo and Prague, and now that I was back for a
visit I wished to pay them back with a little present of
a few American ideas. "Your American ideas," he re-

torted jokingly, "will make you even less popular here than your Serb nationalism did eleven years ago. Drop them while you are here. You'll have more fun shooting wild ducks in the lowlands of the Tamish River near Idvor than clearing up to dullards the American point of view. The duck season is on, and it is a pity to miss a single day. I'll lend you an American gun which is just right for that sort of business." He did, and that gun kept me busy and saved him the trouble of watching my movements. The village notary accompanied me on my shooting tramps; he was an expert fisherman and shot, and spared no pains to please me and—the Fehispan. A two weeks' tramp in the marshes of the Tamish River, chasing the elusive duck, diminished my haste to harmonize the political point of view of the Serbs in the Voyvodina with American ideas.

When the vintage was over, toward the end of September, I made ready to start for Cambridge. I was sorry to leave, because the merry season in Voyvodina is on when the vintage is over and the new wine has ceased fermenting. The golden crops are then all in, and the lazy pigs are fat and round, and ready to be served at wedding-feasts. In other lands it is the springtime when the young man's fancy turns to thoughts of love; in the Serb Voyvodina it is the autumn season which has that mysterious power. It is in the autumn when marriage-bells never cease ringing, and the bagpipes with the merry songs of wedding-feasts stir up the hearts from one end of the Banat plains to the other. But my mother diverted my attention to more serious thoughts, and she assured me that she was even more happy preparing me for my journey to Cambridge than she was when, eleven years before, she was preparing me for my journey to Prague.

A few days prior to my departure the village worthies prepared a fish-supper in my honor. The Tamish fishermen cooked it in their traditional way over a wood fire burning under the open sky. The little supper-party reached the fishermen's hut on the bank of the Tamish River just about sunset. The western sky was all aglow with the golden light of the parting day, and so was the surface of the tranquil Tamish River, made luminous by the image of the western sky. The rest of the landscape looked dark by contrast, excepting the glowing faces of the patient supper-party, who sat around the busy fires and watched the boiling kettles and the broiling pans. At some distance, and standing at the very end of a fisherman's barge, was the dark silhouette of a tall young shepherd, who stood there lonely like some solitary dark spectre hovering over the golden surface of the Tamish River. It was just the spot for one who sought seclusion and longed for quiet meditation. No ripple in the water or in the air disturbed his dreams, if he had any, and I thought that he had. His sheep had been watered, and he had finished his frugal supper long ago, before the light of the day had retired below the distant horizon line of the Banat plains. The silence of the approaching night awakened emotions which only his tuneful flute could express, and suddenly he poured his soul into a melody which surely was not addressed to mere phantoms of the vacuous space. I felt that the quivering air was conveying through the evening silence a message of love to some maiden, who was perhaps just then spinning under some thatched roof of drowsy Idvor and thinking of him. The priest approached me to tell me that the fish was ready and that the feast would soon begin. I told him that my feast had already begun and called his attention to the heavenly melody. He said: "Oh, that's Gabriel, the son of my neighbor Milutin. He entered the village school when you left Idvor, and he finished it long ago. He will be married on St. Michael's day, and what you hear now is his sefdalia (song of sighs) for his future bride, who is over there in our drowsy village." When he jokingly suggested that I might be looking forward to the enjoyment of the sweets of simple pastoral life which were in store for Gabriel, if I had not turned my back on Idvor eleven years before, I answered that perhaps it was not too late to correct the error. The priest looked astonished, and asked me whether I had crossed and recrossed the Atlantic in order to become a shepherd of Idvor. I said nothing, but I knew that Gabriel's melody had disclosed to me another world in which the question "What is Light?" is by no means the most important question. There were other great questions of human life, the answers to which can perhaps be found in Idvor without a knowledge of Maxwell's electrical theory.

VI

STUDIES AT THE UNIVERSITY OF CAMBRIDGE

A LONG-CONTINUED struggle with no let-up will wreck a feeble constitution. It produces in a strong and healthy constitution a tuning-up of continuously rising pitch under the tension of which even the strongest constitution may snap in two. My struggle had been going on for nine years when I was returning to Europe on my way to Idvor, hence my pitch was very high. Nervous tension resulting in a lack of poise was the diagnosis of my ailment, according to my English friend in Lucerne, who urged me to abandon the exploration of the beauties of the Alps and seek the solitude of my native village; otherwise, he said, not even all the guardian angels in heaven could prevent me from breaking my neck. A two months' vacation in the soporific atmosphere of Idvor was a blessing; my pitch was lowered through several octaves, and I did not vibrate violently in response to every impulse that came along. I recognized, for instance, that the Serbs of the Voyvodina could wait a little longer for their political salvation, which I confidently expected from their adoption of the American point of view. I also recognized that to many human beings a knowledge of the modern theories of physics was not indispensable to happiness. There was not a single person in Idvor who cared two straws about these things, and yet most of these good people were happy, as, for instance, Gabriel, who was to be married on St. Michael's day. Gabriel did not know much, I said to myself, but the little knowledge he had was very definite. He knew that he loved the girl he was about to marry, and he also knew that his life,

167

following in the footsteps of his peasant ancestors, had a definite object in view which, as everybody in his village knew, was easily attainable. I knew more than Gabriel did, but my knowledge was not as definite as his. My aim in life was, I thought, much higher than his; but was it attainable? And, if attainable, was it worth the struggle? Two months earlier such a question could not have occurred to me even in a dream. But Gabriel's melody and the dreamy atmosphere of Idvor suggested it.

My mother observed that a change had occurred, but she was not alarmed. I spoke less often of my future plans, and was less anxious about my departure for Cambridge. The wedding celebrations in my native Banat were already ushered in by the gay autumn season, and the beautiful kolo dancers, whirling around the merry bagpipes, engaged my interest much more than when I had come to Idvor two months before. One evening my mother recalled an incident which happened in my early boyhood days and which I remembered well. She said something like this:

"Do you remember when Bukovala's mill with its high conical roof was rethatched?" I said, "Yes," and she continued: "You were then a little shaver, but you certainly remember still the shining tin star which the workmen had planted upon the top of the conical roof after they had finished their work of thatching. The children of Idvor thought that it was a real star from heaven; it looked so bright when the sunlight was shining upon it. One day the tin star disappeared, and everybody wondered how anybody could have climbed up that smooth and steep roof and taken the star away. Old Lyubomir, who loved you so dearly and delighted in making sheepskin coats for you, was sure that it was you, and he suggested that special prayers of thanksgiving be read in church for your miraculous escape. Old Lyubomir was right, as you know, and I always believed that God had saved you for a mission in life much higher than that of young Gabriel, whose happy lot you seem to envy. Blessed America has taught you how to climb a roof much steeper than that of Bukovala's mill, and on its top and all the way up to it you will find many a real star from heaven. You are not far from the top and you cannot stop nor turn back now any more than you could when you saw the peak of Titlis in the distance, but felt too fatigued to finish your climb. Gabriel's magic flute and his mellow sefdalia, song of sighs, have turned your thoughts to things which are now in everybody's mind: to wedding-feasts and kolo dancing, and to other diversions which fill the hearts of Idvor's youth during this merry autumn season. You are dreaming now some of the idle dreams of youth, but when you return to Cambridge you will wake up again and see that all this was a pleasant dream only, which you saw in your restful hours in drowsy Idvor. The real things are waiting for you at Cambridge."

I confessed my weakness and pleaded extenuating circumstances. I tried to persuade her that her tender affection and watchful ministering to what she insisted should be my pleasures and comforts during that summer had transformed a hardy youth into a soft and pampered pet. She answered: "The blacksmith softens his steel before he forges it into a chain; you are just right for the blacksmiths of Cambridge."

When I returned to Cambridge from drowsy little Idvor things looked different from what they had on my former visit two months before. Things which, in my feverish haste, I had scarcely noticed then filled me now with awe. The ancient college buildings inspired a feeling of wonder and of veneration. I saw in them just so many monumental records of the ancient traditions of English learning. I began to understand, I thought, how it hap-

pened that a little nation on a little island in the northern
Atlantic became the leader in the world's empire of intellect, and the cradle of a great civilization. This first
impression made upon me by these ancient monuments
was greatly amplified as soon as I caught even the first
glimpses of the daily activity of Cambridge. The forenoons appeared serious and sombre to an outside observer; everybody wore a black cap and gown and everybody did apparently the same thing, going somewhere
in search of sources of learning and inspiration. The
intellect of Cambridge seemed to be in full action during
the forenoons, and hence the solemn seriousness of the
university town during the early half of the day. But
the scene changed as if by magic when the midday had
passed. The black caps and gowns disappeared, and in
their places white flannel trousers and gaily colored blazers
and caps adorned the college youths and many college
dons. The same youths who in the forenoon, like sombre
monks, were making a pilgrimage to some miracle-work-
ing fountains of wisdom joined in a gay procession in the
afternoon, hastening to the sparkling fountains of athletic
recreation. The intellectual activity of the forenoon was
succeeded by the physical activity of Cambridge in the
afternoon. To a stranger like myself, who knew practically nothing of the famous university town, the change
of scene between morning and afternoon was bewildering.
It looked to me as if I saw a monastic-looking procession
of serious and thoughtful men suddenly changed into gay
groups of lively youths whose only thoughts were on the
games which awaited them. By counting the different
colors of blazers and caps and the coats of arms which
adorned the athletic youths one could easily count the
number of different colleges in the old university. These
colors and coats of arms had a meaning, I thought, and
I asked myself whether they did not, like the ancient
college buildings, record the ancient traditions of the

venerable seat of learning. They certainly did; they were a part of the symbolic language which told the story of the university's customs and traditions. It was clear to me that while at Cambridge my work was to be done in the morning and evening, and my playing in the afternoon, in accordance with the local customs. I stayed at a hotel for several days and watched these external pictures of Cambridge life before I called on Mr. Niven of Trinity and on Mr. Oscar Browning of King's. I wished to get some picture of the daily activities at Cambridge before I presented myself to these learned men, and I got it.

Niven was expecting me and was ready with a programme of work which he had promised me in June, and I gladly accepted it. Both Niven and Browning assured me that at that late date lodgings in any college were out of the question, and that I must get lodgings in the town for one academic year at least. It did not matter, because very many students resided outside of the college buildings. I really preferred it, because I had not come to Cambridge to seek the opportunities offered by its college life; I had come to study physics and find out how Maxwell answered the question "What is Light?" That was the only definite point in the programme which I had brought to Cambridge; the rest was hazy and reminded me often of a Serbian figure of speech which speaks of a goose groping around in a fog to find its way. But I had groped like a goose in a fog when I landed at Castle Garden and finally found my way. The saying, "Where there's a will there's a way," comforted me much.

My residence in lodgings outside of the college precincts had one great advantage. It gave me an opportunity to study English life from what I considered a somewhat novel point of view. It is the point of view which discloses to the foreigner English domestic life through the unique personality of the English landlady. During my eighteen months' stay at the University of Cambridge, I had an opportunity to study her wonderful ways, not only in Cambridge, but also in London, Hastings, Brighton, and Folkestone, where I used to spend my Easter and Christmas vacations. She was the same everywhere: dignified, reticent, punctual, and square; neat and clean in all her ways; willing and anxious to render service, but not a servant; possessing a perfect understanding of her own business, which she minded scrupulously, but avoiding carefully minding anybody else's business.

At Mr. Browning's request a Mr. Ling, the leading tenor of King's College choir, took me around to look for lodgings. He belonged to the town and not to the gown, and was quite anxious to impress me with the many virtues of the town. He transformed our trip into an elaborate inspection tour of the student lodgings, because he was proud of them and considered them a very essential part of the great university. At that time I thought that he, a very enthusiastic townsman, was perhaps exaggerating the importance of this subsidiary instrumentality of the university. But when I got to know the Cambridge landlady and to understand her importance, I became convinced that Mr. Ling was right. I had not been in Cambridge more than a week before I learned the fundamentals of English domestic life, and I admired its wholesome simplicity. My landlady taught me these fundamentals, and in her wonderfully tactful ways she enforced their operation without my being aware that I was led around by her intelligent and forceful hand. I take off my hat to the English landlady, who, in her humble and unostentatious ways, is one of the eloquent interpreters of Anglo-Saxon civilization. She was one of my trusty guides and sympathetic assistants during my strenuous eighteen months at the University of Cambridge.

I started my work at Cambridge unattached to any college. But later I made up my mind to attach myself to King's College, yielding to repeated suggestions from my friend, Mr. Oscar Browning. But I did not change my lodgings. King's had less than a hundred students and many dons. Not one of them was a star in physics, and therefore the college had no attractions for me on account of the learning of its dons. But it had a beautiful chapel and a famous choir. The stained-glass windows of King's College chapel were famous as far back as Cromwell's time and they are still so. Every time I attended service in this glorious chapel I went away feeling spiritually uplifted. I attended regularly, although, as a member of the Orthodox faith, I was excused from all religious services. What the other students, belonging to the established church, considered a stern duty, I considered a rare privilege. The chapel gave me a spiritual tonic whenever I needed it, and I needed it often. I yielded also to Mr. Browning's suggestions to try for a place in the college boat, and succeeded. Rowing was the only exercise which I took at Cambridge after I had become attached to King's, but before that I took long walks, usually with one of the younger dons or with a student who was engaged in the same book work in which I was engaged. They helped me to make myself familiar with the history of Cambridge and of the surrounding country. Everybody in Cambridge took his daily exercise just as regularly as he took his daily bath and food. I followed the universal custom; it suited me well and, besides, that was the best way to get along in Cambridge.

Physical as well as intellectual activity of the students at Cambridge was a matter of daily routine, regulated by customs and traditions. But these regulators were different for different groups of students. The student studying for honors arranged his work differently from the arrangement which suited the needs of a Poll student, that is, the ordinary student who did not aspire to academic honors. Their previous training also had been different. The students who aspired to academic honors in mathematics were quite numerous, more numerous than the students in any other honor class. Cambridge, ever since the time of Newton, had become the nursery of the mathematical sciences in the British Empire. There were about five of these honor groups at Cambridge in those days. Niven advised me to join the honor group in mathematics, the so-called mathematical tripos group, and he picked out a coach for me. Just as one straight line, only, can be drawn through two points, so the line of the student's intellectual activity at Cambridge was fixed when he had picked out the honor class and the tutor or coach to train him for the examinations prescribed for that honor class. To join the honor class in mathematics meant to work alongside of students who expected to become Cambridge *wranglers*. To understand the meaning of this it suffices to know that no greater honor was in store for the ambitious youths in the university than to be a *senior wrangler* or to stroke a victorious varsity boat. The preparations for these glorious honors were just as careful as the preparations of a Grecian youth for participation in the Olympian games. I had no ambition to become a Cambridge wrangler, but Niven pointed out that a prospective physicist who wished to master some day Maxwell's new electrical theory must first master a good part of the mathematical work prescribed for students preparing for the Cambridge mathematical tripos examinations.

"Doctor Routh could fix you up in quicker time than anybody," said Niven with a smile, and then he added cautiously, "that is, if Routh consents to your joining his private classes, and if you can manage to keep up the pace of the youngsters who are under his training." Three months before, when I first called on Niven, and when my pitch was very high, I would have resented this; but

Idvor had lowered my pitch several octaves and I swallowed Niven's bitter pill without the slightest sign of mental distress. My humility pleased him, because it probably relieved him of some anxiety about the question of managing me.

John Edward Routh, fellow of Peterhouse College, was the most famous mathematical coach that Cambridge University had ever seen. In his lifetime he had coached several hundred wranglers, and for twenty-two consecutive years he had coached the senior wrangler of each year. This is really equivalent to saying that a certain jockey had ridden the Derby winner for twenty-two consecutive years. He was a senior wrangler himself in 1854, when great James Clerk Maxwell was second wrangler, and he divided with Maxwell the famous Smith's prize in mathematics. To be admitted by Routh into his private classes was flattering, according to Niven, but to be able to keep up with them would be a most encouraging sign. Niven was anxiously waiting for that sign. Routh accepted me, but gave me to understand that my mathematical preparation was much below the standard of the boys who came to Cambridge to prepare for the mathematical tripos examinations, and that I should have to do considerable extra reading. He also cautioned me that all this meant very stiff work for a good part of the academic year. I went to Cambridge to study physics and not mathematics; but, according to Niven and Routh, my real desire, as far as they could make it out, was to study mathematical physics, and they assured me that my training with Routh, if I could keep the pace, would soon lay a good foundation for that. Lord Rayleigh lectured on mathematical physics and so did famous Professor Stokes (later Sir George Gabriel Stokes); but according to Routh and Niven I was not prepared to attend any of these lectures, and much less to read Maxwell's famous mathematical treatise on his new electrical theory. Niven reminded me once of my first visit to Cambridge, when I had insisted that Cambridge without Maxwell had no attractions for me, and he asked me, jokingly, whether Lord Rayleigh's lectures were good enough for me. I answered that they certainly were, but that, unfortunately, I was not good enough for the lectures. "Next year you will be," said Niven, consoling me; and I, unable to suppress my feeling of disappointment, answered: "Let us pray that the starving jackass does not drop dead before the grass is green again." "What's that?" asked Niven, somewhat puzzled. "That is a free translation of a Serbian proverb, and I am the jackass," said I, and refused to furnish any further explanations. But Niven figured it out correctly in the course of the evening and then laughed heartily. He confessed that Serbo-American humor was somewhat involved and required considerable analysis.

The Cambridge colleges, some nineteen in number, resembled our American colleges in many ways. The career of the Cambridge Poll men was essentially the same as that of our American college boys. But our American colleges had no class of students corresponding to the Cambridge honor men. Referring particularly to the honor men who prepared for the so-called mathematical tripos, they came to Cambridge after graduating at some college outside of Cambridge. For instance, Maxwell came to Cambridge from the University of Edinburgh, and Routh came there from the University College, London. Both of them migrated to Cambridge, because their teachers in mathematics, like illustrious De Morgan, the first mathematical teacher of Routh, were mathematicians of distinction, and discovering in their young pupils extraordinary mathematical talents they developed them as far as they could, and then sent them to Cambridge for further development under the training of famous coaches who prepared them for the mathematical tripos. These teachers were usually former Cambridge wranglers, apostles of the Cambridge mathematical school, and they were always on the lookout for a fresh supply of mathematical genius for the nursery which regarded great Newton as its founder. This was the type of boys which I met in Routh's classes. They did not seem to know as much of Greek and Latin, of history and economics, of literature and physical sciences, as I did, but their training in mathematics was far superior to mine. They were candidates for the mathematical tripos, and no American college of those days had a curriculum which could turn out candidates with the preliminary mathematical training which those boys brought to Cambridge.

Routh had warned me that stiff work was before me for a good part of a whole academic year, if I was to keep up with the young mathematical athletes whom he was training, and he was right. I experienced many moments of despondency and even despair, and I needed all the tonic which King's College chapel could give me; I needed it very often, and I got it. Routh was a splendid drillmaster even for those students who, like myself, had no tripos aspirations. He certainly was a wonder, and everything he did was done with ease and grace and in such an offhand manner that I often thought that he considered even the stiffest mathematical problems mere amusing tricks. Problems over which I had puzzled in vain for many hours he would resolve in several seconds. He was a virtuoso in the mathematical technique, and he prepared virtuosos; he was the great master who trained future senior wranglers. I never felt so small and so humble as I did during the early period of my training with Routh. Vanity and false pride had no place in my heart when I watched Routh demolish one intricate dynamical problem after another with marvellous ease. I felt as a commonplace artist feels when he listens to a Paderewski or to a Fritz Kreisler.

well had no attraction for me. After reading Maxwell's little classic I told Niven that my opinion was, after all, not so funny and strange as he represented it.

A short digression is timely now. I went to Trinity College occasionally to spend a Sunday evening with Mr. Niven. One Sunday evening I walked around the historical Trinity quadrangle, waiting until Mr. Niven returned to his rooms from the evening service in the college chapel. The mysterious-looking light streaming through the stained-glass windows of the chapel and the heavenly music radiating from the invisible choir and organ commanded my attention. I stood motionless like a solitary spectre in the middle of the deserted and sombre quadrangle, and gazed, and listened, and dreamed. Yes, I dreamed of great Newton, the greatest of all Trinity dons; and I saw how, two centuries before, he was treading over the same spot where I was standing whenever he was returning from a Sunday evening service in the very chapel at which I was gazing. I dreamed also of Maxwell, another great Trinity don; and remembered that, five years before, the very same choir and organ to which I was listening had paid their last tribute to this great Cambridge man, when his earthly remains left the grief-stricken university on their last pilgrimage to Maxwell's native Scotland. But I knew that his spirit had remained at Cambridge to inspire forever the coming generations of ambitious students.

I dreamed of other great Trinity College men whose spirits seemed to hover about the sombre quadrangle, rejoicing in the heavenly light and sound which radiated from the historical chapel where Newton and Maxwell worshipped in days gone by. I longed for the day when my alma mater, Columbia College, and other colleges in America, could offer such an inspiring scene to its students; and I wondered how soon that day would come. Niven told me the following story which, he thought, might answer this question:

A don of Magdalen College, Oxford, was asked by an American friend how long it would take to raise, in America, a lawn like the famous lawn of Magdalen College. "I do not know," said the don, "but it took us over two centuries to do it here in Oxford." Niven implied, of course, that it will take much more than two centuries to create at any American college that atmosphere which surrounded me at the Trinity College quadrangle on that memorable Sunday evening. It was the mysterious charm of that atmosphere which held me chained to Cambridge in spite of the fact that I did not believe that the Cambridge tripos method of laying a foundation in mathematical physics was fitting my particular case.

Students shift from university to university in continental Europe, migrating to places where they are attracted by the reputations of teachers who happen to be there. I went to Cambridge because I thought that Maxwell was there. But at Cambridge, and at Oxford too, it was not only the teacher who was there but also the teachers who had lived there during generations long past who determined the choice made by ambitious students. The great teachers in the mathematical sciences when I was there were Lord Rayleigh, the successor of Maxwell; John Crouch Adams, who, with Leverrier in France, shared in the great distinction of calculating from the perturbations in the orbit of Uranus the position of the still unknown planet Neptune; George Gabriel Stokes, the greatest mathematical physicist in Europe at that time, and the occupant of the professorial chair once held by great Newton. But that which brought the students in mathematical sciences to Cambridge was not only the lustre of the reputations of these great professors, but also the existence at Cambridge of a historical educational policy, to the development of which many

ain, so the organization of the physics laboratory at Johns Hopkins by Rowland marks a new and most fruitful era of scientific research in the United States. Rowland's influence had not yet been felt at Columbia College when I was a student there, nor at many other American colleges of those days. But the forward movement soon commenced; and the people of this country do not understand yet as fully as they should how much they owe to the late Henry Augustus Rowland, whom I had the honor of knowing personally and whose friendship I enjoyed for several years. One of the aims of this simple narrative is to throw more light upon some obscure spots of this kind which need more illumination, and particularly upon the work of men like "Rowland of Troy, the doughty knight," as Maxwell referred to him in his verses.

Another historical fact must be mentioned here which is very characteristic of the state of the science of physics in those days, and which is closely connected with the progress of this science as it appeared to me in the course of the last forty years. I mention now another great American physicist whose name, like that of Rowland, I first heard mentioned at Cambridge at that time, and that was Professor Josiah Willard Gibbs, of Yale. I know that many of my young colleagues will find it strange that I never had heard of Lord Rayleigh, of England, before I graduated at Columbia. What will they say when they hear that at that time I never had heard of famous Willard Gibbs, of Yale, New Haven, U. S. A.? Will they charge me with extraordinary ignorance, for which Columbia of those days was to blame? That would be unjust, as the following story will prove. One evening, after dinner, I was enjoying at the University Club, New York, the company of some twelve Yale graduates, and one of them was the learned Professor William Welch, dean of the Johns Hopkins Medical School. He was then president of the National Academy of Sciences. Most of my Yale friends present were of about my age or even older. I offered to wager that the majority of them would fail to give the name of the scientist who, in Doctor Welch's opinion and in mine, was the greatest scientist that Yale had ever graduated. Not one of them mentioned Willard Gibbs. When I mentioned his name they frankly confessed that they had never heard of him before. Neither they nor Yale College of those days were to blame. Did my fellow students at Cambridge, who were training for the mathematical tripos, ever hear of him before they came to Cambridge? If they did, it was by accident, just as I heard of him by accident. Such was the spirit of the times in those days; and it was against this spirit that President Barnard of Columbia took up arms. He considered its existence a national calamity. But I shall return to this point later.

I will now describe the accident just mentioned, because it is closely connected with the main thread of my narrative. In the beginning of the Easter term, the third term of my training under Routh, I had caught up with my class and had spare time for outside reading. Niven was greatly impressed by my enthusiastic eulogies of Maxwell's little book, "Matter and Motion," and he suggested that I take up the reading of another of Maxwell's little classics, "Theory of Heat." It was written with the same elegant simplicity as his "Matter and Motion." This little text-book on heat was the first to give me a living physical picture of the mode of operation by which heat is transformed into mechanical work, an operation which I had watched so often in the Cortlandt Street boiler-room. I had watched it, but I had never dreamed that the operation could be described as Maxwell described it. According to him it may be considered as the resultant action of non-coordinated activities of an immense number of busy little molecules, each of which, as far as hu-

versation. He boasted among the villagers that his reputation as a French scholar had reached the United States
and, *voilà*, had brought me to Pornic. I never denied
it, but on the contrary I often walked through the village streets with the good old *maître d'école* and listened
most attentively to his French accents as if they were
the rarest pearls of wisdom.

When the villagers found out that I was not only an
American but also a student of a great English university,
then the stock of the little schoolmaster rose sky-high.
My landlady informed me that the old curé had become
quite jealous of the little man's rapid rise in the community. An old but renovated Norman castle was a
part of Pornic; it stood on the very edge of the steep coast
and it was inhabited in summer by a rich merchant of
Nantes. The castle had a thick grove of stately old
trees, and there the nightingales revelled. On moonlight
nights I spent many watchful hours listening to their
mellow notes, accompanied by the solemn rhythm of the
Atlantic waves striking gently upon the cliffs of the rocky
coast, which appeared in my imagination, as I listened,
like towering pipes of a giant organ. In daytime I selected lonely spots on the coast and there I spent my
days from early morning till late in the afternoon memorizing my French grammar and vocabulary. Every evening I practised for an hour or so in conversation with my
beloved *maître d'école*. This advanced my knowledge of
French very rapidly and before one month was over I
could converse tolerably well. My circle of acquaintances
expanded rapidly as my knowledge of French increased,
until it took in the nightingale grove, including the family
of the merchant from Nantes. Between my friends in
the nightingale grove and my schoolmaster's garden my
conversation in French became so fluent that it astonished the natives. They pronounced it perfect. But
discounting this enthusiastic estimate by even fifty per

cent I was still secure in my belief that I was enriched by a good knowledge of the language of a great civilization. A two months' visit to Pornic had been my plan; its end was very near, and my trip was a success. I bade good-by to my friends in little Pornic and arrived in Paris on the following day, the fourteenth of July, 1884.

Paris was gay, celebrating the national holiday of France, the anniversary of the storming of the Bastille in 1789. This gave me a chance to see many of the striking characteristics of the gay side of Paris in a single day. The next day, while visiting the great Sorbonne and the Collège de France in the Quartier Latin, I found a great treasure in a second-hand bookshop: La Grange's great treatise, "Méchanique Analytique," first published under the auspices of the French Academy in 1788. La Grange, the Newton of France! There was no student of dynamics who had not heard of his name and of his great treatise. My two months' stay in Pornic had enabled me to appreciate fully the beauty of the language of this great work, and my training with Routh had eliminated many difficulties of the mathematical technique. I was convinced of that in my very first attempts in Paris at deciphering some of its inspiring pages. I describe this short stay in France at some length, because I wish to refer to it later for the purpose of showing how little things can exert a big influence in the shaping of human life.

I had promised my mother to visit her again during that summer, and off I went, deserting without delay the gay scenes of Paris. On my journey to Idvor I wasted no time looking to the right or to the left of my speeding train; villages and towns, rivers and mountains, and the busy folks in the yellow fields who were gathering in the blessings of the harvest season appeared like so many passing pictures which did not interest me. La Grange was talking to me, and I had neither eyes nor ears for

VII

END OF STUDIES AT THE UNIVERSITY OF CAMBRIDGE

When I returned to Cambridge from little Idvor I often thought of my mother's words saying that I was living among the saints of Cambridge. These words sounded like the language which the minstrel of the old Serbian ballads would have used, to convey the meaning which she wished to convey. Whenever I saw one of the great dons of Cambridge, like the famous mathematician Cayley, or the still more famous mathematical physicist George Gabriel Stokes, the discoverer of fluorescence, I asked myself: "Are they the saints of Cambridge?" The answer was in the negative; most of these men were too mobile to pass for saints. One of them, for instance, although quite old and blind, was the stroke of a boat which was very prominent on the river Cam. Its crew consisted of Cambridge dons. When this aged stroke was not rowing he was riding a spirited horse, usually galloping briskly, with his young daughter chasing alongside of him, her long golden hair, like that of a valkyrie, lashing the air as she made strenuous efforts to keep up with her speedy father. It was impossible to associate one's idea of saints with men of that type. But, nevertheless, my mother was right: Cambridge had its saints; their memory was the great glory of Cambridge.

Nature, published in London, was then, as it is to-day, the most popular scientific weekly in the United Kingdom. Many scientists of Cambridge used it as a medium for discussing in a popular way the current scientific events of the day. Among the files of *Nature*, which I consulted

often, I found once a beautiful steel engraving of Faraday, together with a brief account of Faraday's work. It was written by Maxwell, as I found out later. Speaking of the activity of teachers of science, the writer said that they are expected "to bring the student into contact with two main sources of mental growth, *the fathers of sciences*, for whose personal influence over the opening mind there is no substitute, and the material things to which their labors first gave meaning." In the light of this thought I saw that in his two little classics, "Matter and Motion" and "Theory of Heat," Maxwell had brought me into contact with the fathers of dynamical sciences, and that La Grange, in his "Méchanique Analytique," had shown me the men who were the fathers of the science of dynamics, and that for this service I owed them everlasting gratitude.

Jim, the humble fireman in the Cortlandt Street factory, told me once: "This country, my lad, is a monument to the lives of men of brains and character and action who made it." From that day on the name "United States of America" recalled to my mind Washington, Hamilton, Franklin, Lincoln, and the other great men who are universally regarded as the fathers of this country; and when I learned to know and to appreciate them I felt that I was qualified to consider myself a part of this country. Maxwell and La Grange had taught me that Archimedes, Galileo, Newton, Carnot, Helmholtz, and other great investigators had made the dynamical sciences; and from that time on these sciences like monuments recalled to my mind the names of the men who made them. I never saw a man handling a crowbar without remembering that it was the historic lever which in the philosophy of Archimedes served as the earliest foundation for the science of statics. The word *force* always recalled the picture of Galileo dropping heavy bodies from the Leaning Tower of Pisa, and watching their

uniformly accelerated motions, produced by the force which was impelling the falling body to the earth. The picture reminded me that by these ideally simple experiments Galileo had banished forever the mediæval superstition that bodies fall because they are afraid of the vacuum above, and had substituted in its place the simple law of accelerating force, which prepared the foundation for the science of dynamics. I never saw a moving train being brought to a standstill by the frictional reactions of the brakes without seeing in my imagination the image of Newton formulating his great law of equality between physical actions and physical reactions, the crowning point of modern dynamics. These pictures illustrated what Maxwell meant when he spoke of the material things to which the labors of Archimedes, Galileo, and Newton gave a meaning, and when I caught that meaning I felt that I was no longer a stranger in the land of science. Their highest meaning, I knew, was the recognition that the truth which they conveyed was a part only of what my mother called the "Eternal Truth."

My work in Cambridge, guided principally by Maxwell and La Grange, reminded me, therefore, continually of the fathers of the sciences which I was studying and of the material things to which their labors gave a meaning. These thoughts gave me a satisfactory interpretation of my mother's words: "Cambridge is a great temple consecrated to the eternal truth; it is filled with icons of the great saints of science. The contemplation of their saintly work will enable you to communicate with the spirit of eternal truth." My description of the scientific activity of Cambridge had produced this image in her mind, which was dominated by a spirit of piety and of reverence. This spirit, I always thought, is needed in science just as much as it is in religion. It was the spirit of Maxwell and of La Grange.

The atmosphere of Cambridge was most favorable to

the cultivation of a spirit of reverence in scientific thought. At that time, just as to-day, Newton's name was the glory of Trinity College, and the name of Darwin was regarded with the same feeling of reverence at Christ College. Every college at Cambridge had at least one great name which was the glory of that college. These, one may say, were the names of the patron saints of Cambridge; their spirit was present everywhere, and its influence was certainly wonderful. It reminded me of my mother's words: "May God be praised forever for the blessings which you have enjoyed and will continue to enjoy in your life among the saints of Cambridge."

It may seem strange that a Cambridge student of science should have worried so much about interpreting his pious mother's words in terms of his expanding scientific knowledge. But that student was once a Serb peasant in whose early childhood the old Serbian ballads were his principal spiritual food. The central figure of these ballads was Prince Marko, the national hero, who at critical moments of his tempestuous life never appealed for aid to any man. When he needed counsel he asked it from his aged mother Yevrosima, and when he needed help in combat he appealed to Vila Raviyoyla, Marko's adopted sister, the greatest of all the fairies of the clouds. A mother can have a wonderful influence over her boy whose early mental attitude is moulded by impressions of that kind. When she has that influence, then she is her boy's oracle, and no amount of subsequent scientific training will disturb that relationship.

I often think of an old idea which I first conceived while a student at Cambridge. It is this: Our American colleges and universities should have days consecrated to the memories of what Maxwell called the fathers of the sciences, like Copernicus, Galileo, Newton, Faraday, Maxwell, Darwin, Helmholtz. I mention these names, having physical sciences in mind, but similar names can

be mentioned in other departments of human knowledge. Why should not science follow the beautiful example of religion, which has its saints' days? On these memorial days, say Newton's birthday, an address on Newton and his work should tell the young student why Newton is the father of the science of dynamics. Dynamics is not a mere collection of inexorable physical laws which to a young student often sound like dry scientific facts and mute formulæ. Many text-books, unfortunately, represent it that way. It is a record of the life-work of men who lived human lives and became what my mother called "saints of science," because they devoted their life-efforts to the deciphering of divine messages which, through physical phenomena, God addresses to man. The young mind should know as early as possible that dynamics had its origin in the heavens, in the motions of heavenly bodies, and that it was brought to earth by Galileo and Newton when they had deciphered the meaning of the divine message conveyed to them by these celestial motions. The Greeks of old sacrificed to their gods a hecatomb of oxen whenever one of their philosophers discovered a new theorem in geometry, and the philosopher's memory was praised forever. The modern nations should not remain indifferent to the memory of the "saints of science," whose discoveries have advanced so much the physical and the spiritual welfare of man. My life among the saints of Cambridge suggested this idea, and my students, past and present, know that I have always been loyal to it, because I always believed that in this manner every American college and university could raise an invisible "temple consecrated to the eternal truth" and fill it with "icons of the great saints of science." A spirit of reverence for the science which the student is studying should be cultivated from the very start. I observed that spirit among my friends, the mathematical tripos men, at Cambridge; it was there as a part of local tradi-

END OF STUDIES AT CAMBRIDGE

tions. I certainly felt its influence, and the longer I stayed
at Cambridge the more I felt convinced that "Cambridge
is a great temple consecrated to the eternal truth." This
enabled me to recognize while still at Cambridge that
nothing was more characteristic of the mental attitude
of many scientific men in America and in England at that
time than their reverence for the "saints of science" and
their strong desire to build great temples "consecrated
to the eternal truth." Maxwell was one of their leaders,
and the best illustration of that mental attitude. I have
already referred to this in my short allusion to the Cambridge craving for scientific research, and I shall now attempt to describe a much wider intellectual movement
of which this craving was a local manifestation only. I
felt the force of its current during my Cambridge days,
and I recognize to-day that at that time I moved along
following more or less unconsciously the stream-lines of
this current.

The completion of the mathematical training under
Routh recommended by Niven was approaching its end,
and I was satisfied with its results. I could follow without much effort the lectures of Stokes and Lord Rayleigh,
and I could handle the mathematics of Maxwell's theory
of electricity with considerable ease; but I did not understand his physics.

President Barnard, of Columbia College, said once in
an address of fifty years ago that a young student in
America at that time lacked a "knowledge of visible
things and not information about them—knowledge acquired by the learner's own conscious efforts, not crammed
into his mind in set forms of words out of books." His
statement fitted admirably my own case; I lacked that
knowledge of visible things which one gets from his own
conscious efforts; I had no knowledge of physics acquired
from my own conscious efforts in a physical laboratory.
Neither Columbia College nor any other college in the

United States, with very few exceptions, offered at that time this opportunity to the student. I suspected that this was the real secret of my inability to understand Maxwell's physics; I longed for work in a real physical laboratory and made preparations to enter the Cavendish Laboratory at Cambridge. But I learned, in the beginning of 1885, that Lord Rayleigh had given up the directorship of this laboratory, and that a Mr. J. J. Thomson of Trinity College had been appointed as his successor, the same Thomson who is to-day Sir John Joseph Thomson, Master of Trinity College, and the leading physicist in the world. The new director was only twenty-eight years of age in the year of his appointment—at the end of 1884. Although a second wrangler in the mathematical tripos test of 1880, he was four years later already a sufficiently famous experimental physicist to be appointed director of the Cavendish Laboratory. The new director was only two years older than myself, but he was already a famous experimental physicist, whereas I had never had a physical apparatus in my hand. What will he think of me, thought I, when I present myself to him and ask for permission to work as a mere beginner in the Cavendish Laboratory! I blushed when I thought of it, and I was afraid that I should blush even more when he compared me to his younger students who had already acquired much skill in physical manipulations. The failure of my competition with boys and girls in the speed tests of punching biscuits in the Cortlandt Street cracker factory came back to my memory; and I bemoaned, just as I did in Cortlandt Street nine years before, my hard luck of having had no earlier training. Many an American college student of physics bemoaned in those days his lack of early laboratory training. When I say this I am touching the principal point of my narrative; it is the point at which my narrative begins to sail on the back of a wave which started actually when Johns Hop-

kins University was organized, in 1876, but the motive power of which had been gathering long before that, perhaps at the same time when the motive power of the Cambridge movement in favor of scientific research was gathering, resulting, as it had, in the establishment of the Cavendish Laboratory. But I must resume the thread of my story and return later to the point just mentioned.

My lack of what Barnard called "knowledge of visible things . . . acquired by the learner's own conscious efforts . . ." gave me much anxiety; and I often thought that it would, perhaps, be better to go to some other university where the director of the physical laboratory was an older man, who would not notice my age as much as would the new and extremely young director of the Cavendish Laboratory. That thought, however, did not console me much, because I was very much attached to Cambridge and did not wish to give up what my mother called "life among the saints of Cambridge." Just then, as if by an act of kind providence, a letter from President Barnard of Columbia College reached me, enclosing a letter of introduction to John Tyndall, the famous physicist, colleague and successor of Faraday in the direction of the Royal Institution. Barnard informed me that Columbia had received a generous sum of money from Tyndall, representing a part of the net proceeds from his famous course of public lectures on light, which he had delivered in the United States in 1872–1873; that the income of this sum would be given as a fellowship to a Columbia graduate to assist him in his study of experimental physics; that the fellowship would be called a John Tyndall Fellowship, netting over five hundred dollars annually; and that he and Rood, professor of physics at Columbia, considered me a suitable candidate. Unexpected things of this kind happen every now and then, and when they do they certainly encourage the belief that there is such a thing as luck.

promote scientific education in this country." Tyndall delivered his famous course of six lectures on light in Boston, New York, Philadelphia, Baltimore, and Washington. Joseph Henry, as secretary of the Smithsonian Institution and president of the National Academy of Sciences, took them under his personal direction. The success of these lectures surpassed even the most sanguine expectations. At the farewell dinner to Tyndall some of the wisest scientific intellects of the land were heard, and their words indicated clearly what was the uppermost thought in the minds of the scientific men of the United States when they invited Tyndall. I quote here some of the words spoken by these men.

President Barnard of Columbia, the first American expounder of the undulatory theory of light, said:

I say, then, that our long-established and time-honored system of liberal education . . . does not tend to form original investigators of nature's truths. . . .

Among the great promoters of scientific progress . . . how large is the number who may, in strict propriety, be said to have educated themselves? Take, for illustration, such familiar names as those of William Herschel, and Franklin, and Rumford, and Rittenhouse, and Davy, and Faraday, and Henry. Is it not evident that nature herself, to those who will follow her teachings, is a better guide to the study of her own phenomena than all the training of our schools? And is not this because nature invariably begins with the training of the observing faculties?

The moral of this experience is, that mental culture is not secured by pouring information into passive recipients; it comes from stimulating the mind to gather knowledge for itself. . . . If we would fit man properly to cultivate nature . . . our earliest teachings must be things and not words.

Doctor John William Draper, the world-renowned American investigator of the laws of radiation from hot bodies, said:

Nowhere in the world are to be found more imposing political problems than those to be settled here; nowhere a greater need of scientific knowledge. I am not speaking of ourselves alone, but also of our Canadian friends on the other side of the St. Lawrence. We must join together in generous emulation of the best that is done in Europe. . . . Together we must try to refute what De Tocqueville has said about us, that communities such as ours can never have a love of pure science.

Andrew White, President of Cornell, said:

I will confine myself to the value, in our political progress, of the spirit and example of some of the scientific workers of our day and generation. What is the example which reveals that spirit? It is an example of *zeal*, zeal in search for the truth . . . of *thoroughness*—of the truth sought in its wholeness . . . of *bravery*, to brave all outcry and menace . . . of *devotion* to duty without which no scientific work can be accomplished . . . of *faith* that truth and goodness are inseparable.

The reverence for scientific achievement, the revelation of the high honors which are in store for those who seek for truth in science—the inevitable comparison between a life devoted to the great pure search, on the one hand, and a life devoted to place-hunting or self-grasping on the other—all these shall come to the minds of thoughtful men in lonely garrets of our cities, in remote cabins of our prairies, and thereby shall come strength and hope for higher endeavor.

Tyndall responded in part as follows:

It would be a great thing for this land of incalculable destinies to supplement its achievements in the industrial arts by those higher investigations from which our mastery over nature and over industrial art itself has been derived. . . . To no other country is the cultivation of science, in its highest form, of more importance than to yours. In no other country would it exert a more benign and elevating influence. . . . Let chairs be founded, sufficiently but not luxuriously endowed, which shall have original research for their main object and ambition. . . . The willingness of American citizens to throw their fortunes into the cause of public education is, as I have already stated, without parallel in my experience. Hitherto their efforts have been directed to the practical side of science. . . . But assuredly among your men of wealth there are those willing to listen to an appeal on higher grounds. . . . It is with the view of giving others the chance that I enjoyed, among my noble and disinterested German teachers, that I propose, after deducting, with strict accuracy, the sums which have been actually expended on my lectures, *to devote every cent of the money which you have so generously poured in upon me to the education of young American philosophers in Germany.*

What a splendid example to the men of wealth to whom Tyndall was appealing! We shall see later that the appeal was not made in vain.

But the sentiments expressed at this dinner were echoes, only, of Tyndall's thundering voice, to which America listened spellbound when he delivered the last of his course of six lectures on light. In the last part of this lecture, called "Summary and Conclusions," he first erected what my mother would have called "a temple consecrated to the eternal truth" which we call light, and in that temple he placed what she would have called "the icons of the saints of the science" of light. The names of Alhazan, Vitellio, Roger Bacon, Kepler, Snellius, Newton, Thomas Young, Fresnel, Stokes, and Kirchhoff stood there like so many icons of saints which one sees on the altars of orthodox churches. In this he surpassed, I thought, even Maxwell and La Grange, and that was saying a great deal. He stood in the middle of that temple and challenged the statement once made by De Tocqueville that "the man of the North has not only experience but knowledge. He, however, does not care for science as a pleasure, and only embraces it with avidity when it leads to useful applications." Tyndall proceeded to draw a clear distinction between science and its applications, pointing out that technical education without original investigations will "lose all force and growth, all power of reproduction," just "as surely as a stream dwindles when the spring dies out." "The original investigator," said Tyndall, "constitutes the fountainhead of knowledge. It belongs to the teacher to give this knowledge the requisite form; an honorable and often difficult task. But it is a task which receives its final sanctification when the teacher himself honestly tries to add a rill to the great

JOSEPH HENRY (1799–1878)

JOHN TYNDALL (1820–1893)
From a photograph taken about 1885

stream of scientific discovery. Indeed, it may be doubted whether the real life of science can be fully felt and communicated by the man who has not himself been taught by direct communion with nature. We may, it is true, have good and instructive lectures from men of ability, the whole of whose knowledge is second-hand, just as we may have good and instructive sermons from intellectually able and unregenerate men. But for that power of science which corresponds to what the Puritan fathers would call experimental religion in the heart, you must ascend to the original investigator."

Many more passages could be quoted from Tyndall's "Summary and Conclusions" of his American lectures. Suffice it to say here that the cause of scientific research in this country never had a more eloquent advocate than Tyndall. The message which he delivered in his American lecture tour in 1872–1873 was heard and heeded in every part of the United States and of the British Empire. It is no exaggeration to say that the response to this call was the movement for scientific research in American colleges and universities which dates from those memorable years. It was in its earliest days under the leadership of the famous Joseph Henry, President Barnard, and other American scientists who had associated themselves in the National Academy of Sciences which was chartered by an act of Congress in 1863.

I shall try to show in the course of this narrative that it was the greatest intellectual movement in the United States, producing results of which nobody could even have dreamed fifty years ago; and the end is not yet in sight.

Tyndall had called my attention to volume VIII of *Nature*. The article on Faraday I had read before, but there were a large number of other communications advocating strongly the stimulation of scientific research in colleges and universities. Tyndall's "Summary and

Conclusions" had aroused a deep interest in my mind
for these things, and besides, they furnished a most welcome sidelight upon the Cambridge movement which, as
described above, I had felt before I met Tyndall.   The
University of Cambridge was severely criticised in these
communications by some Cambridge dons themselves on
account of the alleged entire absence of the scientific research stimulus.   One of these criticisms is so characteristic of the feeling of Cambridge in 1873 that it deserves
a special reference.   It is in volume VIII of *Nature* and is
entitled: "A Voice from Cambridge."   A very brief abstract follows:

> It is known all over the world that science is all but dead in Eng-
> land. By science, of course, we mean that searching for new knowledge
> which is its own reward. . . . It is also known that science is per-
> haps deadest of all at our universities. Let any one compare Cam-
> bridge, for instance, with any German university; nay, with even some
> provincial offshoots of the University of France. . . . What, then, do
> the universities do? They perform the functions, for too many of
> their students, of first-grade schools merely, and that in a manner
> about which opinions are divided; and superadded to these is an enor-
> mous examining engine, on the most approved Chinese model, always
> at work. . . .

Not even President Barnard could have uttered a more
severe criticism! The most forcible appeal was made by
the president of the British Association for the Advancement of Science at its meeting in Bradford, in September,
1873. This I also found in volume VIII of *Nature*. These
stirring appeals were published several months after
Tyndall's lecture tour in the United States, and they
all sounded to me like so many echoes of the thundering
voice with which he delivered the "Summary and Conclusions" of his American lectures.

These studies, recommended by Tyndall, gave me a
view of science which I did not have before. I caught a
glimpse of it from the books of Maxwell and La Grange,

to which I referred above. The realms of science are a strange land to a youth who enters them, just as the United States was a strange land to me when I landed at Castle Garden. Maxwell, La Grange, and Tyndall were the first to teach me how to catch the spirit of the strange land of science, and when I caught it I felt as confident as I did in Cortlandt Street after I had read and understood the early historical documents of the United States. I knew that soon I should be able to apply for citizenship in that great state called science. These were the thoughts which I carried with me when I started out for my second visit to Tyndall.

When I called on Tyndall again, a month or so after my first visit, I took along a definite plan for my future work. This pleased him, because he had advised me that every youth must think through his own head, the same advice which was given me some years later by Professor Willard Gibbs, of Yale. I assured Tyndall that my second reading of the "Summary and Conclusions," his sixth American lecture, had cleared my vision, and that I knew perfectly what my next step should be. He was much amused when I told him how, eighteen months before, I had wandered into Cambridge like a goose into a fog, and asked me where I got that expression. I told him that it was a Serbian saying, and he looked perfectly surprised when I told him that I was a Serb by birth.

"Well, I did not decipher you as quickly as you said I did. I thought," said he, referring to my habit of emphasizing the sound of the letter r in my pronunciation, "that you were a native American of Scotch ancestry." "Why not of Irish?" asked I, entering into his jocose mood. "Ah, my young friend," said he, with a merry twinkle in his eye, "you are too deliberate and too cautious to suggest the Irish type. I do not know what I would have thought had I seen you when you wandered into Cambridge 'like a goose into a fog.'"

He was evidently much impressed by my careful analysis of his "Summary and Conclusions" and of its effect upon the minds of American and English scientists. Seeing that he enjoyed informal conversation and encouraged it, I told him of my Alpine experiences in Switzerland and of the anxiety I caused to my English acquaintance because I was far from being "too deliberate and too cautious." "Well," said he, "I might have suspected an Irish ancestry if I had met you in Switzerland twenty months ago. But you have changed wonderfully since that time, and if you keep it up the goose that came to Cambridge may be quite a swan when it departs from Cambridge."

I informed Tyndall that Maxwell's glowing account of Helmholtz, which I had seen in Campbell's life of Maxwell, and in *Nature*, to which he had referred me, had decided me to migrate from Cambridge to Berlin and take up the study of experimental physics in Helmholtz's famous laboratory. He looked pleased, and referring good-naturedly to my goose simile again, he said jokingly: "You are no longer a goose in a fog. Let Helmholtz decide whether you are a swan or not." Then, growing more serious, he added: "You will find in the Berlin laboratory the very things which my American and British friends and I should like to see in operation in all college and university laboratories in America and in the British Empire. In this respect the Germans have been leading the world for over forty years, and they have been splendid leaders." This, then, was the reason, I thought, why, twelve years before, Tyndall said to his New York friends: "I propose . . . to devote every cent of the money which you have so generously poured in upon me to the education of young American philosophers in Germany."

I ventured to address to the very informal Tyndall the following informal question: "Since in your opinion

I am no longer a goose in a fog, you will have no objection if I apply to the Columbia authorities to send me as their 'young American philosopher,' as their first Tyndall fellow, to Berlin, will you?" "No, my friend," said he, "I have already urged you to do so. Remember, however, that a Tyndall fellow must never permit himself to wander like a goose in a fog, but must strive to carry his head high up like a swan, his body floating upon the clear waters of stored-up human knowledge, and his vision, mounted on high, searching for new communications with the spirit of eternal truth, as your mother expressed it so well." He liked my mother's expressions, "temple consecrated to the eternal truth," and "the icons of the great saints of science."

I will add here that Tyndall's mental attitude toward science appeared to me to be the same as my mother's mental attitude toward religion. God was the great spiritual background of her religion, and the works of the prophets and of the saints were, according to her faith, the only sources from which the human mind can draw the light which will illuminate this great spiritual background. Hence, as I said before, her fondness for and her remarkable knowledge of the words of the prophets and the lives of saints. The "eternal truth" was, according to my understanding at that time, the sacred background of Tyndall's scientific faith, and the works of the great scientific discoverers, their lives, and their methods of inquiry into physical phenomena were the only sources from which the human mind can draw the light which will illuminate that sacred background. He nourished that faith with a religious devotion, and his appeals in the name of that faith were irresistible. His friends in America and in England, who were glad to have him as their advocate of the cause of scientific research, had the same faith that he had, and they nourished it with the same religious devotion. I know to-day, and I suspected it at that time, that this faith was kindled and kept alive in the hearts of those men both here and in the British Empire by the light of the life and of the wonderful discoveries of Michael Faraday, and by the prophetic vision which led this great scientist to his discoveries. He was their contemporary and his achievements, like a great search-light, showed them the true path of scientific progress.

My last visit to Tyndall took place toward the end of the last, that is, the Easter, term, and when I returned to Cambridge I informed my friends that at the end of the term I would migrate to Berlin. It was not necessary for me to assure them how badly I felt to leave what they often heard me call "the saints and the sacred precincts of Cambridge"; they knew of my reverence for the place and they also knew my reasons for that reverence. They understood my reverent devotion to the memory of Newton, but they did not quite understand my similar devotion to the memory of Maxwell. How could they? None of his classics were necessary in order to solve the problems usually served before the candidates for the mathematical tripos honors. Neither could they understand my admiration for La Grange, who, in their opinion, was only an imperfect interpreter of Newton. Helmholtz they appreciated more, but the exalted opinion which Maxwell had of Helmholtz had not yet penetrated among my mathematical chums at Cambridge. They were sorry to lose me, they said, but they did not envy me, because they did not see that Berlin had anything which Cambridge did not have. This never was the opinion of Maxwell and it was not at that time the opinion of Tyndall.

Tyndall was the only physicist that I had ever met who had known Faraday personally. He was Faraday's co-worker in the Royal Institution for many years, and to him and Maxwell I owe my earliest knowledge of Faraday's wonderful personality. Tyndall conducted me into that knowledge by word of mouth, and his conversation about Faraday's personality and scientific temperament thrilled me. I told him that I had bought in a Cambridge second-hand book-shop three volumes of Faraday's "Electrical Researches" for three shillings, and Tyndall remarked: "Faraday is still quite cheap at Cambridge." Then, after some meditation, he added: "Read them; their story is just as new and as stirring to-day as it was when these volumes were first printed. They will help you much to interpret Maxwell." He presented me with a copy of his story, "Faraday as a Discoverer," which closes with the words:

"Just and faithful knight of God."

In this book Tyndall drew the same picture of Faraday which Campbell had given me of Maxwell. One can imagine what it meant to the world to bring these two spiritual and intellectual giants into personal contact during the period of 1860–1865, when Maxwell was professor at King's College, London, and Faraday was at the Royal Institution, where he had been for nearly sixty years. It was significant that at the close of that period, that is, in January, 1865, Maxwell. in a letter to an intimate friend, said this:

"I have a paper afloat, with an electromagnetic theory of light, which, till I am convinced to the contrary, I hold to be great guns."

A very strong claim made by the most modest of men! The paper was presented during that year to the Royal Society and was "great guns." It marks, like Newton's discovery of the law of gravitation and his formulation of the laws of dynamics, a new epoch in science. In Maxwell I saw a Newton of the electrical science, but I confess that in those days nothing more substantial than my youthful enthusiasm justified me in that opinion. I was aware that my knowledge of Faraday's discoveries and of Maxwell's interpretation of them was quite hazy, and I made up my mind to get more light before I started out for Berlin.

The summer vacation was on and I decided to take Faraday's "Electrical Researches" to Scotland, the land of Maxwell. In the preface to his great—and to me, at that time, enigmatic—electrical treatise Maxwell modestly had stated that he was an interpreter, only, of Faraday. But I was delighted when I heard Tyndall's suggestion that Faraday would help me to interpret Maxwell. Perhaps, thought I, the invigorating air of Maxwell's native Scotland would help me to catch some of the ideas which Maxwell had caught when he was reading Faraday. I selected what I thought would be a quiet and secluded spot, the island of Arran. It belonged to the Duke of Hamilton, and I was told that his grace had imposed so many restrictions upon his tenants that the island had become an ideal spot for those who sought seclusion. I found there a neat little inn at Corrie. It was surrounded by several tiny cottages for summer visitors who took their meals at the inn. It was popular with people from Glasgow, Greenock, and Paisley. Every one of the visiting families was blessed with numerous daughters. They were very athletic and played tennis from early morning till late in the afternoon, interrupted now and then by swimming contests in the frigid waters of the Firth of Clyde. In the evening there was lively dancing—not easy-going waltzing, but the real fling and reel of the strenuous Highland type. "What a sturdy race this is," I said to myself, as I watched the dancers working themselves up into a frenzy of rhythmic movements, one hand resting upon the hip, the other raised high up in the air, while their joyful limbs were pumping up and down in perfect rhythm as if they were busy pulling up from mother earth all the earthly joys stored up there for mortal man. The whole scene was particularly thrilling

to me when a piper came along and furnished the music.
The bagpipes reminded me of my native Idvor, and made
me feel at home in bonny Scotland before I had been
much over a week in Arran. The Scotch and the Serbs
have many things in common, and I always believed
that somewhere back in the history of Iran they must
have belonged to the same tribe. I am told that at the
Macedonian front the Scotch and the Serbian soldiers
got along beautifully, as if they had known each other
from time immemorial, and they had little use for the
other races assembled there. I got along at Corrie as if
I had known the Scotch all my life. But that had its
disadvantages also. I came to Corrie looking for seclusion
where, undisturbed, I could communicate with Faraday.
But the lively lassies from Glasgow, Greenock, and Paisley, the tennis and the swimming contests, the fascinat-
ing sound of the bagpipes accompanying the stirring
Highland dances—all these things whispered into my
ear: "Faraday can wait, but your friends here cannot."
Then I remembered a passage in one of Maxwell's letters,
given in Campbell's life of Maxwell, which said: "Well,
work is good and reading is good, but friends are better."
What a splendid excuse for joining the lassies and the
lads at Corrie and revelling in the healthful pursuits of
their youthful exuberance! Besides, said I to myself,
have I not accomplished enough during my eighteen
months' drilling under Routh, Maxwell, La Grange, Rayleigh, Stokes, and Tyndall to deserve a complete change
of mental and physical activity? When a person looks
for an excuse to do what he or she likes to do a splendid
excuse can always be found, and so I bade a temporary
farewell to Faraday's "Electrical Researches," and joined
the playful activities of my Corrie friends, challenging
them to go the limit. In tennis and swimming I held
my own, but the Highland reels floored me every time,
until Madge, one of the sturdy lassies from Greenock,

by persistent private instruction finally succeeded in initiating me into the mysteries of the Highland rhythm. Glen Sannox, near Corrie, with its rich bed of heather, watched me often by the hour making many futile efforts to catch this rhythm and make my limbs obey it. Nobody else watched these efforts in lonely Glen Sannox excepting Madge, and she, I told her, had more fun than a Bosnian gypsy training his bear. I can still hear the slopes of Glen Sannox echoing the clear notes of her ringing laughter, whenever I made an awkward and clumsy movement in my persistent efforts to master the Highland fling or reel. She could not help it, and I did not mind it, because I had made up my mind to do the trick or die. Finally I did it, not very well, but well enough for a fellow who was not a Scotchman, and Madge presented me with my portrait in pencil, which she drew during the intermissions between my efforts to master the art of the Highland dances. That was my reward and it was a very good one; she was a most promising young artist who had won several prizes in the Greenock art school. The memory of this experience always recalled to my mind the thoughts which went through my head at that time—the thoughts, namely, that Scotch originality, individuality, and sturdiness are hard to follow, not only when a foreigner meets these wonderful qualities in the mental activity of a Scot, like the mental activity of a Maxwell, but also in physical activity like that displayed in the national dances of Scotland. One does not appreciate fully the wonderful qualities of the Scot until he tries to master the theory and the practice of the Highland fling or reel. Maxwell's electrical theory, I thought, might be just as different from other electrical theories as the Highland dances are different from the dances of other nations. I found out later that my guess was not very far from the truth.

Several years ago I was driving through the streets of

London, visiting England again after an absence of many years. Suddenly I saw a crowd watching a Scotch dancer. The dancer was a young woman in Highland costume, and she was dancing the sword dance exquisitely; her husband was playing the bagpipes, marching up and down with all the swagger of the Scotch Highlander. I stopped my cab, got out, and watched. The memories of Corrie and Oban and of the gathering of the clans there which I witnessed while at Arran came back, and I was thrilled. Presently the dancer reached me in her tour soliciting voluntary contributions. I threw a sovereign into her plate and she looked surprised and asked me whether I had not made a mistake. "Yes," said I, "I did make a mistake when I went out with only one sovereign in my pocket. If I had two you should have them both." "Are you a Scotchman, sir?" she asked jokingly, and when I said "No" she smiled and said: "I did not think you were." She knew that there was a fundamental difference between a Scot and a Serb.

After I had been at Corrie for about a month a letter arrived from my mother, written by my oldest sister, telling me how happy she was that I had decided to spend my summer in Scotland for the purpose of meditating over the life and the work of one of the greatest "saints of science." I meant Faraday when I wrote to her. She also told me that Idvor was fearfully dusty on account of a long-continued drought, and that the crops were poor and the vintage prospects even poorer, and that Idvor was not a very cheerful place during that summer for anybody who wished to meditate free from complaints of grumbling neighbors. "Berlin, I am told, is much nearer to Idvor and when you are there you can always run down to Idvor, much more easily than you can now," she said, closing her letter, in which logic and motherly love vied with each other to furnish her with a consolation for my absence from Idvor during that summer.

My mother's letter made me feel guilty and it called for a reconsideration of my first resolution, adopted a month earlier, which authorized me to bid a temporary farewell to Faraday's "Electrical Researches"; and I passed another resolution rescinding my first. But the question arose, how to carry it into effect. The answer was obvious: bid good-by to Corrie. My friends, however, suggested a less obvious but certainly a much more agreeable answer. "Go up and live in the Macmillan homestead, and read your Faraday there in the morning and come down to Corrie for dinner, late in the afternoon," suggested Madge, and the suggestion was adopted without a dissenting voice on the part of my young friends.

The Macmillan homestead was a very humble old cottage located half-way between Corrie and the top of Goat Fell Mountain, the highest point on the island of Arran. An old crofter and his wife lived there, leading one of the most frugal existences that I had ever seen anywhere. They were willing to furnish me with lodging and simple breakfast, consisting of tea and oatmeal porridge with some bread covered with a thin layer of American lard. I did not object; I was prepared to take up low living and high thinking for the love of Michael Faraday. Communion with Faraday from early morning until four in the afternoon, and after that any play that came along, with plenty of dancing in the evening, was a splendid combination. Practically one solid meal a day, my dinner at the Corrie inn, supplied the fuel for all this activity, and it did it satisfactorily. How could I complain? The man whose wonderful scientific discoveries I was absorbing each day started life as a bookbinder's apprentice, and the founder of the great Macmillan publishing-house was born and passed his boyhood days in the humble cottage where I was lodging. I was sure that in their youth they never had more than one solid meal a day and they prospered. My rapid absorption and di-

gestion of the mental food which Faraday offered I attributed to my avoidance of superfluous physical food, but I must confess that I was quite hungry when dinner was served at the Corrie inn, and I enjoyed it immensely.

I never understood the full meaning of low living and high thinking as well as I did while I was a lodger at the Macmillan homestead. My thinking machinery, I thought, never worked better, and even my vision, always very good, seemed to be better than ever before. On exceptionally clear days I was sure that from the high elevation of the Macmillan cottage, on the slope of Goat Fell Mountain, I could see the beautiful Firth of Clyde as far as Greenock and Paisley, and at times even the gray and gloomy edifices of Glasgow seemed to loom up in the distance. I bragged about it, but my friends at Corrie met my bragging by informing me, jokingly, that any Scotchman can see much farther than that. One of them, a pupil of Sir William Thomson at the University of Glasgow, met my bragging by the epigrammatic question: "Can you see in Faraday as far as Maxwell, the Scotchman, saw?" I never bragged again about my vision while I was in Scotland. I was certain, however, that from the Macmillan homestead on the slopes of Goat Fell Mountain I obtained a deeper view into Faraday's discoveries than I could have obtained in any other place. I seldom mention the names of Faraday and Maxwell without recalling to memory the beautiful island of Arran and the humble Macmillan homestead on Goat Fell Mountain.

VIII

STUDIES AT THE UNIVERSITY OF BERLIN

EVERY period in the history of mankind had its revelation in science. Some periods were most fortunate in this respect. The first half of the nineteenth century saw the great scientific revelation called the Principle of Conservation of Energy, and considered it its greatest glory. Our own American philosopher, Benjamin Thompson, of Woburn, Massachusetts, known in Europe as Count Rumford, was one of several early prophets in science who foresaw the advent of this great dynamical doctrine. Its importance to mankind cannot be overestimated. I am sure that many a scientific man of those days felt grateful to heaven for the blessing of having lived during the age when that great revelation was received by mankind. The scientific men of to-day are grateful for having lived during the second half of the nineteenth century, when the great electromagnetic theory was revealed to man. Its importance, likewise, cannot be overestimated. But there is a radical difference in the historical progress of these two nineteenth-century revelations in science. The existence of the first was intuitively foreseen and may be said to have existed in one form or another in the minds of many scientific men long before it received its final form of statement. Its formulator, Helmholtz, thought that he was not announcing anything new, but was only stating his own view of something that was already well known. After his announcement, in 1847, every scientific man accepted the revelation as an almost self-evident truth. The electromagnetic

theory of light and of matter had a different history. It was born as a dim vision in the mind of a single man, Faraday, and nearly fifty years elapsed before it was formulated by Maxwell and experimentally demonstrated by Hertz. It was only then that the world began to understand that a great scientific revelation had appeared to man. To-day we know that new physical concepts requiring a new language for their expression had to be created in the minds of scientific men before the modern electromagnetic doctrine could be revealed to the world. The first glimpses of that revelation I caught on the slope of Goat Fell Mountain, and two years later I saw in Berlin what I believed to be a clear outline of its meaning.

When I look back to those days and consider how few were the physicists who had caught this meaning even twenty years after it was stated by Maxwell in 1865, I wonder whether it is possible to-day to convey that meaning to people who are not trained physicists. I think it is, and I believe that the attempt should be made, because the electromagnetic doctrine is to-day recognized to be the very foundation of all our knowledge of physical phenomena. I also think that one of the best methods of conveying that meaning is to describe my early attempts which failed to catch it.

Faraday's discoveries in the electrical science during the first half of the nineteenth century attracted world-wide attention and admiration. I knew that much at Arran, and I also knew of the rapid growth of the practical applications of his discoveries, to telegraphy, to generation of electrical power for electrical lighting, electrical traction, and electrochemical work, and finally to telephonic transmission of speech. The world understood that all these wonderful things, which contributed so much to the comforts of mankind, came from those sources in the realm of abstract science which were opened up by Faraday's discoveries. Scientific research began to assume a different aspect even in the eyes of the captains of industry who in those days showed lamentable indifference to science which did not promise immediate tangible returns. The advocates of scientific research, like Tyndall and his American and British friends, pointed with pride to Faraday's work whenever a question arose concerning the practical value of research in the domain of the so-called abstract physical sciences. This helped very much to arouse in this country and in Great Britain a deeper interest in what Andrew White called "strength and hope for higher endeavor."

But Tyndall's and Maxwell's descriptions of Faraday and of his work convinced me that Faraday's exalted position among his contemporaries like Maxwell, Henry, Tyndall, and Barnard was due not so much to the immediate practical value of his electrical discoveries, great as that value certainly was, as it was to the clear vision with which he searched for and revealed new morsels of the *eternal truth*. It was clear to me even at that time that inventions are the handwork of mortal man and that, though at first they appeal to us, as they ought to, as wonderful creations of human ingenuity, their ultimate fate is to become more or less commonplace. The telegraph and the telephone, the dynamo and the motor, the light of the electrical arc and of the incandescent filament, had lost much of their awe-inspiring character even at the time when I was a student at Cambridge. Inventions grow old and are superseded by other inventions, and, being the creation of the constructive schemes of mortal man, are themselves mortal. But the laws which the stars and the planets obey and have always obeyed in their paths through the heavens are unchangeable; they never grow old, and therefore they are immortal; they are a part of the *eternal truth*. We do not know of any natural processes by which eternal things have been evolved. Their existence is the best philosophic proof

From a photograph by John Watkins, London

MICHAEL FARADAY

Reproduced from Volume II of "The Scientific Papers of James Clerk
Maxwell," edited by W. D. Niven. By permission of the publishers,
The University Press, Cambridge

that back of all this changeable visible world there is the unchangeable, the eternal divinity. Archimedes, Galileo, and Newton co-operated in the discovery of immutable laws, and thereby revealed to mortal man morsels of the *eternal truth*. Oerstedt, a hundred years ago, discovered a morsel of the eternal truth when he discovered the magnetic force which is produced by the motion of electricity. Discoveries of immortal things and of the immutable laws which direct the mission of their immortal existence are themselves immortal. Their discoverers are, and deserve to be, immortal. Tyndall and Maxwell were the first to show me that Faraday occupied a distinguished place among such immortals as Archimedes, Galileo, Newton, and Oerstedt.

The closing sentence of Maxwell's biographical sketch of Faraday, in vol. VIII of *Nature*, referred to above, reads as follows:

We are probably ignorant even of the name of the science which will develop out of the materials we are now collecting, when the great philosopher next after Faraday makes his appearance.

To me these prophetic words indicated that Maxwell had something in his mind which was not explicitly expressed in Faraday's discoveries, but which enabled Maxwell to speak like a prophet. The words of a prophet are not always easy to understand. I discovered later that, when the world with the aid of the Hertzian experiments had caught Maxwell's meaning, then a new and wonderful epoch in the history of the physical sciences was inaugurated. Its end is not yet in sight. This inauguration I witnessed during my student days in Berlin. It is, I believe, of considerable interest to record here how the scientific world, as I saw it at that time, appeared to be preparing to receive the great revelation which was delivered to it on that historic inauguration day in 1887.

My communion with Faraday on the island of Arran

began my own preparation for this inauguration day by developing gradually in my mind new physical concepts, which I discovered later to be fundamental physical concepts in the modern views of physics. Long before I had finished my reading of Faraday's "Experimental Researches in Electricity," I began to understand why Tyndall, referring to them, said: "Read them; their story is just as new and as stirring to-day as it was when these volumes were first printed. They will help you much to interpret Maxwell." The same statement is true to-day, and therefore I proceed now, with much trepidation, to tell a part at least of that story as briefly as I can, in order to describe, even if it be quite inadequately, Faraday's relation to the present great epoch of modern physics, the epoch of the electromagnetic view not only of *light* but also of *matter*.

The gradual development of this view was due to the gradual development of new physical concepts which were born in Faraday's mind and existed there as a poetical vision; but in Maxwell's mind they appeared as physical quantities having definite quantitative relations to other well-known physical quantities, which a physicist can measure in his laboratory. In every creative physicist there is hidden a metaphysicist and a poet; but the physicist is less apt to persist in his occasional errors as metaphysicist and poet, because the creations of his speculative mind and of his poetical vision can be subjected to crucial experimental tests.

Faraday's "Experimental Researches in Electricity," published in three thick volumes, looked like very long reading. But my studies at Arran soon convinced me that no reading is long which continually stirs up the interest of the eager reader. Faraday was a pioneer in science, and the descriptions of his explorations read like tales from a new world of physical phenomena, full of poetical visions which his discoveries suggested to his

imagination. It must be said, however, that in spite of his wonderful imagination and his free use of it, no investigator ever succeeded better than Faraday in drawing a sharp line of division between the new facts and principles which he had discovered and the visions which his imagination saw in the still unexplored background of his discoveries. For instance, his discovery that a perfectly definite and invariable quantity of electricity is, as we express it to-day, attached to every valency of an atom and molecule, expresses a physical law which his experiments revealed and which he illuminated with all the light of his brilliant intellect. But when this new and precious morsel of the eternal truth had been disclosed by his experiments, then Faraday the scientist stepped aside, and Faraday the poet disclosed his visions about the constitution of matter suggested by what I called at Arran the atomic distribution of electricity in material bodies.

A man who discovers one of the most remarkable facts in modern science, namely, that in every atom and molecule there are definite and equal quantities of positive and negative electricity, and that the forces between these electricities are by far the largest known forces which keep together the components of chemical structures, cannot, if he has the imagination of a discoverer, refrain from asking the question: "What is matter?" The reader of Faraday's "Experimental Researches in Electricity" rejoices whenever Faraday, the poet and prophet, asks an apparently speculative question of this kind, because he knows that he will be thrilled by the poetical fancy which dictates Faraday's answer. Faraday's new facts and principles revealed by experiment are steeped in the honey of his fancy; they are rich food made delicious by the flavor of his poetical imagination, even when that flavor leaves the ordinary mortal guessing as to its exact meaning.

Two other questions Faraday often approached in these researches; they may be stated as follows: What is electricity? and, What is magnetism? He discovered that motion of magnetism produces electrical forces in a manner similar to that in which, according to Oerstedt's discovery, motion of electricity produces magnetic forces. This remarkable reciprocal relation between electricity and magnetism stirs up the imagination, and makes it eager to look behind the curtain which separates the region of the revealed truth from that which is still unrevealed. It was undoubtedly this eagerness of the explorer which encouraged Faraday to approach the questions, What is electricity? and, What is magnetism? Faraday never gave a final answer to these questions, but his magnificent efforts to find this answer gave birth to new ideas which are the foundation of our modern electromagnetic view of physical forces. One of the great pleasures of my life has been the contemplation of the gradual unfolding of this new view; and if in the course of this simple narrative I succeed in describing some of its beauties, I shall consider that this narrative was not written in vain.

Since, as explicitly stated by Faraday, electricity and magnetism are known by the forces, only, which they exert, it was plain to him, as his books, "Experimental Researches in Electricity," testify, that the first question which must be answered was the question: How are the forces between electrical charges and between magnetic charges transmitted through the intervening space—the same way as gravitational forces, or are they transmitted in a different way? In his unceasing efforts to answer this question Faraday made a radical and fundamental departure from the view of the natural philosophers of his time. He stood alone and devoted a very large part of his experimental work and of his philosophical thought to the justification of his position. He stood alone for a

very long time, because he was formulating a radically new physical concept which the world knows now to be one of the most fundamental concepts of the electromagnetic science of to-day; and it was difficult for his contemporaries and for his students of forty years ago, including myself, to understand him. In an address on Faraday by Helmholtz, which I read during my student days in Berlin, the following sentence refers to Faraday's difficulty just mentioned:

It is generally very difficult to define by a general statement a new abstraction, so that no misunderstandings of any kind can arise. The originator of a new concept of that kind finds, as a rule, that it is much more difficult to find out why other people do not understand him than it was to discover the new truths.

It was very consoling to me to find out in Berlin from no less an authority than Helmholtz that I was not the only poor mortal who was guessing in vain about the exact meaning of Faraday's visions.

Newton's law of gravitation enables the astronomers to calculate accurately from a simple mathematical formula the motion of celestial bodies, without any assumption concerning the mechanism by which gravitational force is transmitted from one body to another body at a distance, say, from the sun to the earth. Newton's formula says nothing about the time of transmission. The action can be assumed to be direct action at a distance and therefore instantaneous. Experience seemed to indicate that this assumption is correct, because no detectable errors are committed when one assumes that gravitational force travels with infinite velocity. Faraday refused to accept this belief in direct action at a distance for electric and magnetic forces. A few words, only, will suffice to describe how Faraday attempted to eliminate the belief in this direct action at a distance for electrical and magnetic forces. These attempts will al-

ways be recorded in history as the first steps in the development of the modern electromagnetic science.

Faraday, starting from points in the electrical and in the magnetic charges, drew numerous curves which indicated at every point in space the direction of the electric or of the magnetic force, and in that manner the whole space surrounding the charges he divided geometrically into *tubular filaments which he called the lines of force.* Every one of these filaments was constructed in accordance with a simple rule, so that it indicated at every point in space not only the direction but also the intensity of the force. A specific example, often employed by me at Arran, will illustrate this. A conducting sphere, say of copper or brass, is charged with positive or with negative electricity. When that charge is in equilibrium it is, as was well known, all on the surface of the sphere and uniformly distributed. Its force of attraction or repulsion, for electrical charges in the space outside of the sphere, is obviously along radii drawn from the centre of the sphere. These radii, drawn in every direction and sufficiently numerous, envelop little cones the vertices of which are at the centre of the sphere. Adjust the size of the cones in such a way that the area of the section of every one of them with the sphere is the same, and make their total number proportional to the charge on the sphere. These little cones are then in this particular case the Faraday lines of force, because their direction gives the direction of the electrical force, and their number per unit area of the surface of any concentric sphere is proportional to the electrical force at any point of the surface of this concentric sphere. According to this picture there are attached to each little element of the total charge a definite number of these conical filaments or lines of force, and each element of the charge on the sphere is nothing more than the terminal of these filaments. When the charge on the sphere is increased or diminished

the number of these filaments is also increased or diminished proportionately, and therefore they are more densely or less densely packed in the space which they occupy.

Should the charge on the sphere be set in motion, then the filaments or lines of force attached to it would also move. Thus far I followed Faraday, but went no farther; if I had gone just a little farther I should have met Maxwell. But, unfortunately for me, this simple picture which I constructed, in order to aid my understanding of Faraday's "Experimental Researches in Electricity" over which I pondered at Arran, suggested nothing more than a mere geometrical representation of the electrical force which the charged sphere exerts at any point in space. It conveyed no additional information which a simple mathematical formula, well-known at that time, did not convey. Additional information, however, was added by Faraday's imagination, which introduced here what I and many other mortals at that time considered a strange hypothesis. He described the hypothesis at great length in his books, and here is a brief statement of it:

Faraday claimed that all electrical and magnetic actions are transmitted from point to point along his lines of force; and, impelled by a remarkable intuition, he insisted that his lines of force are not mere geometrical pictures but that they had a real physical existence, and that there was something like muscular tension along these lines of force tending to contract them, and a pressure perpendicular to them tending to expand them; and that these tensions and pressures give the same numerical value for the mechanical force between the charges as that calculated from Coulomb's law, but with the fundamental difference, which Faraday pointed out, that his hypothesis demands a definite finite time for the transmission of electrical and magnetic forces; whereas according to the hypothesis of direct action at a distance, which Coulomb's law neither favors nor opposes, these forces are transmitted instantaneously. The question of the velocity of transmission of electrical and of magnetic forces through space became, therefore, a crucial question in the decision between the old view and Faraday's view.

In a letter addressed to Maxwell in 1857, and quoted by Campbell, Faraday said:

I hope this summer to make some experiments on the time of magnetic action . . . that may help the subject on. The time must probably be short as the time of light; but the greatness of the result, if affirmative, makes me not despair. Perhaps I had better have said nothing about it, for I am often long in realizing my intentions, and a failing memory is against me.

This letter was written ten years before Faraday's death, and nothing was ever reported about the result of the experiment planned by him. We know, however, that the result which he expected from the experiment was obtained thirty years later by Hertz, a pupil of Helmholtz.

I imagined at Arran that I could hear Faraday say:

Where the lines of magnetic force are there is magnetism, and where the lines of electric force are there is electricity.

Faraday's answer to the questions, "What is electricity?" and, "What is magnetism?" was, therefore, according to my understanding at that time, that they were manifestations of force; and where these manifestations exist there is electricity and there is magnetism, in the sense that there are pressures and tensions which are the result of a certain state of the space which may be called the electrical or the magnetic state. Faraday's visions, as I found them nearly forty years ago, disclosed in his "Experimental Researches in Electricity," went even so

far as to suggest that matter itself consists of centres of
force with lines of force proceeding from these centres
in every direction to infinite distances, and where these
lines are there is the body; in other words, every material
body, like every electrical and every magnetic charge,
extends to infinity by means of its lines of force; and hence
all material bodies are in contact, explicitly denying the
existence of ether. No mortal man ever suggested a bolder
conception! And yet to-day we know that a conception
regarding the structure of matter very similar to that
first conceived by Faraday is rapidly gaining universal
recognition, not merely as a new metaphysical specula-
tion but as the logical and inexorable demand of experiment. But when Faraday told me all these strange things
as I listened attentively on the slope of Goat Fell Mountain at Arran, I could not see anything in them except
geometrical pictures and a lot of what appeared to me
like pure metaphysics in the background of simple geometrical structures. Although I was sure that Faraday's
metaphysics had some definite physics back of it, I was
unable to disentangle it from the hypothetical notions
which I did not understand clearly. Maxwell, I thought,
must have disentangled that physics, and I often thought
of my Scotch friend at Arran who asked me the question:
"Can you see in Faraday as far as Maxwell, the Scotchman, saw?"

When I came to Berlin my head was full of Faraday's
lines of force starting at electrical and magnetic charges
and winding in all sorts of shapes through space, like
stream lines which start from the sources of a river and
follow it in its flow toward the ocean. The physical facts
and principles which Faraday discovered stood out sharply
defined like the bright stars in the firmament of a clear
and quiescent summer night; but the conception of the
new view of attracting and repelling electric and magnetic forces, which he represented graphically by his lines

of force, endowed with strange physical powers residing in pressures and tensions, left in my mind impressions which made me feel that my faith in the new doctrine was not very strong. Faith without conviction is a house built upon sand. Helmholtz said once:

I know too well how often I sat staring hopelessly at his descriptions of the lines of force, their number and their tensions.

Little I thought during my journey from Arran to Berlin in October, 1885, that two years later all the nebulous notions in my perplexed mind would lift like the mist before the early rays of a sunny autumn morning. I continued my studies of Faraday during my first year in Berlin, reserving for that purpose the necessary time for extra reading. What did the physicists of Berlin think, I wondered, of Faraday's tubes or lines of force?

I went to Berlin to study experimental physics with Hermann von Helmholtz, the famous professor of physics at the University of Berlin, the formulator of the principle of conservation of energy, and the first interpreter of the meaning of color both in vision and in music and speech. He was then the director of the Physical Institute of the university. His title, conferred upon him by the old Emperor, was Excellenz, and the whole teaching staff of the institute stood in awe when the name of Excellenz was mentioned. The whole scientific world of Germany, nay, the whole intellectual world of Germany, stood in awe when the name of Excellenz von Helmholtz was pronounced. Next to Bismarck and the old Emperor he was at that time the most illustrious man in the German Empire.

I had letters of introduction to him from President Barnard of Columbia College, and also from Professor John Tyndall of the Royal Institution. Professor Arthur Koenig, the right-hand man of Helmholtz and the senior instructor in the Physical Institute, took me to the office of Excellenz von Helmholtz and introduced me as Herr Pupin, a student from America, and the proposed John Tyndall fellow of physics of Columbia College. I was awarded the fellowship three months later. Koenig bowed before his master as if he wished to touch the ground with his forehead. I bowed American fashion, that is, with a bow of the head which did not extend below my shoulders, the same kind of bow which was practised at the University of Cambridge at that time, and I called it the Anglo-Saxon bow; it was entirely different from Koenig's bow. Helmholtz seemed to notice the difference and he smiled a benevolent smile; the contrast evidently amused him. He had much Anglo-Saxon blood in his veins; his mother was a lineal descendant of William Penn. It was understood in Berlin that he was the most "hoffähig" (presentable at court) scientist in the German Empire.

He received me kindly and showed deep interest in my proposed plan of study. His appearance was most striking; he was then sixty-four years of age, but looked older. The deep furrows in his face and the projecting veins on the sides and across his towering brow gave him the appearance of a deep introspective thinker, whereas his protruding, scrutinizing eyes marked him a man anxious to penetrate the secrets of nature's hidden mysteries. The size of his head was enormous, and the muscular neck and huge thorax seemed to form a suitable foundation for such an intellectual dome. His hands and feet were small and beautifully shaped, and his mouth gave evidence of a sweet and gentle disposition. He spoke in the sweetest of accents, and little, but his questions were direct and to the point. When I told him that I never had an opportunity to work in a physical laboratory and had paid exclusive attention to mathematical physics, he smiled and suggested that I should make up this deficiency as soon as possible. "A few experiments successfully carried out usually lead to results more important than all mathematical theories," he assured me. He then requested Professor Koenig to map out for me a suitable course in the laboratory and to look after me. Koenig did it, and I shall always be grateful to the sadly deformed and extremely kind little man with bushy red hair and distressingly defective eyesight, which he tried to correct with the aid of enormous spectacles employing lenses of extraordinary thickness. Helmholtz was always mellow-hearted to little Koenig, partly because, I think, Koenig reminded him of his own son Robert, who was deformed in hand and foot and back, but had the magnificently shaped head of his distinguished father.

During my first year's study in Berlin I attended Helmholtz's lectures on experimental physics. They were most inspiring, not so much on account of the many beautiful experiments which were shown, as on account of the wonderfully suggestive remarks which Helmholtz would drop every now and then under the inspiration of the moment. Helmholtz threw the search-light of his giant intellect upon the meaning of the experiments, and they blazed up like the brilliant colors of a flower garden when a beam of sunlight breaks through the clouds, and tears up the dark shadows which cover the landscape on a cloudy summer day. These lectures were attended not only by students in physics, mathematics, and chemistry, but also by medical students and army officers. The official world, and particularly the army and navy, paid close attention to what Excellenz von Helmholtz had to say; and I had much reason to believe that they consulted his scientific opinions at every step. I have often been called upon to correct the opinion that Helmholtz was a pure scientist par excellence. There is no doubt that his great work dealt principally with fundamental problems in scientific theory and in philosophy; but there is also no doubt that, like many other German scientists, he

HERMAN VON HELMHOLTZ
From a painting by L. Knaus

was much interested in the application of science to the solution of problems which would advance the industries of Germany. His earliest career is associated with his invention of the ophthalmoscope. The optical glass industry of Germany was being developed by some of his former students, who led the world in geometrical optics, a part of physics to which Helmholtz devoted much attention in his younger days.

One day I was on my way to the institute; in front of me walked a tall German army officer, smoking a big cigar. . When we reached the entrance of the institute the officer stopped and read a sign which said: "Smoking is strictly forbidden in the institute building." He threw his cigar away and walked in. I recognized Crown Prince Frederick in the officer. Two years later he became Emperor of Germany and ruled for ninety days. I watched his footsteps and saw that he entered Helmholtz's office and stayed there over an hour. He undoubtedly consulted the great scientist on some scientific problem which was then interesting the German army and navy.

Helmholtz's personality was overpowering and seemed to compel one's interest in problems in which he was interested, and at that time his principal interest was outside of the electromagnetic theory. Nevertheless, I kept up my interest in Faraday, which interest I brought with me from Arran; but I found no opportunity to ascertain Helmholtz's opinion concerning Faraday. Finally the opportunity came toward the end of my first year at the University of Berlin.

Gustav Robert Kirchhoff, the famous discoverer, formulator, and interpreter of the science of spectrum analysis, and the founder of the theory of radiation, was at that time professor of mathematical physics at the university. He was considered the leading mathematical physicist of Germany. His contributions to the electrical theory occupied a very high place. The most important of these was undoubtedly his theory of transmission of telegraphic signals over a thin wire conductor stretched on insulated poles, high above the ground. It was a magnificent mathematical analysis of the problem, and it showed for the first time that theoretically the velocity of propagation of these signals along the wire is equal to the velocity of light. The university catalogue announced that he was to deliver a course of lectures on theoretical electricity during the first term of my residence at the university. I attended the course and waited and waited, but waited in vain to hear Kirchhoff's interpretation of Faraday and Maxwell. At the close of the semester the course ended and the electromagnetic theory of Faraday and Maxwell was referred to on two pages only, out of two hundred; and the part so honored was not, even according to my opinion at that time, the essential part of the theory. In this respect the lectures were disappointing, but nevertheless I was most amply rewarded for my pains. I never heard a more elegant mathematical analysis of the old-school electrical problems than that which Kirchhoff developed before his admiring classes. That was the last course of lectures which he delivered; he died in the following year, and was succeeded by Helmholtz as temporary lecturer on mathematical physics.

Helmholtz was rather reserved and could not easily be approached by his students, unless they had some physical problem or a question which was unquestionably worthy of his attention. I made up my mind to ask him, when suitable opportunity presented itself, why Kirchhoff in his lectures paid so little attention to Faraday and Maxwell. It was a very significant sign of those days and I did not understand its meaning. Professor Koenig threw up his hands in holy horror when I informed him of my intention, and prophesied that all kinds of dire consequences would result from my daring proposition;

pointing out that such a question would betray a lack of respect on my part both for Kirchhoff and for Helmholtz. Koenig himself could not answer my question except to say that he did not see why the German school of physics should worry much about the English school, particularly when there was a radical difference between the two in the realm of the theory of electromagnetic phenomena. I admitted that if Kirchhoff was the spokesman of the German school then there was a radical difference, intimating however, in the mildest possible way that, in my humble opinion, the difference counted in favor of the English school. I really did not know enough to express that opinion, but I did it under provocation. Koenig flushed up and there would have been quite a lively verbal contest if Helmholtz had not entered my room at that very moment, like a *deus ex machina*. He was making his customary round of visits to the rooms of his research students, in order to find out how their work was moving along. Both Koenig and I looked somewhat perplexed, betraying the fact that we had been engaged in a heated argument, and Helmholtz noticed it. We confessed that we had had a lively discussion; when he learned the subject of our discussion he smiled and referred us both to an address which he had delivered before the Chemical Society of London, five years before. It is entitled, "Recent Developments in Faraday's Ideas Concerning Electricity." The same day saw me with two volumes of Helmholtz's addresses in my hands analyzing his Faraday address. I felt as I went on with this study as if the heavy mist were lifting which had prevented me from seeing a clear view of Faraday's and Maxwell's ideas. Tyndall's fame for clearing up obscure points in physical science was deservedly great, but when I compared Helmholtz's interpretation of Faraday and Maxwell with that which Tyndall gave me in his book entitled "Faraday as Discoverer," I marvelled at Helm-

of electrical charges through conductors) does not stop
at the surface of the conductor, but continues in the non-
conducting space beyond as motion of Faraday's lines of
force, as *motion of electricity*. The extension of the meaning of the word electrical current, just described, was,
according to Helmholtz, the cardinal difference between
the old electrical theories and the Faraday-Maxwell electromagnetic theory, and Helmholtz declared in favor of
the last. I applauded Helmholtz and took off my hat
to his clear vision of things which other people, including
myself, failed to see. But can any one blame ordinary
mortals, who were always accustomed to look upon the
electrical current as motion of electrical charges in conductors, when they failed to see that the electrical current
can take place even in a vacuum where there are no electrical charges at all, and therefore no motion of them?
That was the physical concept which found its way so
slowly into minds polarized by preconceived notions even
after Helmholtz's lucid explanation. This is substantially
all there is in the Faraday-Maxwell electromagnetic theory
as I gathered it directly from the Helmholtz address.
But there is another very important element which I
ought to describe here.

A corollary of Maxwell's extension of the meaning of
electrical current, which Helmholtz did not mention explicitly but which I soon found in Maxwell, is this: Electrical charges move because a force acts upon them; similarly the number of Faraday's lines of force, passing
through any surface in space, increases or diminishes because there is a force acting upon them. Wherever there
is an action there is an equal and opposite reaction, according to the most fundamental law of Newton's dynamics.
Hence space, including the vacuum, must react when
Faraday's lines of force (that is, when the electricity represented by them) move through it. But if this reaction
really exists in space, how can it be expressed? Faraday

and Maxwell devoted much thought and many experimental investigations in search for a definite answer to this question, and they found it.

Faraday showed by experiment that if the charged sphere is immersed in an insulating fluid, say an insulating mineral oil, or in a solid insulator like rubber, or even if a piece of an insulator is brought near it, then the reacting force for a given charge on the sphere is smaller than when the sphere is surrounded by a vacuum; or, in other words, liquid and solid insulators are more *permeable* to the electrical lines of force (that is, to electricity) than a vacuum is. Therefore, an electrical force which is acting in order to increase the charge on the sphere and, as a result, increase the number of lines of force through the surrounding space, will experience the less reaction the more permeable the surrounding medium is. The reaction of an insulator against the action of an electrical force appears therefore as a reaction against the passage of electricity, that is, of electrical lines of force, through it. That picture of the process has stayed with me ever since my Berlin days.

The same line of reasoning which I followed above, regarding electrical lines of force, leads to similar results with regard to the magnetic lines of force. The reaction of the medium against an increase of the electrical and of the magnetic lines of force through it was the second new physical concept introduced into the electrical science by Faraday and Maxwell.

The Faraday-Maxwell electromagnetic theory extended the well-known electrical and magnetic actions and reactions from conductors to non-conductors, including the vacuum. If this theory is correct, then electromagnetic disturbances will be propagated from their source to all parts of space, and not along conductors only, by definite waves travelling at a definite velocity.

Maxwell's calculation showed that electromagnetic

Hungarian school. I would have liked nothing better than to tell him how Maxwell answered the question: "What is Light?"

In the beginning of August of that summer I was in Idvor again, carrying with me the two volumes of Helmholtz's addresses. My mother received me with a heart which she described as overflowing with blessings which my visit and the visit of God's grace upon Idvor was pouring into it. The golden harvest was all in, and it was the richest that Idvor had seen for many a year; the grapes in the old vineyards were beginning to ripen, and the peach-trees among the rows of vines in the vineyards were heavily loaded with the juicy fruit of ambrosial flavor; the melons in the endless melon patches looked big and flourishing, and suggested that at any moment they might burst with the fulness of their exuberant prosperity. The dark-green corn-fields seemed to groan under the heavy load of the young ears of corn, and the pasturelands alongside of the corn-fields were alive with flocks of sheep, carrying udders which reminded one of the abundance of milk, cream, and cheese such as Idvor had seldom seen. All these things my mother pointed out to me, and she assured me that by the grace of God she was enabled to be a bountiful hostess to me, because she had everything in great abundance which she knew I always liked. Melons, cooled at the bottom of a deep well; grapes and peaches picked before sunrise and covered up with vine-leaves to keep them cool and fresh; young corn picked late in the afternoon and roasted in the evening in front of a wood fire; cream from sheep's milk supplied by the blessed sheep the day before. All these were sweet and delicious things; but have you ever tasted them when their sweetness is flavored by the love of an indulgent mother? If you have not, then you do not know what sweetness is. I warned my mother that her hospitality might transform me, as three years before, into a pampered pet who would be too slow to return to Berlin. Reminding me of the story which she had told me two years before, describing my climb up the steep and slippery roof of Bukovala's mill in search of a star, she said: "You have done much climbing during the last two years, and I know that in your climbing you have found several real stars from heaven. One of them is now in Berlin and no sweets in Idvor will keep you away from it." She guessed right, undoubtedly because she observed with what joy I kept up, during that vacation, my reading of Helmholtz's addresses.

Many a night during that summer I spent in my mother's vineyard sleeping on sheepskins under the open sky and looking at the stars at which I looked fifteen years before, when I helped the herdsman to guard the village oxen during the starlit summer nights. I remembered the puzzles which I tried to solve at that time concerning the nature of sound and of light, succeeding in the case of sound and failing in the case of light. I rejoiced at the feeling that I had finally succeeded in finding from Faraday and Maxwell through Helmholtz that sound and light resembled each other, one being a vibration of matter, and the other a vibration of electricity. The fact that I did not know what electricity is did not disturb me, because I did not know what matter is. Nobody knows the exact nature of these even to-day, except, as Faraday suggested, that they are manifestations of force. David's nineteenth Psalm, which I recited so often fifteen years before during my training in herdsmanship, conveyed a different meaning, and so did Lyermontoff's line which says that "star speaketh to star." They certainly spoke to me during those glorious August nights, when, covered with sheepskins, I lay in my mother's vineyard and amid the deep silence of slumbering earth I listened to their heavenly tales. The more

the heart-beat of every other star and of every living thing, even of the tiniest little worm in the earth, she answered:

"Faraday's science is that part of my religion which is described in the words addressed to God by King David:

" 'Whither shall I go from thy spirit? Or whither shall I flee from thy presence?

" 'If I ascend up into heaven, thou art there: if I make my bed in hell, behold, thou art there.'

God is everywhere, and where he is, there is every part of his creation." Her religion taught her how to catch the spirit of science, and I was always certain that science can teach us how to catch the spirit of her religion.

IX

END OF STUDIES AT THE UNIVERSITY OF BERLIN

I CONFESS that when I first arrived in Berlin I brought with me old prejudices, which were annoying, to say the least. The Teutonism in Prague, when I was a school-boy there, had made lasting impressions upon my young mind; they were with me when I landed at Castle Garden. Early impressions are very persistent and cannot be obliterated by time alone. Christian's father, the innkeeper of West Street, and his friends, the hardy Friesland sailors who taught me how to handle the paint-brush, drew me closer to the German heart, and I found it much less grasping than I thought it was. But the Frieslander of those days had no great love for the Prussian. Bilharz, the idealist of Cortlandt Street, gave me a more intimate knowledge of the German temper, and helped much to dispel many of my early prejudices. But Bilharz displayed decided dislike for the Prussians. The few German friends whom I had during my "greenhorn" days were southern Germans, and they did not appear to be very friendly to the idea of a united Germany under Prussian hegemony. These early experiences encouraged me in the belief that the Prussians were probably responsible for the Teutonism which I disliked. This belief was strengthened by Bismarck's anti-Russian and anti-Serbian, but strongly pro-Austrian, policy at the treaty of Berlin in 1878. He protested, I knew, that he would not sacrifice the bones of a single Pomeranian grenadier for all the Balkans; but I did not believe him. Hence the

uncomfortable feeling of being in an enemy country, when I first came to and settled down in Berlin.

The Teutonism of Prague, more than anything else, was responsible for it. Racial antipathy is one of the saddest of psychic derangements; and, although it is a repulsive product of modern nationalism, the world does less than nothing to get rid of its insidious poisons. European civilization is being destroyed by it. I suffered from its evil effects during the early days of my life in Berlin. Helmholtz, Koenig, and all the officers in the Physical Institute showed me every kindness and consideration, and that prevented me from turning around and speeding back to Cambridge as soon as the first breath of the atmosphere of Berlin gave me an acute attack of anti-Teutonism. My German landlady and her friends, as well as the German students I met in the lecture-rooms, struck no responsive chord in my heart, because it was out of tune with my surroundings. I remained a stranger in a cold, strange land. A young Scotch friend of mine, a graduate of the University of Glasgow, appeared on the scene, some time after I had become settled in Berlin. He kept his promise, given me at Arran, to join me in Berlin. He stayed at the university for one semester only and heard lectures on Roman law. He looked like a northern Apollo: tall and erect, the pink of youth radiating from his handsome face, and the locks of purest gold adorning a lofty brow, which made you believe that you were looking at a young Sir Walter Scott. His deepblue eyes knew of no suspicions, and his heart had never been touched by the poison of racial antipathy. He loved the world and the world loved him. His knowledge of German was very poor, and yet everybody loved to talk to him. Even the stern Schutzman (policeman), stirred up to white heat by too noisy a rendering of American and Scotch college songs in the slumbering streets of Berlin, was as gentle as a dove when the blue-eyed young

Scot stood in front of him and greeted him with a honey-hearted smile. My landlady, quite an aged person, as well as her young boarders, begged me to bring him to dinner as often as possible. "Yes, do bring him," said a sarcastic young fräulein; "you look quite human and almost handsome when he is around." There was much truth in what she said; the poison of racial antipathy did not operate in me when he was present. He made friends on every side among the German students, and when I saw how he warmed up to them and how they warmed up to him I began to thaw out myself. Helmholtz and dear little Koenig were the first persons in Berlin who helped me to forget that Europe was made up of different races who lived in eternal suspicion of each other. After that, following the example of my Scotch friend, I began to rid myself of the poisonous infection which I received from the Teutonism in Prague; but it was a slow process. Helmholtz's address on Faraday was so warm and so generous to Faraday as well as to Maxwell, and so wonderfully just, that I began to question the justice of my anti-Teutonic prejudices.

The two volumes of Helmholtz's addresses and public speeches which I enjoyed so much during that summer in my mother's vineyard made me almost repentant. My mother knew of my anti-Teutonic sentiments and never approved of them. One day we drove to visit my younger sister, who lived about fifteen miles from Idvor. On the way we passed through a large village, Echka, having a mixed population of German, Rumanian, and Serb peasants. There was a striking contrast in the appearance of the houses, of the people, and of their methods of moving about in the pursuit of their daily work. The German peasants were far ahead of the Rumanians as well as of the Serbs. My mother called my attention to it, but I made no comment. Presently we passed the stately Roman Catholic church of the village, which

looked like a cathedral. It was built, I was told, by the German peasants of Echka, and my mother told me that it was crowded on Sundays and holidays, and that the priest was a very learned and a very good man. When we passed the Orthodox church, which was quite small and insignificant-looking, my mother said: "Would you not feel ashamed if St. Sava came down to earth again and after seeing that splendid German church looked at this hut which is called the Orthodox church? But small as it is you will never find it filled except at some weddings or at memorial services for some departed rich person, when people expect much feasting."

Again I made no comment, because I was opposed to "alien intruders" myself, as some people called the German colonists; and my mother looked disappointed. Just then we saw two peasant girls carrying river water in shining copper vessels. These vessels were suspended at the ends of a long flexible staff which was nicely balanced on the shoulder of each young carrier, so that one vessel was in front and one behind her. The first girl was a blonde with slippers on her feet; a simple dark-blue dress covered her youthful figure and displayed the successive phases of her rhythmical movement. It was synchronized with the swinging motion of the bright copper vessels, which moved up and down like a double pendulum, bending the flexible shaft around its point of support on the shoulder of the fair carrier. The copper vessels, although filled to the brim, did not spill a single drop of water; the perfect adjustment of the swinging motion of the carrier to that of the swinging shaft produced this admirable result. The girl, the staff, and the shining vessels stood in a beautiful harmonic relation to each other. They reminded one of the harmonics in a sweet musical chord. It was a beautiful sight, and I said so. My mother, noticing my sudden burst of enthusiasm, sounded a warning. "She is a German girl," she said,

"and she certainly is lovely. Her heart and soul are in her job. But if you find one like her in Berlin, remember your promise; you must marry an American girl if you wish to remain an American, which I know you do."

She evidently had become a little alarmed at the thought that her praises of the Germans might cause my sentiments to swing too far the other way. The second water-carrier was a barefooted and gaudy-looking lassie, who stepped along any old way and marked her track with frequent splashes of water from the copper vessels. "She is a wild Rumanian," exclaimed my mother; "she can dance like a Vila, but she hates her job of carrying water. You will never find one like her in Berlin. The Germans have no use for people who do not love their daily duties." My mother was a great admirer of the thrifty and industrious German colonists in Banat, whom she always recommended as models to the peasants of Idvor. When she heard my praises of Helmholtz and my confession of racial antipathy to the Germans she put up many powerful arguments which were most convincing. They had a wonderful effect.

When I returned to Berlin from Idvor things looked more inviting, and my landlady remarked that I looked much more cheerful than I did a year before, when I arrived from Scotland. In another year, she suggested jokingly, I might look as cheerful as a real Prussian, particularly if I should succumb to the charms of a Prussian beauty. Remembering the promise that I had given to my mother about marrying an American girl, I said to my landlady: "Never! I have already pledged my word to one who is nearer to my heart than any Prussian beauty could ever be." "Ach, Herr Pupin, you have changed most wonderfully," exclaimed the landlady, and then she added in a whisper: "Just think of it! To get a confession on the first day of your return which I could not get before in nearly a year! I understand now why you

were always so distant to the young ladies in my pen-
sionat." But the change of feeling, speeded up by my
mother, and noticed by my landlady, was speeded up
almost as effectively by another Serb.

A Bosnian Serb with the name of Nikola had a fine
cigarette shop on Unter den Linden, the principal avenue
of Berlin. It was within a stone's throw from the Imperial palace, and the highest aristocracy of Berlin patron-
ized it. He was a rough diamond, and would stand no
nonsense from any prince or count. If they found fault
with his famous Turkish cigarettes he did not hesitate
to tell them to buy them somewhere else. But he prospered, he said, because these German aristocrats never
resented straight talk from man to man. He laughed at
me, when I mentioned to him my suspicions and antip-
athies; and begged me to pass with him, from time to
time, an hour or so in his store, and watch his German
customers. I did, and profited much. The Prussian aristocrats had no racial antipathy against a Serb, if their
apparently genuine affection for Nikola had any meaning. Nikola never left them in any doubt as to his pride
of being a Serb.

Half-way between Nikola's store and the Imperial
palace was an old chop-house, called Habel, dating from
the time of Frederick the Great. Frederick's generals
always stopped there for a glass of wine, when they returned from an audience with the king. The custom
persisted and was still in existence when I was a student
in Berlin. Nikola often invited me to early luncheon at
this chop-house, and there we saw the great generals
and marshals of the German Empire, sitting around a
long and separate table and taking a glass of wine after
returning from the Imperial palace, from their daily audience with old Emperor William. It was a wonderful
sight; those tall, broad-shouldered, deep-chested, brainy,
and serious-minded Teuton warriors inspired tremendous

respect. Nikola assured me that he knew many of them personally, they being his customers, and that as human beings they were as gentle as doves. "Many a time I called them down when they joked about my cigarettes, and they submitted without a murmur. Do you call that arrogance?" asked Nikola, throwing out his chest and trying to look as stern and as imposing as any of the generals present.

Once he took me to an avenue where Moltke used to walk and showed me the great field-marshal, who was then eighty-six years old, but still as straight as an arrow. "Did you ever see a more modest and thoughtful or a more spiritual-looking man anywhere?" asked Nikola, and I confessed that I had not. "Then stop your talk about Prussian pride!" exclaimed Nikola. On another occasion we walked to the park and he showed me Bismarck, riding on horseback, a friend and an adjutant accompanying him. Nikola saluted him and so did I, and Bismarck saluted back graciously. "Does he look like a brute, or like a fool who would try to convert by force all the Slavs into Germans?" asked Nikola, poking fun at my anti-Teutonic suspicions. "No," said I, "I do not think he does; in fact, I think he looks very much like Helmholtz, except that there is much less spirituality in his face than in that of the great scientist." "Helmholtz!" exclaimed Nikola, "even he would lose his saintly expression, if he had to carry the load of the whole empire upon his shoulders, the socialists on the top of his load pushing it one way, and the clericals at the bottom pushing it the other way."

Nikola was born in Bosnia when the Turks ruled supreme, and hence he was not much of a scholar; but he was a careful listener, and always thought through his own head; his judgment was remarkable, I thought. He knew who's who and what's what in Berlin better than many a foreign diplomat there. He used to joke about

it, saying that his knowledge was expected of him, because he was the next-door neighbor of the great Kaiser. The Serbs of Banat did not seriously dislike the German colonists there, nor did the colonists dislike them, and they delighted in speaking the Serb language. They called each other "komshiya," neighbor. The Serbs, in general, use this word when they refer to a German in a friendly way. Nikola always referred to the great Kaiser as his "komshiya"; many of his customers knew that and enjoyed it hugely. They returned the compliment and often addressed Nikola with the Serbian word "komshiya." "Come and see my komshiya," said he one day to me, and there I stood for the first time in front of the Imperial palace and waited for the old emperor to show himself at the window. He did that almost every day about noontime when the guards marched by on their daily parade. Presenting arms and looking straight at the old emperor, they marched by like a single body animated by a single heart and a single soul, and they spanked the ground with their vigorous goose-step, the rhythmic strokes of which could be heard quite a distance away through the ringing cheers of the enthusiastic crowd. "Do you know what that means?" asked Nikola. I answered "No," and he said: "It means that every German looks up to his fatherland for orders, and the perfect rhythm of that goose-step means that every German will obey these orders and finish on time any job for the good of the fatherland that may be assigned to him. It is the symbol of German unity." That was Nikola's unique interpretation; I never heard anybody else interpret it that way. But Nikola had a lively imagination and he evidently wished me to get a favorable interpretation of everything the Germans did.

Between my young Scotch friend, my mother, Nikola and my professors in the Physical Institute, I soon forgot the unpleasant memories of the Teutonism in Prague

and Berlin no longer looked to me like a Thraenenthal, a valley of tears, as my old friend Bilharz in Cortlandt Street would have called it. I soon found myself enjoying warm personal friendships of German fellow students and of the professors, and it was a very fortunate thing; it was providential. Nothing but the love of God and the friendship of man can give that spiritual power which one needs in moments of great sorrow. One day in the beginning of winter, of that year, a letter arrived from my sister, telling me that my saintly mother was no longer among the living. I vowed on that day that her blessed memory should be perpetuated as far as an humble mortal like myself could do it. Twenty-seven years later the Serbian Academy of Sciences announced that the income of a foundation in memory of Olympiada Pupin would be expended annually to assist a goodly number of poor schoolboys in Old Serbia and Macedonia.

The vanishing of a life which is an essential part of one's own life produces a mysterious shift of the direction of one's mental and spiritual vision. Instead of searching for light which will illuminate the meaning of things in the external physical world, as the vision of young people usually does, it begins to search for light which will illuminate the meaning of what is going on in the internal world, the spiritual world of our soul. The question "What is Light?" was no longer the most important question of my thoughts after my mother's death. The question "What is Life?" dominated for a long time my thoughts and feelings. I became introspective, and, being a somewhat temperamental person, like most Slavs, might have lost my way forever in the labyrinth of all sorts of metaphysical structures of my own creation. Providence came to my rescue. Two American students with aspirations in science similar to mine joined the Physical Institute. One of them, a Harvard graduate, the late Arthur Gordon Webster, was the very distinguished professor of physics at Clark University; the other, a Johns Hopkins man, Joseph Sweetman Ames, is now the director of the physical laboratory at Johns Hopkins and a worthy successor to the famous Henry Augustus Rowland. Their truly American enthusiasm and directness prevented me from relapsing into the drowsy indefiniteness, sometimes called idealism, of a temperamental and sentimental Slav. They told me many wonderful tales of the higher endeavor in science at Harvard and at Johns Hopkins. The new Jefferson Physical Laboratory at Harvard was a wonder, according to Webster; and Ames never grew weary of extolling the beauties of Rowland's wonderful researches in solar spectra, and I never grew weary of listening to them. At times, however, I wondered why these two men had ever come to Helmholtz when they were so well off at home. Ames wondered, too, and he returned to Rowland at the end of the year; but Webster stayed, although in my presence he never admitted unreservedly that the Physical Institute in Berlin was very much better than anything they had at Harvard. Webster's and Ames's testimony convinced me that the great movement in the United States for higher endeavor in science was making rapid progress and I longed to finish up my studies in Berlin and return to the United States. After my mother's death Europe attracted me much less.

A new physical science was attracting much attention in Germany at that time, the science of physical chemistry. Helmholtz was very much interested in it. I had read his latest papers on the subject and they reminded me of what I had seen in Maxwell's book on heat about Willard Gibbs of Yale. I soon discovered that the alleged German fathers of the new science were anticipated by Gibbs by at least ten years. Remembering the charge of De Tocqueville that the American democracy had never done anything for abstract science, I made a careful note of my find. It was a clean-cut little discovery, I thought, and Helmholtz admitted it. He suggested even that I might find material in it for a research leading to a doctor dissertation. I embraced the suggestion and started an experimental research, at the same time studying the theories of Gibbs, Helmholtz, and other authorities, mostly German, on physical chemistry. The more one penetrates the depths of any problem the more he yields to the belief that this problem is the most important problem in the world. This happened to me; and the Faraday-Maxwell electromagnetic theory was shelved, temporarily, on account of my interest in physical chemistry, and particularly on account of the prospect of finding there a doctor dissertation, which I finally did.

At the end of the first semester and at Webster's suggestion he and I, in the spring of 1887, went to Paris for a short visit. We wished to see what physical science was doing at the Sorbonne and at the Collège de France, and to compare the academic world of Paris with that of Berlin. We stayed there three weeks and learned quite a number of novel and interesting things. The architectural beauties of Paris as well as its art galleries and museums made a profound impression upon me. As a record of a magnificent old civilization Paris, I thought, was incomparably ahead of Berlin. The spirit of Laplace, La Grange, Fourier, Ampère, Arago, Fresnel, Foucault, and Fizeau was very much alive in the ancient halls of the Sorbonne and of the Collège de France. The background of a former glorious period of physical science in France was much more impressive in Paris than the corresponding background in Berlin. But for every one of the great savants in physical and mathematical sciences, who were active in Paris at the time of my visit, like Poincaré, Hermite, Darboux, Appell, Lippmann, one could name several in Berlin. And there was nobody in Paris who, in my opinion, could measure up to Helmholtz, Kirchhoff, and DuBois Reymond. There was no states-man there of Bismarck's caliber, and no general like Moltke. I saw no warriors who looked like the mag-nificent fellows whom Nikola first exhibited to me at the long table in Habel's. General Boulanger was very much in the limelight. I saw him at a great official reception, and I should have felt very sorry if the destiny of France had been intrusted to him. The physical and chemical laboratories were rather poorly equipped and compared unfavorably with the corresponding laboratories in Ber-lin. The draped statues in the Place de la Concorde, testifying to France's grief for the loss of Alsace-Lorraine, completed the picture of Paris in my mind, which was anything but cheerful. France, I thought, had not yet recovered completely from her wounds of 1870–1871 and I felt sorry. Two years earlier I had passed through Paris on my way from Pornic to Idvor and had carried away a much more cheerful picture. But at that time my observations, covering barely two days, did not see much and, besides, I did not know Berlin at that time and could make no comparisons. If Paris reflected the spirit of France and Berlin that of Germany, then France, I thought, was a falcon with broken wings and Germany was a young eagle that had just discovered the wonder-ful power of its pinions. The wonderful intellectual and physical vigor of the new empire impressed powerfully every foreign student at the University of Berlin when I was a student there. This gave me much food for thought and I searched for explanations.

There was one explanation which always appealed to me much on account of its simplicity. I heard it from a very learned German. This was his story: The German iron always contained phosphorus, including also the great deposits of iron which the Germans had found

Alsace-Lorraine. The only good iron that Germany had prior to 1880 was that in the Iron Chancellor. Hence, Germany could not build up a steel industry, and without it no great industrial development is possible in any country. A miracle happened; a young Englishman, a clerk in a London police court, made a discovery which was destined to give Germany its great steel industry. This was Sidney Gilchrist Thomas, who discovered the so-called "basic Bessemer" process. It made iron containing phosphorus easily available for the manufacture of iron and steel products. This started the modern steel industry of Germany in the early eighties. Many a street in the towns of the German steel districts was named in honor of Gilchrist Thomas. "This," said my informant, "is the power which, as you express it, the young German eagle has discovered in its pinions." I suspected that the object of his story might have been to discourage an opinion on my part that the remarkable vigor of Germany was derived from the weakness of France. Hence I looked up the data of his story, but I found them correct. Years ago I told this story to the late Andrew Carnegie, and he agreed with my German informant. To-day I am convinced that neither the great works of Krupp, nor the great German navy, nor many other things which have happened since my Berlin days, would have been possible without the start which was made with the aid of Gilchrist Thomas.

Another remarkable assertion from the same informant made a lasting impression. According to him, united Germany would not have endured very long, if it had not been for the rapid rise of the German steel industry and of other German industries which followed in its wake. The organization of Germany as an economic unit secured the organization of Germany as a political unit. He summed it up by saying that Bismarck and Moltke had raised the structure of the German Empire, but that Gilchrist Thomas had built a steel ring around it which prevented it from falling to pieces. He added then a corollary to this startling statement, and I repeat it here in the form of a question. If the scientific research of a young clerk in a London police court, who studied chemistry in a London evening school, could do so much for Germany, how much can one reasonably expect from the great research laboratories of the German universities and technical schools? This, according to my informant, had become a national question in Germany. This information reminded me that the great movement in Great Britain and in the United States for higher scientific research was also present in Germany, but in a much more advanced form. My informant called my attention to Werner von Siemens's pioneer work in this German movement.

Ernst Werner von Siemens was at that time, next to Helmholtz, the most admired scientist in the German Empire. He was the head of a great electrical plant in the heart of Berlin, and was known everywhere to possess a splendid combination of talents in abstract science and engineering. Men of that type were quite rare in those days, and they are very rare even to-day. I heard a great deal about him in a course of lectures on electrical engineering which I attended at the Polytechnic School of Berlin. I saw him several times, when he called at the Physical Institute on his friend and relative by marriage, Excellenz von Helmholtz. His remarkable appearance made a strong impression upon me, and I longed to see his great plant, where all kinds of electrical things were made, from the finest electrical precision instruments to the largest types of dynamos and motors, many of them his own inventions. As a sign of special favor Helmholtz gave me a note of introduction to his distinguished friend, who received me graciously and gave me to an official who took me around the great electrical plant the first that I had ever seen. The impression which it made upon my mind was certainly wonderful, but not more wonderful than the impression which the great personality of Siemens had made upon me. The more I learned about him the more I became convinced that no industrial organization ever had a presiding genius of greater attainments than Siemens. His attitude toward abstract science and its relation to the industries is best described by mentioning here a fact which is of great significance in the history of physical science. He founded in that year, 1887, the great Physical-Technical Institute, and presented it to the German nation; Helmholtz was its first president. The modern science of radiation rests upon a foundation first laid by Kirchhoff and greatly strengthened by additional experimental data obtained in this institute under the guidance of Helmholtz. Planck, the successor of Kirchhoff at the University of Berlin, already in office before I left Berlin, was undoubtedly inspired by these experiments when he formulated his great law of radiation which forms to-day the last word in the science of radiation, a great science which justly bears the mark "made in Germany," just as the electro-magnetic theory bears the mark "made in England." The Physical-Technical Institute will always stand as a memorial to the man who preached in Germany the doctrine of the closest co-operation between abstract science and the industries. Germany adopted it first; the United States adopted it many years later. Helmholtz and Siemens always represented to me the highest symbol of this co-operation.

Bismarck and Moltke, Helmholtz and Siemens, were the great power which the young German eagle had discovered in his pinions; and he flew as he had never flown before, and his flight astonished me when I was a student in Berlin. He who wants to know the real Germany of the eighties should study the lives of Bismarck and

Moltke, of Helmholtz and Siemens. They, I firmly believed at that time, were the leaders of the German constructive thought and action; they were the fathers of united Germany just as Washington and Hamilton, Franklin and Jefferson, were the fathers of this country. But would the spiritual influence of the fathers of united Germany produce a German Lincoln? I knew the historical background of the Declaration of Independence and also its historical foreground too well to answer this question in the affirmative. Extraordinary men can do extraordinary things, but the course of a nation's destiny will always be guided not by transient efforts of one or even of several extraordinary men of a given period, but by the persistent power of the nation's traditions.

My visit to Paris was to supply me with more knowledge of the academic world of France, and also with some fresh food for thought relating to my problem in physical chemistry, and it did in a measure. But the current of thought which was started by some of the strongest mental stimuli which I received in Paris had nothing to do with either physical chemistry or with academic France; it ran into German channels which I described above. These were the channels which ran through the minds of most university men in Germany, and in these channels every problem in art, science, and literature was viewed at that time from the standpoint of German economic and political unity. My German scientific friends, particularly those in eastern Prussia, where I spent the summer vacation of 1887, would rather discuss those problems than the problems in physical chemistry or in the electromagnetic theory. It took me some time after my return from Paris to get back completely to my research in physical chemistry. But no sooner had I gone back to it than the irresistible power of the current of big events, following each other in quick succession, took me away from it again. I shall describe them in their his

torical order, but only in so far as they are related to the
main thread of my narrative.

One of the many sources of inspiration at the University
of Berlin was the Physical Society which met
once a month at the Physical Institute. The research
students of the institute were admitted to these meetings,
and one can imagine what an inspiration it was to
them to see and to hear the scientists like Kirchhoff, the
great mathematical physicist, DuBois Reymond, the
great physiologist, Hoffman, the great chemist, and Helmholtz,
the greatest of them all. I often imagined while
attending these meetings and listening to the learned
remarks of these scientific giants, that I was a lucky mortal
who by some strange accident had found himself suddenly
among the great heroes in Walhalla. Helmholtz
usually presided, and his impressive physiognomy suggested
a Wotan presiding at a gathering of the Teuton
gods in Walhalla. Whenever I hear Wagner's Walhalla
motif I am reminded of those memorable scenes in the
Physical Institute in Berlin, the scenes of victory of the
immortal mind of man over mortal matter.

At one of those meetings, which took place toward
the end of 1887, many scientific giants of the university
were present and Helmholtz presided. There was an
atmosphere of expectancy as if something unusual was
going to happen. Helmholtz rose and looked more solemn
than ever, but I noticed a light of triumph in his eyes;
he looked like a Wotan gazing upon the completed form
of heavenly Walhalla, and I felt intuitively that he was
about to disclose an unusual announcement, and he did.
Referring to Doctor Heinrich Hertz, a former pupil of
his and at that time professor of physics at the Technical
High School in Karlsruhe, Helmholtz solemnly announced
that he would describe some remarkable experimental
results which Hertz had obtained by means of very rapid

electrical oscillations. He then described in his inimitable way a preliminary report which Hertz had sent him, pointing out, in a most lucid manner, the bearing of these experiments upon the Faraday-Maxwell electromagnetic theory, and affirming that these experiments furnished a complete experimental verification of that remarkable theory. Everybody present was thrilled, particularly when Helmholtz closed with a eulogy of his beloved pupil, Hertz, and with a congratulation to German science upon the good fortune of adding another "beautiful leaf to its laurel wreath." That thrill soon reached the physicists in every physical laboratory in the world; and for a number of years after that memorable announcement most investigators in physics were busy repeating the beautiful Hertzian experiments. The radio of to-day is an offshoot of those experiments.

This is no place to go into a detailed description of what Hertz did. The fundamental idea underlying his beautiful research and its relation to the Faraday-Maxwell far-reaching electromagnetic theory can be described in very simple terms. The wonderful achievements of radio broadcasting alone, to say nothing of other much more important achievements, demand this description. That idea, like the tiny seed hidden in a beautiful flower, lay hidden in Faraday's visions and in Maxwell's wonderful, but, to most ordinary mortals, enigmatic interpretation of them. Hertz, guided by his great teacher, Helmholtz, caught the hidden seed and out of it grew a physical embodiment of the Faraday-Maxwell theory, represented by ideally simple apparatus, operating in an ideally simple way. The apparatus and its operation are now the heart and soul of a new art, the radio art, a beautiful daughter of the beautiful mother, the Faraday-Maxwell electromagnetic science. The following description of Hertz's apparatus and of its operation was the theme of popular lectures and of many conversation which I had with my friends who were not physicists by profession. It represents quite closely the simple picture which I carried away in my mind from that memorable meeting of the Berlin Physical Society thirty-six years ago.

Two equal metal spheres A and B, each twelve inches in diameter, and each carrying copper rods C and D, are placed as indicated in the diagram given here. At E is an opening of about three-tenths

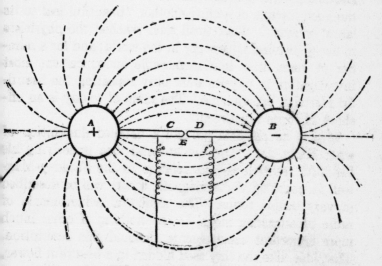

THE HERTZIAN OSCILLATOR

of an inch in length, the so-called *air-gap*. By means of two wires e and f, connected to an electrical machine, the spheres are charged, one receiving a positive electrical charge denoted by the (+) sign, and the other a negative one, denoted by the (−) sign. The air-gap E insulates one sphere from the other, and its function is to make it possible for the electrical machine to increase the two charges until a very high electrical tension is reached. When the electrical tension between the two charges, acting through the air-gap E, is sufficiently high, then the insulating power of the air-gap is overstrained and suddenly it breaks down and becomes conductive and permits the two charges to rush toward each other. The conductivity of the air-gap suspends the action of the charging machine. A large current passes then between the two spheres along the rods and through the air-gap E which is heated by the current to white heat. It becomes then a very good conductor and permits the charges to pass through it easily. The collapse of the air-gap is reported by the sharp crack of the electrical spark which is due to the very sudden heating and expansion of the air in the air-gap produced by the passage of the electrical current. It is a miniature lightning. The two charges reunite, the spheres are discharged, and after that the air-gap E recovers quickly from its breakdown and becomes an insulator again. The process is then repeated by the action of the machine and a rapid succession of sparks can be maintained, each one of them announcing by the crack of the spark the reunion of the charges that had been pulled apart and forced to the surfaces A and B by the action of the electrical generator.

All this was known long before Hertz. The first experiment of this kind I saw in Panchevo in my boyhood days, when my Slovenian teacher Kos explained to me the theory of lightning according to the views of Benjamin Franklin, a theory which clashed with the St. Elijah legend of Idvor and nearly proved me guilty of heresy. But there was something in these electrical discharges that Benjamin Franklin did not know, and that knowledge was first suggested by another great American scientist, a scientist even greater than Benjamin Franklin was in his day.

As far back as 1842 our own Joseph Henry performed experiments similar to those performed by Hertz, and he inferred, prophetically, that the discharge was oscillatory. Nobody ever suggested this idea before, but Henry's experiments permitted such an inference. Its oscillatory character was then demonstrated mathematically in 1853 by Professor William Thomson of Glasgow, and his calculation was proved to be correct by many experimental tests covering a period of over twenty-five years, and thus the electrical oscillator, similar to the one employed by Hertz, became a well-known apparatus.

What, then, was the novel element in the Hertzian work? It was, broadly speaking, his demonstration that the space surrounding the oscillator (the spheres with their rods) participates in the electrical oscillations in perfect agreement with the Faraday-Maxwell theory; a participation which was foreign to all previous electrical theories. In other words, he detected in the old electrical-oscillation experiments a new action, never detected nor even dreamed of before. He discovered the electrical waves in the space outside of the oscillator. Remembering the impression which Helmholtz's lecture on Faraday made upon my mind, I was certain at that time that nobody in Continental Europe but one of Helmholtz's pupils like Hertz could have predicted that there was in these well-known electrical oscillations a new action, an action demanded by the Faraday-Maxwell theory. A simple analogy will, I trust, help much to illustrate the new action which Hertz expected when he started out to search for an experimental test of the modern electromagnetic theory. No scientific expedition ever started out in search of scientific treasures and returned with a richer load.

Here is the analogy:

If by the force of our fingers we deflect the ends of the prongs of a tuning-fork and then let go, the prongs will return to their normal position after performing a number of vibrations of gradually diminishing amplitude. The state of rest is reached when the energy of bending, produced by the work of our fingers, has been expended, partly in overcoming the internal friction in the tuning-fork, partly in overcoming the reactions of the surrounding medium, the air; this last effect results in sound-waves which are radiated off into space. The stiffness and the mass of the prongs of the fork determine the period of vibration, that is, the pitch of the fork.

I confess that in the course of my life since my Berlin days I afforded considerable amusement to my friends whenever I tried to explain to them the Hertzian experiments by appealing to what I considered a well-known action of the tuning-fork. Some of them objected on the ground that this action is just as difficult to understand as the action of the Hertzian oscillator. I met this objection by describing to them the action of the reed in Serbian bagpipes which I watched when I was a boy, and understood sufficiently well to recognize later in the action of the tuning-fork a performance similar to that of the reed in the Serbian bagpipes. I understood the tuning-fork because I understood the reed. An educated American, I claimed, should find no difficulty in understanding the action of a simple mechanism which an uneducated Serbian peasant boy understood.

The Hertzian electrical oscillator, described above, acts like the tuning-fork. The process of pulling apart the two charges, the positive from the negative, and of forcing them to the surface of the spheres by the action of the electrical machine, is a parallel to the process of deflecting by the pressure of our fingers the prongs of the tuning-fork from their normal position. In one case the tuning-fork by its elastic stiffness reacts against the bending of the prongs. In the electrical case the electrical lines of force in the space surrounding the oscillator react against the action of the machine which crowds them into this space by stretching and compressing them. This is the picture of the action of the lines of force which Faraday gave me on the island of Arran, but I did not understand it. In the picture the dotted curves are the Faraday lines of force and the arrow-heads indicate the direction of the electrical force. The Hertzian oscillator, and what Helmholtz had told me before, made Faraday's language and thoughts much more intelligible. The work done by the machine is all expended upon the stretching and compressing of the lines of force into the space outside of the spheres, that is, upon the *electrification of that space*.

Compare now the motion of the tuning-fork, after the pressure of the fingers has been removed, to the electrical motion when the air-gap has broken down and the action of the electrical generator suspended. The prongs are driven back to their normal position by the elastic reaction due to the bending; but when they reach that position they are moving with a certain velocity, and their momentum carries them beyond that position; they move on until the energy of the moving mass has been expended in the work of bending the prongs in the direction opposite to that of the original bending. The prongs begin then to move back in the opposite direction, starting the second cycle of motion. The same line of reasoning will carry us into the third and fourth and every succeeding cycle of motion. It is obvious that these cycles will follow each other during equal intervals of time, which gives a definite pitch to the tuning-fork. A periodic motion of this type is called an oscillation or vibration; and it is clear that it is a periodic transformation of the energy of elastic bending into energy of motion of the mass of the prongs including the surrounding air, and vice versa. The motion is finally reduced to rest when the energy of bending, produced at the start by the work of the fingers, has been used up. The question, what has become of that energy? is very important in this connection. The answer is: It is used up partly in overcoming internal friction and *partly in overcoming the reactions of the surrounding air, which result in sound-waves.* A sound-wave is a short name describing the physical fact that in the air there are compressions and dilatations alternating at periodically recurring intervals. The production of sound-waves in the air is a proof that the air in the space surrounding the tuning-fork participates in the motions of the tuning-fork.

A perfectly analogous experiment was performed by Hertz with his electrical oscillator, and his principal object was to find whether the electrical field, that is, the electrified space surrounding the oscillator, reacted as did the air driven by the vibrating tuning-fork; if it did it would develop electrical waves. If these electrical waves actually existed, what did Hertz expect them to be? In the description of the oscillator and of its action, given above, two things only were mentioned: the action of the electrical machine which charges the oscillator and the reaction of the lines of force against the tensions and pressures which crowd them into the surrounding space. The electrical waves can, therefore, be nothing else than periodic variations of the tensions and pressures in the lines of force, that is to say, periodic variations in the destiny of the lines of force in the space surrounding the oscillator. This was what Hertz had found.

The breakdown of the air-gap in the electrical oscillator and the consequent suspension of the action of the electrical generator is analogous to the removing of the pressure of the fingers from the prongs of the tuning-fork. The electrical charges on the spheres with the lines of force attached to them, strained by tensions and compressions, are released, and they move toward each other through the conducting air-gap. Just as the prongs of the tuning-fork, after the pressure of the fingers has been removed, cannot remain in the strained position in which they have been bent, so the electrical lines of force, after the insulating air-gap has broken down and the action of the machine been suspended, cannot remain in the position to which they are stretched; they contract, and hence their positive terminals on one sphere and the negative on the other move toward each other. The motion of the strained lines of force with their terminals, the charges on the spheres, has a momentum. Maxwell was the first to show that the momentum of the moving electrical lines of force is equal to the number of magnetic lines of force which, according to Oerstedt's discovery, are produced by the motion of the electrical lines of force.

The motion of the electrical lines of force has not only momentum but also energy. Employing Faraday's mode of expression we can say that the electrical energy of the stretched electrical lines of force is thus transformed into energy of the electrical motions. This is perfectly analogous to the passage of the elastic energy of the bent prongs of the tuning-fork into the energy of motion of the moving mass of these prongs. Again, just as the momentum of the moving mass of the tuning-fork bends the prongs in the opposite direction and continues this bending until that motion has disappeared, so the momentum of the moving electrical lines of force will stretch again the electrical lines of force and continue this stretching until the energy of motion has disappeared, when the two spheres are charged again, but in the direction which is opposite to that in the beginning. A new cycle of electrical motion is then started again by the stretched electrical lines of force, repeating itself in an oscillatory fashion until the original electrical energy, produced by the charging electrical machine, has disappeared.

But where has the energy gone? This question is just as important in this case as it was in the case of the tuning-fork. The old electrical theories answered this question one way, and Maxwell, inspired by Faraday, answered it in another. The old theories maintained that there is no other electrical motion except the motion of the charges along the conducting surface of the spheres and the rods. They paid no attention to the motion of the lines of force, because they knew nothing about them. Their vision did not see the lines themselves but only their terminals, the charges. Hence, according to the old theories, all of the energy imparted by the machine is transformed into heat in the conducting parts of the oscillator.

Hertz was the first to prove that a part of the energy is radiated off into space, in a similar manner as the energy of a tuning-fork is radiated off in the form of sound waves. He detected in the space surrounding the oscillator the presence of electrical waves, that is, periodically recurring variations of the density of the electrical lines of force; he measured their length, and, having calculated the period of his oscillator, he divided the wave-length by the period and obtained the velocity of propagation. It came out, in his earliest experiments, roughly equal to the velocity of light, as the Faraday-Maxwell theory had predicted. The waves were reflected and refracted by insulators denser than air, and all these and other effects Hertz demonstrated to follow the laws which hold good for light, supporting admirably Maxwell's theory that light is an electromagnetic disturbance. Even this preliminary report which Hertz had sent to Helmholtz convinced everybody that the Faraday-Maxwell electromagnetic theory had triumphed, and that our knowledge of electromagnetic phenomena had been wonderfully extended. Subsequent experiments by Hertz and others added more and more laurels to this first victory.

That meeting of the Physical Society in Berlin was what I always considered the inauguration day of the electromagnetic theory. Prior to that day the theory existed in all its beautiful completeness, but it dwelt on high in the celestial heights of Faraday and Maxwell. Continental physicists needed the guidance of a Helmholtz to reach these heights. After that day it came down to earth and lived among mortal men and became part of their mode of thought. It was a heavenly gift which Hertz brought down to earth. Everybody was convinced that the science of light had become a part of the science of electricity.

This new knowledge was the second great revelation of the nineteenth century. The wonderful things which followed in its wake, even before the nineteenth century had closed, testify to the greatness of that revelation.

I have often asked myself the question, Why did not our Joseph Henry, who discovered the oscillatory electrical motions and operated with apparatus similar to that employed by Hertz, pursue his studies further than he did in 1842? and why did not Maxwell, the formulator

of the modern electromagnetic science, perform those
ideally simple experiments which Hertz performed? The
knowledge of the electrical oscillator was the same in
1865 as in 1887, and Maxwell undoubtedly had that knowledge. History offers an answer to these questions and
this answer throws a splendid light upon the character
of these two great scientists.

Soon after 1842 Joseph Henry resigned his professorship at Princeton College, and bade good-by to his laboratory where he had made several of his splendid discoveries,
and where in 1832 he had constructed and operated the
first electromagnetic telegraph, one of the practical results
of his great discoveries. This happened long before Morse
had ever been heard of. Henry's fame among men of
science was very great and promised to grow even greater
if he continued his scientific researches. He was still in
his prime, only a few years over forty. But a patriotic
duty called him to Washington, where the Smithsonian
Institution waited for his skilled hand to organize it
and to defend it against the scheming politician. This
duty tore him away from his beloved laboratory, and
he spent the rest of his life, over thirty years, in Wash
ington as secretary of the Smithsonian Institution, a
originator of most of the national scientific bureaus o
which this country is proud to-day. He was also the firs
president of the National Academy of Sciences, char
tered by Congress in 1863, thanks to his efforts. Physica
science under his leadership had rendered valuable ser
vice to the country during the Civil War, and the con
gressional charter to the National Academy of Science
was a graceful recognition of this service. I have already
pointed out Joseph Henry's splendid efforts for the ad
vancement of scientific research in this country and shal
return to it later. He was a great scientist, but he wa
also a great patriot; his country stood first and his own
scientific achievements and fame stood second in hi

heart. That, I am sure, was the reason why he did not pursue any further than he did his researches of electrical oscillations. I will mention here that one of the most gratifying results of my humble efforts was the naming of an electrical unit after his name. My colleague, the late Professor Francis Bacon Crocker of Columbia University, joined me most enthusiastically in these efforts; and the Electrical Congress in Chicago in 1893, at which Helmholtz presided, adopted the name Henry as the unit of electrical inductance; the unit Farad was named in honor of Faraday. No other electrical units are in more frequent use than the Farad and the Henry, particularly in the radio art. No other men contributed to this art as much as Faraday and Henry did.

Maxwell resigned his professorship at King's College, London, at the end of 1865, soon after he had communicated to the Royal Society his great *memoir* on the electromagnetic theory. The electromagnetic theory of light which, as I pointed out before, he had called "great guns" in a letter addressed to a friend, was the climax of it. He retired to his country place, Glenlair, in Scotland, and for five years he was free to devote his entire time to study and meditation. That was the highest joy of his life. But the Duke of Devonshire, a loyal Cambridge man, had presented the university with a goodly sum of money for the building and equipment of a physcal laboratory. It was to be named the Cavendish laboratory, after Lord Cavendish, the Duke's illustrious ancestor, who had devoted his life to electrical science. This gift was the Duke's response to the Cambridge movement in favor of scientific research. Maxwell was called to Cambridge to become the director of the new laboratory, and he responded, knowing well that, from that moment on, most of his time would be devoted to organization and administration. Duty to his university, and to the cause of scientific research in Great Britain, stood higher in his heart than the experimental demonstration of his great theory; that was certainly one of the reasons why Maxwell did not perform those ideally simple experiments which Hertz performed. But as director of the Cavendish laboratory he had trained a number of men, in order to prepare them to push on the line of advance where he had left it; and one of them, in particular, was soon to take the leadership in the rapid development of the Faraday-Maxwell electromagnetic theory.

The examples of Henry and of Maxwell must have been in Andrew White's mind when in 1873 he spoke those memorable words which I quoted before and will quote here again:

I will confine myself to the value, in our political progress, of the spirit and example of some of the scientific workers of our day and generation. What is the example which reveals that spirit? It is an example of *zeal*, . . . of *thoroughness*, of *bravery*, . . . of *devotion to duty* without which no scientific work can be accomplished, . . . of *faith* that truth and goodness are inseparable.

The Hertzian experiments created quite an upheaval in the research programme of the Physical Institute everybody seemed anxious to drop his particular subject of research and try his hand at the Hertzian waves. Several candidates for the doctor's degree yielded, but resisted and returned to my problem in physical chemistry, and plodded along as if nothing had happened. was very anxious to finish my research, get my doctor's degree, and return to the United States. But I soon found out that there are currents in human life which can influence the course of life of a young scientist much more powerfully than even a new and powerful current of thought in physical sciences.

During the first two months of 1888, Nikola, the Bosnian Serb, began to look worried. He informed me confidentially that he had received bad news about the health of his great "komshiya," the aged Kaiser. The audiences at the palace were separated by longer and longer intervals, and Habel's long table began to look deserted; the old generals with their splendid uniforms were conspicuously absent and the historic chop-house began to look commonplace. The daily parades of the guards were finally suspended, and there were no expectant crowds in front of the Imperial palace. The gay life of Unter den Linden became very much subdued. Finally the historic event occurred: the great emperor died on March 9, 1888. Berlin went into mourning and prepared for a funeral such as Germany had never seen before. "I have secured a balcony for you and your friends right over my store," said Nikola; "I want you and your friends to see the funeral procession as my guests." His grief over the death of the old emperor was really pathetic. He wanted me and my American friends to see the great procession which, according to his gloomy forebodings, was to mark the first step downward in the wonderful development of the German Empire. When, consoling him, I pointed out the well-known virtues of Crown Prince Frederick, he took hold of his larynx and his gesture indicated that he expected the death of the Crown Prince from his incurable malady. "What then?" I asked him. He answered: "Ask your Bismarck and Moltke, Helmholtz and Siemens; they are your oracles, perhaps they can answer your question; no ordinary mortal can."

Nikola had never met my American friends whom he mentioned in his invitation, but he had heard a great deal about them. My classmate at Columbia, A. V. Williams Jackson, now the distinguished Orientalist and professor at Columbia University, was at that time at the University of Halle, studying with the great Orientalist, Professor Geltner. He had visited me in Berlin and I returned his visit by spending with him a week-end at Halle. This was shortly before the great Kaiser's death.

Jackson's mother and two sisters were there on a longer
visit, and for two days I felt that I was back in New York
again, and I was supremely happy. On the way back to
Berlin I could not dismiss from my mind the memory
of my mother's words: "You must marry an American
girl if you wish to remain an American, which I know you
do." Ever since my return from Halle, I could hear these
words ringing in my ear no matter where I was, in my
lodgings, in the laboratory, in the lecture-rooms, or even
in Nikola's store. Nikola had read my thoughts, and
when he mentioned my American friends he meant Jackson and his mother and sisters at Halle. Well, they came,
they saw, and they conquered. One of Jackson's sisters
went to Italy during that spring and I followed; she returned to Berlin to join her mother and I followed; she
went to the island of Norderney, in the North Sea, to
spend a part of the summer season, and I followed. The
Faraday-Maxwell electromagnetic theory and the Hertzian experiments, my research in physical chemistry, and
the learned essays of Helmholtz and Willard Gibbs, and
of all the other fathers of physical chemistry, disappeared
from my mind as if they had never been there. The only
problem that could find a place there was the question
Will she accept me? She finally did, and I made a bee-
line for New York. in order to find out how soon I could
get a job there.

The Columbia authorities were organizing at that time
a new department in the School of Mines, the Department of Electrical Engineering, and they were glad to
see me and consult me about it. It was to start its work
a year from that time, that is, the end of September
1889. I was offered a position in it as "Teacher of Mathematical Physics in the Department of Electrical Engineering." A very long title, indeed, but such it was
and an interesting bit of history is attached to it. I accepted gladly and hurried back to Europe proud as

peacock. My fiancée and her family met me in London and I was married in the Greek church, according to the rites of the Orthodox faith the faith of my mother and of all my ancestors.

"Marriage gives that fulness to life which nothing else can give," said Helmholtz when I saw him again in Berlin and informed him that I was married and that I had been promised an academic position at Columbia College. He approved my dropping the experimental research and substituting in its place a mathematical research in physical chemistry. This research was finished in the early spring and I sent it to Helmholtz who was then in Baden-Baden. He telegraphed: "Your successful effort approved and accepted." Never before nor since did I ever receive a telegram which made me more happy. The examinations gave me no serious trouble, and in the late spring of that year I had my doctor's degree and became a citizen in the world of science. The three theses which, according to old German custom, every candidate seeking promotion to the dignity of a doctor of philosophy must frame and defend publicly are given here, in order to show my final mental attitude which was formulated by my scientific studies in Europe.

I. Instruction in Physics in the preparatory schools should be as much as possible a practical one.

II. The Thermodynamic methods of Gibbs, von Helmholtz, and Planck form the most reliable foundation for the study of those physical processes which we cannot analyze by ordinary dynamics.

III. The Electromagnetic Theory of Light deserves more attention than it has received so far in university lectures.

Usually these theses, appended to German doctor dissertations, are not taken very seriously either by the candidate, who is to be promoted, or by anybody else; but I took my theses very seriously. The first summed up President Barnard's doctrine relating to scientific instruction, which I described before in connection with my description of the American movement favoring scientific research in American colleges and universities; the second summed up my admiration for the new science of physical chemistry first started by our own Josiah Willard Gibbs; and the third summed up my love for the Faraday-Maxwell electromagnetic science. On these three questions in physical science I had, I thought, quite clear and definite ideas; and that gave me much confidence that I was about to return to the United States sufficiently equipped to render service in return for some of the many favors which I had received.

As the ship which carried me back to the United States entered New York Harbor I saw on my right Castle Garden; it looked the same as it did fifteen years before, when I first entered on the immigrant ship, and it reminded me of that earlier day. I said to my bride, who was standing by my side, that I did not carry much more money into New York Harbor than I did fifteen years before when I first looked upon Castle Garden, and yet I felt as rich as a Crœsus. I felt, I told her, that I owned the whole of the United States, because I was sure that the United States owned me; that I had an ideal American bride, who had assured me that I had lived up to the standards of an ideal American bridegroom; and that I had a fine position in a great American institution and strong hopes of filling it to everybody's satisfaction. I enumerated all these and other things to my bride and wound up by saying, jokingly: "I have also some prospects which modesty prevents me from mentioning," and then I added: "These are the only worldly goods with which I thee endow."

X

THE FIRST PERIOD OF MY ACADEMIC
CAREER AT COLUMBIA UNIVERSITY

THE new "Department of Electrical Engineering in
the School of Mines of Columbia College" had announced
its courses of instruction quite a number of months before I arrived in New York. The late Francis Bacon
Crocker, at that time the newly appointed instructor in
electrical engineering and my future colleague and life-
long friend, had been consulted with regard to these
courses, and he was most liberal to the theoretical side,
which was to be my share of the instruction. He attached
much importance to the fundamental theory, although
he was a practical engineer. The new department was
to be independent of the other scientific departments.
We had some difficulty, however, in maintaining that
independence; the older departments of engineering
showed a disposition to claim some right of guardianship
over the new infant department. For instance, many
chemists thought that electrical engineering was largely
chemistry on account of the storage batteries, the galvanic
cells, and the electrochemical processes which formed an
important part of the electrical operations in the early
history of applied electricity. Others asserted that, since
mechanical engineering attended to the design and the
construction of electromagnetic generators and to the
power plant which furnished the driving power, electrical
engineering was, therefore, largely mechanical engineering.

Crocker and I maintained that there is an electrical
science which is the real soul of electrical engineering,

and that every other abstract science or its application
was an incident only in electrical engineering. We won
out in spite of the fact that at other institutions of higher
learning in the United States electrical engineering was
taught in the departments of physics or of mechanical
engineering. But it was not an easy matter in those days
to persuade people that the electrical science with its
applications was then, or that it ever would be, big enough
to need a department of its own, like, for instance, civil
engineering.

A small brick shed, a temporary structure, had been
built at Columbia College to accommodate the new department. The students called it the "cowshed," and
the boy who invented the name did not indulge in any
stretching of his imagination. It certainly looked like a
cowshed. The laboratory equipment consisted of a
dynamo, a motor, and an alternator, with some so-called
practical measuring instruments. When I compared the
facilities of the new "Department of Electrical Engineering at Columbia College" with that of the Polytechnic
School in Berlin, I felt somewhat humbled, but not discouraged. I said to Crocker: "Our guns are small and
few in number; the men behind the guns will have to expand much beyond their present size if this department
is to make any impression upon the electrical art."
"Pupin," said Crocker, "you have no idea how rapidly
a young fellow grows when he tries to teach a new subject to poorly prepared beginners."

Crocker and I were given to understand that any additional equipment during the first year would have to
be bought from contributions outside of the university.
We raised some money by giving a course of twelve popular lectures for which we charged ten dollars per person.
Each lecture lasted two hours; we were somewhat dubious
about their quality, and so we provided a generous quantity. We raised in this manner three hundred dollars

and bought additional equipment, but no two young scientists ever worked harder to earn three hundred dollars. The experience, however, was worth many times that amount. Our audience consisted of business men and lawyers, who were either interested in the electrical industries, or expected to become interested. They had hardly any previous scientific training. It took much judgment and skill to talk science to these people without shooting much above their heads. Every one of them believed that the electrical science was in its infancy, and that most of its useful applications were obtained empirically by a rule of thumb. When we told them that the electrical science was one of the most exact of all physical sciences, some shook their heads and exhibited considerable scepticism. One of them asked me: "Doctor, do you know what electricity is?" "No," said I, and he added another question: "Then how can you have an exact science of electricity when you do not even know what electricity is?" To this I retorted: "Do you know what matter is? Of course you do not, nor does anybody else know it, and yet who will deny that there are exact sciences relating to material things? Do you deny that astronomy is an exact science?" It is a difficult thing to make unscientific people understand that science studies first and foremost the *activities of things and not their ultimate nature.*

In that first course of public lectures I found it necessary to devote much of my exposition to the correction of erroneous notions lodged in the minds of my audience. When I told that audience that no electrical generator generates electricity, because electricity was made by God and, according to Faraday, its quantity in the universe is constant, and that for every positive charge there is an equal negative one, most members of my audience were inclined to think that I was talking metaphysics. "Then what does it generate?" asked one of my hearers. I answered: "It generates motion of electricity, and by that motion it furnishes us with means of doing useful work like telegraphy, telephony, and electrical lighting." Then I added: "The electrical science studies the forces which make electricity move against the reactions of the bodies through which it moves; in the overcoming of these reactions the moving electricity does useful work." Illustrations from dynamics of material bodies did not help very much, because my audience had hardly any knowledge of even the elements of Newton's great work, although Newton considered these elements obvious truths. All they knew about Newton was that he had "discovered gravitation." When I told them that Newton had discovered the law of gravitational action and not gravitation itself, they thought that I was splitting hairs. I was never quite sure that those good people had carried away much knowledge from my lectures, but I was quite sure that they had left much knowledge with me. In trying to straighten out their notions I straightened out my own very considerably. Crocker was right when he said: "You have no idea how rapidly a young fellow grows when he tries to teach a new subject to poorly prepared beginners." That was the real profit from our first course of public lectures.

Every cultured person is expected to have an intelligent view of literature, of the fine arts, and of the social sciences, which is as it should be. But who has ever thought of suggesting that culture demands an intelligent view of the primary concepts in fundamental sciences? If cultured people had it, there would be no need to renew periodically the tiresome topic of the alleged clash between science and religion, and there would be much more straight thinking about things in general. Every child in the public schools should be made perfectly familiar with the simple experiments which illustrate th fundamental elements of Newton's divine philosophy, as Milton calls science. Barnard, Joseph Henry, Andrew White, and the other leaders of scientific thought in the United States, who started the great movement in favor of higher scientific research and of a better scientific education, had a difficult up-hill pull, because people in high places lacked an intelligent view of science. A famous lawyer, a trustee of a great educational institution, looked surprised when I told him, over thirty years ago, that one cannot teach science without laboratories both for the elementary and for the advanced instruction. He actually believed that graduate schools in science needed only a lot of blackboards, chalk, and sponges, and a lecturer who could prepare his lectures by reading books. He believed what he thought would suit him best, namely, that a university should be built on the top of a heap of chalk, sponges, and books. These instrumentalities are cheaper than laboratories, and that appeals to many university trustees. The teacher who can lecture from books and not from his experience in the laboratory is also much cheaper. But heaven help the country which trusts its destiny to cheap men operating with cheap instrumentalities. I gave that trustee a lecture by reciting the sermon which Tyndall preached in the "Summary and Conclusions" of his famous lectures of 1872–1873. I was bold enough to deliver several of these lectures to men in high places. Some liked them and some did not, but they all agreed that I had my own opinions upon the subject and was not afraid to express them.

The American Institute of Electrical Engineers had heard of my somewhat novel opinions regarding the teaching of the electrical science in its bearing upon electrical engineering, and it invited me to give an address upon the subject at its annual meeting in Boston, in the summer of 1890. The address was entitled "Practical Aspects of the Alternating Current Theory." It was a eulogy of the electrical science, and particularly of Faraday, Maxwell, and Joseph Henry on the purely scientific side, and of the technical men who were developing the system of electrical power distribution by alternating electrical forces. I noticed that my audience was divided into two distinct groups; one group was cordial and appreciative, but the other was as cold as ice. The famous electrical engineer and inventor, Elihu Thomson, was in the friendly group, and he looked me up after the address and congratulated me cordially. That was a great encouragement and I felt happy. Another man, a well-known physicist and engineer, also looked me up, and asked me whether I really expected that students of electrical engineering could ever be trusted to swallow and digest all the mathematical stuff which I had presented in my address. The "mathematical stuff" to which he referred was a very elementary theoretical illustration. I thought of my chums, the tripos youngsters at Cambridge, and of their wonderful capacity for swallowing and digesting "mathematical stuff," but said nothing; the man who was addressing me was one of those people who had a small opinion of the capacity and willingness of our American boys to "swallow and digest" just as much "mathematical stuff" as their English cousins do.

A short time prior to my return to Columbia College in 1889, a bitter polemic had been carried on in the New York newspapers concerning the two methods of electrical power distribution, the *direct* and the *alternating* current method. The New York interests favored the first and another group, including the Westinghouse Company, supported the alternating current method. The opponents of the latter method called it the "deadly alternating current," and did their best to discredit i They actually succeeded, I was told, in persuading th State authorities to install an alternating current machin at the Sing Sing prison, to be used in electrocutio

When in my address at Boston I recited my eulogy of the alternating current system I did not know of this bitter polemic, but when I heard of it I understood the chilliness among a part of my audience.

In the following autumn I was made to understand that my address in Boston had made a bad impression, and that it had offended the feelings of some *big* men who were interested in the electrical industries. I could not help seeing the glaring hint that the new "Department of Electrical Engineering at Columbia College" was to suffer from the fact that one of its two instructors was accused of an unpardonable "electrical heresy." The great and mighty person who broached this matter to me suggested that perhaps the easiest way out of this difficulty was my resignation. "Very well," said I, "I will certainly resign if the trustees of Columbia College, who appointed me, find me guilty of a scientific heresy." The trustees never heard of this incident, but my colleague Crocker did, and he said in his characteristic manner: "There are many persons to-day who would not hesitate to burn the witch of Salem, but no persons of that kind are on the board of trustees of Columbia College." Crocker was a Cape Cod man and he had a very soft spot for the witch of Salem.

The notion among many captains of industry that the electrical science was in its infancy, and that it worked by the rule of thumb, made it possible to launch an opposition of that kind against the introduction of the alternating current system of electrical distribution of power. Tesla's alternating current motor and Bradley's rotary transformer for changing alternating currents into direct were available at that time. The electrical art was ready then to do many of the things which it is doing to-day so well, if it had not been for the opposition of people who were afraid that they would have to scrap some of their direct current apparatus and the plants for manufacturing it, if the alternating current system received any support. A most un-American mental attitude! It was clear to every impartial and intelligent expert that the two systems supplemented each other in a most admirable manner, and that the advancement of one would also advance the other. Men like Elihu Thomson and my colleague Crocker knew that, but ignorance and false notions prevailed in the early nineties, because the captains of electrical industries paid small attention to highly trained electrical scientists. That explains why in those days the barbarous steel cables were still employed to drag cars along Third Avenue, New York, and why in 1893 I saw the preparatory work on Columbus Avenue, New York, for installing additional barbarous steel ropes to drag street-cars. But, fortunately, electrical traction came to the rescue of Columbus Avenue.

During the summer of 1893 I had the good fortune to meet, quite often, William Barclay Parsons, the distinguished engineer, the future builder of the first New York subway, and to-day the distinguished chairman of the Board of Trustees of Columbia University. He passed the summer vacation at Atlantic Highlands, and I at Monmouth Beach, and we used the same steamboat in our occasional trips to New York. His head was full of schemes for the solution of the New York rapid-transit problem, but I observed that his ideas were not quite clear on the question of the electrical power transmission to be employed. A very few years later his ideas had cleared wonderfully. He had visited Budapest in 1894 and had seen there surface cars operated electrically and most satisfactorily by an underground trolley. It was a most instructive object-lesson, but how humiliating it was to the engineering pride of the great United States to consult little Hungary in electrical engineering! The electrical power transmission system employed to-day in the New York subways is practically the same which had been proposed to and accepted by Parsons, the chief engineer, not so many years after our trips to New York, in 1893; it is the electrical power transmission consisting of a combination of the alternating and direct current systems. No fundamentally novel methods were employed which did not exist at the time when the alternating current machine was installed at Sing Sing for the purpose of electrocuting people by the "deadly alternating current." In less than five years a radical change in popular notions had taken place about a matter which was well understood from the very first by men of higher scientific training, like Stillwell, the chief engineer of the Niagara Power Company, and Sprague, the well-known pioneer in electrical traction, the inventor of the multiple unit system, without which our subway would be practicably impossible.

Four historical events, very important in the annals of the electrical science in the United States, had happened in rapid succession between 1890 and 1894. The first was the successful electrical transmission of power between Lauffen and Frankfurt, in Germany, in 1891; it employed the alternating current system. The second was the decision of the Niagara Falls Power and Construction Company to employ the alternating current system for the transmission of its electrical power; Professor Henry Augustus Rowland, of Johns Hopkins University, as consulting expert of the company, favored this system; another consulting scientific expert, the famous Lord Kelvin, favored the direct current system. The third historical event was the consolidation of the Edison General Electric Company with the Thomson-Houston Company of Lynn, Massachusetts. This consolidation meant the end of the opposition to the alternating current system on the part of people who were most influential in the electrical industries. No such opposition could exist in an electrical corporation where Elihu Thomson's expert opinion had any weight. The fourth historical event was the Electrical Congress at the World Exposition in Chicago, in 1893. Helmholtz came over as an official delegate of the German Empire, and was elected honorary president of the congress. The subjects discussed at that congress, and the men who discussed them, showed that the electrical science was not in its infancy, and that electrical things were not done by the rule of thumb.

Once I asked Professor Rowland whether anybody had ever suggested to him resigning from Johns Hopkins University on the ground that in favoring the alternating current system for the Niagara Falls Power Transmission plant he had made himself liable to a charge of heresy. "Heresy?" said he; "I thought that my heresy was worth a big fee, and when the company attempted to cut it down the courts sustained my claim." An interesting bit of history is attached to this. When the Niagara Power and Construction Company objected to the size of the fee which Rowland charged for his services as scientific adviser, and asked for a reduction, the matter was referred to the court. During Rowland's cross-examination the defendant's lawyer, the late Joseph Choate, asked him the question: "Who, in your opinion, is the greatest physicist in the United States?" Rowland answered without a moment's hesitation: "I am." The judge smiled, but agreed with the witness, and his agreement was in harmony with the opinion of all scientific men. Rowland justified his apparently egotistical answer by the fact that as a witness on the stand he was under oath to speak the truth; he certainly spoke the truth when he testified that he was the leading physicist in the United States.

Rowland's interest in the electrical science and its technical applications helped much to dissipate the notion, entertained by many, that it was empirical and still in its infancy. Bogus inventors always encouraged this superstition. The attention which Rowland and his former pupil, the late Doctor Louis Duncan, devoted to electrical engineering at Johns Hopkins University helped much to raise the status of electrical engineering. When the new General Electric Company was organized by the consolidation of the Edison General Electric Company and the Thomson-Houston Company, Elihu Thomson became the chief scientific adviser of the new corporation, and its highest court of appeals in scientific matters. I remember telling my colleague, Crocker, that if the Thomson-Houston Company had contributed nothing else than Elihu Thomson to the new corporation it would have contributed more than enough. Thomson, in my opinion, was the American Siemens, and Rowland was the American Helmholtz, of the new era in the history of American industries—the era of close co-operation between abstract science and engineering. With these two men among the leaders of the electrical science and the electrical industry in the United States, the senseless opposition to the alternating current system of power distribution began to wane. It vanished quickly after the Electrical Congress of 1893. The first visible result of the co-operation between abstract science and the technical arts was the splendid power plant at Niagara Falls, and later the electrical power distribution system in the New York subways, in which the alternating and the direct current systems supplemented each other most admirably.

The scientific spirit of Rowland's laboratory and lecture-room was felt everywhere in the electrical industries; it was felt also in our educational institutions. His and his students' researches in solar spectra and in other problems of higher physics made that spirit the dominating influence among the rising generation of physical science in America. It was universally acknowledged that Johns Hopkins was a real university. The intellectual movement in favor of higher scientific research, first inaugurated by Joseph Henry, President Barnard of Columbia College, and Doctor John William Draper, in the early seventies, was marching on steadily under the leadership of Rowland when I started my academic career at Columbia, thirty-four years ago, and he led on like a "doughty knight of Troy," as Maxwell used to call him. It was the spirit of Johns Hopkins which inspired the generation of the early nineties in its encouragement of the movement for the development of the American university. Some enthusiasts at Columbia College went even so far as to advocate the abolition of the college curriculum and the substitution of a Columbia University for Columbia College; I was not among these enthusiasts, because I knew only too well the historical value of Columbia College and of other American colleges. What would the University of Cambridge be without its ancient colleges? College lays the foundation for higher citizenship; the university lays the foundation for higher learning.

Speaking for physical sciences I can say that in those days there was no lack of trained scientists who could easily have extended the work of the American college and added to it a field of advanced work resembling closely the activity of the European universities. Most of these men had received their higher academic training in European universities, and quite a number of them came from Johns Hopkins. But there were two obstacles: first, lack of experimental-research facilities; second, lack of leisure for scientific research. Rowland and his followers recognized the existence of these obstacles, and demanded reform. Most of the energy of the teacher of physical sciences was consumed in the lecture-room; they were pedagogues, "pouring information into passive recipients," as Barnard described it. My own case was a typical one. How could I do any research as long as I had at my disposal a dynamo, a motor, an alternator and a few crude measuring instruments only, all intended

HENRY AUGUSTUS ROWLAND (1848–1901)
First Director of the Physics Laboratory of Johns
Hopkins University

By courtesy of the Columbia University Library

JAMES CLERK MAXWELL (1831–1879)
First Director of the Cavendish Laboratory at
Cambridge University

to be used every day for the instruction of electrical-engineering students? When the professor of engineering died, in the summer of 1891, a part of his work, theory of heat and hydraulics, was assigned to me. The professor of dynamics died a little later, and his work also was transferred to me. I was to carry the additional load of lecture-room work temporarily, but was relieved from it, in part only, after several years. As a reward my title was advanced to adjunct professor, with an advance of salary to two thousand five hundred dollars per annum. But in return for this *royal* salary I had to lecture three to four hours each forenoon, and help in the electrical laboratory instruction in the afternoons. While this pedagogic load was on my back scientific research could not be seriously thought of. My young colleagues in other colleges were similarly situated. This overloading of young scientists with pedagogic work threatened to stunt, and often did stunt, their growth and also the growth of the rising American university. "Let chairs be founded, sufficiently but not luxuriously endowed, which shall have original research for their main object and ambition," was the historic warning which Tyndall addressed to the American people in 1873, but in 1893 there was little evidence that it was heeded anywhere outside of Johns Hopkins University. But there they had Rowland and a number of other stars of the first magnitude who had succeeded Joseph Henry, Barnard, and Draper as leaders of the great movement in favor of higher scientific research. In 1883 Rowland delivered a memorable address as vice-president of one of the sections of the American Association for the Advancement of Science. It was entitled, "A Plea for Pure Science," and described the spirit not only of Johns Hopkins of those days but also of all friends of higher learning in science. That spirit was advocated here by Tyndall in 1872–1873, and under Rowland's leadership it was bound to win our battle for higher ideals in science. The people of the United States owe a great debt of gratitude to Johns Hopkins for the leadership in that great movement which, as we see to-day, has produced a most remarkable intellectual advancement in this country. Nearly thirty years ago I heard Rowland say in a public address: "They always say in Baltimore that no man in that city should die without leaving something to Johns Hopkins." When he said it he knew that Johns Hopkins was very poor. It is poorer to-day than ever, and no rich man in the United States should die without leaving something to Johns Hopkins, the pioneer university of the United States.

Rowland said once that lack of experimental facilities and of time was not a valid excuse for neglecting entirely scientific research. I agreed with that opinion; neglect breeds indifference, and indifference degenerates into atrophy of the spirit of inquiry. The alternating current machine of the electrical engineering laboratory at Columbia was free in the evenings, and so was my time; that is, if my wife should not object, and, being a noble and unselfish woman, she did not object. With the assistance of several enthusiastic students, among them Gano Dunn, to-day one of the most distinguished engineers in the United States, I started investigating the passage of electricity through various gases at low pressures, and published two papers in the *American Journal of Science*. I soon discovered that most of my results had been anticipated by Professor J. J. Thomson, of Cambridge, who, in all probability, had received his inspiration from the same source from which I had received mine. He not only had anticipated me but, moreover, he showed a much better grasp of the subject than I had, and had much better experimental facilities. I decided to leave the field to him, and to watch his beautiful work from the outside. It was a wise decision, because it prepared me to understand the epoch-making discoveries in this field which were soon to be announced, one in Germany and one in France. I turned my attention to another field.

I must mention, however, one of the results which Thomson had not anticipated and which created quite an impression among astronomers. I noticed a peculiar appearance in the electrical discharge proceeding from a small metal sphere which was located in the centre of a large glass sphere containing air at low pressure. The discharges looked very much like the luminous corona of the sun which astronomers observe during eclipses, and which was always a mysterious puzzle in solar physics. Pasting a tin-foil disk on the glass sphere, so as to hide the metal sphere and see only the discharge proceeding from it, I photographed the appearance of the discharge and obtained the pictures given opposite page 294. The resemblance of these photographs to those of the two types of the solar corona is most striking. This is what I said about it at that time:

"The bearing which these experimental results may have upon the theory of the solar corona I prefer to leave to others to decide. That they may prove a suggestive guide in the study of solar phenomena seems not unreasonable to expect."

In a communication read later before the New York Academy of Sciences I was much bolder, having previously discussed the subject with my friends at Johns Hopkins and with the late Professor Young, the famous astronomer at Princeton. I soon found myself advocating strongly the electromagnetic theory of solar phenomena. A German professor, Ebert by name, a well-known authority on electrical discharges in gases, took me very seriously indeed, which was very flattering, but he claimed priority. I had no difficulty in establishing my priority through the columns of *Astronomy and Astrophysics*, one of whose editors was George Ellery Hale, to-day the distinguished director of Mount Wilson Observatory. I was indeed fortunate to make his acquaintance during that period when both he and I were very young men. His influence prevented me from running wild with my electromagnetic theory of solar phenomena. Thanks to the splendid astro-physical researches at the Mount Wilson Observatory in California under Doctor Hale's direction, we know to-day that enormous electrical currents circulate on the surface of the sun, and we know also from other researches that negative electricity is shot out from all hot bodies, even from those not nearly as hot as the sun, and that the solar corona is, in all probability, closely related to this electrical activity on the sun.

After giving up the subject of electrical discharges in gases I looked around for another problem of research which I could manage with my meagre laboratory facilities. Rowland had found distortions in an alternating current when that current was magnetizing iron in electrical power apparatus. This distortion consisted of the addition of higher harmonics to the normal harmonic changes in the current. This reminded me of harmonics in musical instruments and in the human voice. Helmholtz was the first to analyze the vowels in human speech by studying the harmonics which they contained. The vowel o, for instance, sung at a given pitch, contains in addition to its fundamental pitch—say one hundred vibrations per second—other vibrations the frequencies of which are integral multiples of one hundred, that is two, three, four, . . . hundred vibrations per second. These higher vibrations are called harmonics of the fundamental. Helmholtz detected these harmonics by the employment of acoustical resonators; it was an epoch making research. I proceeded to search for a similar procedure for the analysis of Rowland's distorted alternating currents, and I found it. I constructed electrical

ECTRICAL DISCHARGES REPRESENTING TWO TYPES OF SOLAR CORONA

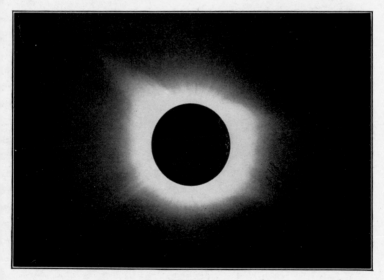

SOLAR CORONA OF 1922
Photographed by the Lick Observatory Expedition to Australia

resonators based upon dynamical principles similar to those in the acoustical resonators employed by Helmholtz. These electrical resonators play a most important part in the radio art of to-day, and a few words regarding their operation seem desirable. In fact, there is to-day a cry from the Atlantic to the Pacific on the part of millions of people who wish to know what they are really doing when they are turning a knob on their radio-receiving sets in order to find the correct wave length for a certain broadcasting station. I am responsible for the operation, and I owe them an explanation of it.

The mass and form of an elastic body, say a tuning-fork, and its stiffness determine the pitch, the so-called *frequency* of vibration. When a periodically varying force, say a wave of sound, acts upon the tuning-fork, the maximum motion of the prongs will be produced when the pitch or frequency of the moving force is equal to the frequency of the tuning-fork. The two are said then to be in resonance, that is, the motion of the fork resonates to or synchronizes with the action of the force. Every elastic structure has a frequency of its own. The column of air in an organ-pipe has a frequency of its own; so has the string of a piano. One can excite the motion of each by singing a note of the same frequency; a note of a considerably different frequency excites practically no motion at all. Acoustical resonance phenomena are too well known to need here any further comment. There are also electrical resonance phenomena very similar to those of acoustical resonance. If you understand one of them there is no difficulty in understanding the other.

If an electrical conductor, say a copper wire, is coiled up so as to form a coil of many turns, and its terminals are connected to a condenser, that is to conducting plates which are separated from each other by insulating material, then the motion of electricity in that conducting circuit is subject to the same laws as the motion of the prongs of a tuning-fork. Every motion, whether of electricity or of matter, is determined completely by the force which produces the motion, and by the forces with which the moving object reacts against the motion. If the law of action of these several forces is the same in the case of moving matter as in the case of moving electricity, then their motions also will be the same. The moving forces are called the *action* and the opposing forces are called the *reaction*, and Newton's third law of motion says: *Action is equal to the opposing reaction.* I always considered this the most fundamental law in all physical sciences. It is applicable to all motions no matter what the thing is which moves, whether ponderable matter or imponderable electricity. Twenty-six years ago a student of mine, Albert R. Gallatin, brother of the present park commissioner of New York, presented a large induction coil to the electrical laboratory at Columbia College in recognition of my services to him, because, he said, this formulation of the fundamental law in the electrical science, which I have just given, made everything very clear to him. This was most encouraging to a young professor, and it goes without saying that ever since that time he and I have been warm friends. He is a banker and I am still a professor, but the interest in the fundamental principles in physical sciences are a strong bond of union between us.

The electrical force which moves the electricity in the circuit, just described, experiences two principal reactions. One reaction is due to the lines of electrical force which, attached to the electrical charge on the condenser plates, are crowded into the insulating space between these plates. This reaction corresponds to the elastic reaction of the prongs of the tuning-fork, and follows the same law. In the case of the tuning-fork the *elastic reaction is proportional to the displacement* of the prongs from their normal position; in the electrical case the reacting force is proportional to the electrical charges which have been pulled apart, the negative from the positive, and driven to the plates of the condenser. Call this separation *electrical displacement*, and the law can be given the same form as above, namely: *The reacting force is proportional to the electrical displacement*. The greater the distance between the plates, and the smaller their surface, the greater is the reaction for a given electrical displacement. By varying these two quantities we can vary the electrical yielding, the so-called capacity, of the electrical condenser. This is what you do when you turn the knob and vary the capacity of the condenser in your receiving set.

The moving prongs have a momentum, and a change in the momentum opposes a reacting force, the so-called inertia reaction, which is equal to the rate of this change. This was discovered by Galileo over three hundred years ago. We experience the operation of this law every time we bump against a moving object. The Irish sailor who, after describing the accident which made him fall from the mast, assured his friends that it was not the fall which hurt him but the sudden stop, appreciated fully the reacting force due to a rapid change of momentum. Every boy and girl in the public schools should know Galileo's fundamental law, and they would know it if by a few simple experiments it were taught to them. But how many teachers really teach it? How many of my readers really know that law? Just think of it, what an impeachment it is of our modern system of education to have so many intelligent men and women, boys and girls, ignorant of so fundamental a law as that which Galileo discovered so long ago!

The moving electricity has a momentum. The magnetic lines of force produced by this motion are a measure of this momentum. Their change is opposed by a reacting force equal to the rate of this change. This was discovered by Faraday nearly a hundred years ago. The larger the number of turns in the coil of wire the larger will be the momentum for a given electrical motion, that is, for a given electrical current. But how can anybody understand very clearly this beautiful law, discovered by Faraday, who does not understand Galileo's simpler discovery? The fact that electricity, just like matter, has inertia, and that both obey the same law of inertia, is one of the most beautiful discoveries in science. Whenever I thought that so many intelligent and cultured people knew nothing about it I rebelled against the educational system of modern civilization.

The motion of electricity in the conductor described above overcomes reacting forces which follow the same laws as the motion of the elastic prongs of the tuning-fork. The motion of one has, therefore, an analogy in the motion of the other. In an electrical circuit having a coil and a condenser the moving electricity has a definite inertia and a definite electrical stiffness; hence it will have a definite pitch or frequency for its vibratory motion, just like a tuning-fork; it will act as a resonator. It is obvious, therefore, that an electrical resonator, the pitch of which can be adjusted by adjusting its coil or its condenser or both, is a perfect parallel to the acoustical resonator. By means of an electrical resonator of this kind, having an adjustable coil and an adjustable condenser, I succeeded in detecting every one of the harmonics in Rowland's distorted alternating currents, in the same manner in which Helmholtz detected the harmonics in the vowel sounds, but with much greater ease, because the pitch of an electrical resonator can be very easily and accurately changed by adjusting its coil and condenser. There are millions of people to-day who are doing that very thing when they are turning the knobs on their radio receiving sets, adjusting them to the wave-length of the transmitting station. The expression, "adjusting them to the pitch or frequency of the transmitting station," is much better, because it reminds the operator of the analogy existing between acoustical and electrical resonance. The procedure was inaugurated thirty years ago in the "cowshed" of old Columbia College. I called it "electrical tuning" and the name has stuck to it down to the present time. The word "tuning" was suggested by the operation which the Serbian bagpiper performs when he tunes up his bagpipes, which I watched with a lively interest in my boyhood days. Those early impressions had made acoustical and electrical resonance appear to me later as obvious things.

The results of this research were published in the *American Journal of Science* and also in the *Transactions of the American Institute of Electrical Engineers for* 1894. They, I was told, had never been anticipated; and they confirmed fully Rowland's views concerning the magnetic reaction of iron when subjected to the magnetic action of an alternating current. When Helmholtz visited this country in 1893, I showed him my electrical resonators and the research which I was conducting with their assistance. He was quite impressed by the striking similarity between his acoustical resonance analysis and my electrical resonance analysis, and urged me to push on the work and repeat his early experiments in acoustical resonance, because my electrical method was much more convenient than his acoustical method.

Helmholtz was always interested in the analysis as well as in the synthesis of vibrations corresponding to articulate speech. The telephone and the phonograph were two inventions which always enjoyed his admiring attention. During his visit in America he looked forward with much pleasure to meeting Graham Bell and Edison. The simplicity of their inventions astonished him, because one would hardly have expected that a simple disk could vibrate so as to reproduce faithfully all the complex vibrations which are necessary for articulation. He spent a Sunday afternoon as my guest at Monmouth Beach and in the course of conversation I told him what impression the telephone had made upon me when I first listened through it. It happened during the period when I was serving my apprenticeship as greenhorn, and when I was trying hard to master the articulation of the English language. The telephone plate repeated perfectly everything spoken at the other end, and I said to myself: "These Americans are too clever for me; they can make a plain steel plate articulate much better than I can ever expect to do it with all my speaking organs. I had better return to Idvor and become a herdsman again." Helmholtz laughed heartily and assured me that the articulating telephone plate had made a similar impression upon him, although he had spent several years of his life studying the theory of articulation. "The phonograph disk is just as clever as the telephone disk," said Helmholtz, "perhaps even more so, because it has to dig hard while it is busily talking."

My scientific friends in New York saw in the construction of my electrical resonator and in its employment for selective detection of alternating currents of definite frequency a very suitable means for practising harmonic telegraphy, first suggested by Graham Bell, the inventor of the telephone. They finally persuaded me to apply for a patent and I did so. I often regretted it, because it involved me in a most expensive and otherwise annoying legal contest. Two other inventors had applied for a patent on the same invention. One of them was an American, and the other a French inventor, and each of them was backed by a powerful industrial corporation. A college professor with a salary of two thousand five hundred dollars per annum cannot stand a long legal contest when opposed by two powerful corporations; but it is a curious psychological fact that when one's claim to an invention is disputed he will fight for it just as a tigress would fight for her cub. The fight lasted nearly eight years and I won it. I was declared to be the inventor, and the patent was granted to me. But a patent is a piece of paper worth nothing until somebody needs the invention. I waited a long time before that somebody came, and when he finally showed up I had almost forgotten that I had made the invention. In the meantime I had nothing but a piece of paper for all my pains, which nearly wrecked me financially.

Just about that time the newspapers reported that a young Italian student by the name of Marconi, while experimenting with Hertzian waves, had demonstrated that a Hertzian oscillator will send out electrical waves which will penetrate much longer distances when one of its sides is connected to earth. "Of course it will," said I, "the grounded oscillator takes the earth into closer partnership." When as a herdsman's assistant on the pasturelands of my native Idvor I stuck my knife into the ground and struck its wooden handle, I knew perfectly well that the ground was a part of the vibrating system, and that the sound-producing stroke was taken up by the ground much better than when I struck the knife-handle without sticking the knife into the ground. But I also knew that unless the boy who was listening pressed his ear against the ground he would not hear very much. It was, therefore, quite obvious to me that the best detector for a Hertzian oscillator which is grounded must be another Hertzian oscillator which is also connected to the ground. Grounding of the sending and of the receiving Hertzian oscillators was in fact the fundamental claim of the Marconi invention. Marconi, in my opinion, was unwittingly imitating the young herdsmen of Idvor when, figuratively speaking, he stuck his electrical knives into the ground for the purpose of transmitting and receiving electrical vibrations, but the imitation was a very clever one; very obvious indeed as soon as it was pointed out, like all clever things.

Every now and then we are told that wireless signals might be sent some day to the planet Mars. The judgment of a former herdsman of Idvor considers these suggestions unscientific for the simple reason that we cannot get a ground on the planet Mars and, therefore, cannot take it into close partnership with our Hertzian oscillators. Without that partnership there is no prospect of covering great distances. A very simple experiment will illustrate this. Scratch the wood of a pencil and ask your friends who are sitting around a table whether they hear the scratching. They will say "No." Put the pencil on the table and scratch it again; your friends will tell you that they can hear it faintly. Ask them to press their ears against the table and they will tell you that the scratching sound is very loud. In the third case the pencil, the table, and the ears of your friends are all one closely interconnected vibratory system. Every herdsman of Idvor would interpret correctly the physical meaning of this experiment. "If Marconi had waited just a little longer I should have done his trick myself," I said jokingly to Crocker, and then I temporarily dismissed the matter from my mind as if nothing had happened. But I was fairly confident that my electrical resonators would some day find a useful application in this new method of signalling, and Crocker was even more hopeful than I was. I turned my attention to another problem and would have completed its solution, if my work had not been interrupted by the announcement of a most remarkable discovery made in Germany, I mean the discovery of the Roentgen rays.

I cannot describe the effects of this epoch-making discovery without referring again to great Helmholtz. It was due to his initiative that Hertz took up the research of electrical oscillations, which suggested to Marconi their technical application. This started a new technical art, wireless telegraphy, which developed into the radio art. Without Helmholtz, not only the experimental verification of the Faraday-Maxwell electromagnetic theory but also the radio art might have been delayed quite a long time. I shall point out now that the great discovery of the Roentgen rays also was due in a great measure to the initiative of Helmholtz.

While in Berlin I was conducting a research upon vapor pressures of salt solutions. For this purpose I needed the assistance of a clever glass-blower. A Herr Mueller was recommended to me by the people of the Physical Institute. I paid frequent visits to him, not only because I liked to watch his wonderful skill in glass-blowing, but also because he knew and entertained me often with the history of a remarkable physical research which had been carried out by Doctor Goldstein, a Berlin physicist, under the auspices of the German Academy of Sciences, Herr Mueller, the glass-blowing artist, assisting.

The motion of electricity through rarefied gases was first extensively studied in Germany in the fifties and sixties by several investigators. Hittorf was one of them, and I mention him here for reasons given later. The English physicists took up the subject a little later, and among them Crookes did the most distinguished work. His tubes with a very high vacuum gave brilliant cathode rays, first discovered by Hittorf, which produced among other things the well-known phosphorescence in vacuum tubes made of uranium glass. In spite of the surpassing beauty of the electrical phenomena in vacuum tubes revealed by Crookes's experiments, no final and definite conclusions could be drawn from them toward the end of the seventies. But he was undoubtedly the first who correctly inferred that the cathode rays were small electrified particles moving with very high velocity. This inference proved to be of very great importance. In 1893

Lord Kelvin said: "If the first step toward understanding the relations between ether and ponderable matter is to be made, it seems to me that the most hopeful foundation for it is knowledge derived from experiment on electricity in high vacuum." This was the very opinion which Helmholtz had formulated fifteen years earlier, and he persuaded the German Academy of Sciences to make a special grant for a thorough experimental review of the whole field of research relating to electrical motions in high vacua. Doctor Goldstein was selected to carry out this work. Mueller was his glass-blower. The most important result of this work was the discovery of the so-called *Canal Rays*, that is, motion of positive electricity in the direction opposite to the motion of negative electricity the latter being the cause of the *cathode rays*. To get that result Mueller had to make innumerable vacuum tubes of all sorts of shapes. He told me that if all these tubes could be resurrected they would fill the house in which his shop was located. "But the grand result was worth all the trouble, and I am proud that I did all the glass-blowing," said Mueller, with a triumphant light in his eyes, and his beaming countenance testified that he felt what he said. He was an artisan who loved his craft and, judging from his remarkable knowledge of all the vacuum-tube researches which had been conducted up to the time of his co-operation with Doctor Goldstein, I inferred that he was a unique combination of the science and the art involved in the job which he was doing for Doctor Goldstein. Mueller was the first to arouse my interest in the results of vacuum-tube researches, and I always considered him one of my distinguished teachers in Berlin. New knowledge is not confined to the lecture-rooms of a great university; it can often be found in most humble shops, treasured by humble people who are quite unconscious that they are the guardians of a precious treasure. Mueller was one of these humble guardians.

The importance of Goldstein's work was due principally to the fact that it brought into the field three other German physicists of great acumen. The first one was Hertz. Several years after he had completed his splendid experimental verification of the Faraday-Maxwell electromagnetic theory, he showed that the cathode rays penetrated easily through thin films of metal, like gold and aluminum foil, although these films were perfectly opaque to ordinary light. It was a novel and most important contribution to our knowledge of cathode rays, and would have been followed up by more additional knowledge if Hertz had not died on January 1, 1894, at the age of thirty-six. Helmholtz died several months later. Science never suffered a greater loss in so short an interval of time. Helmholtz met with an accident on the ship on his return trip from the United States in 1893. He never completely recovered, although he lectured at the University of Berlin until a few days before his sudden death in the midsummer of 1894. Autopsy revealed that one side of his brain was and had been in a pathological state for a long time, but nobody had ever observed that his intellectual power had shown any signs of decay. It is a pity that he did not live another two years; he would have seen what he told me during his visit here he longed to see, and that is an electrified body moving at a very high velocity suddenly reversing its motion. That, he thought, might furnish a direct experimental test of the mobility of ether. The discovery described below furnished such a body.

Hertz's work was continued and greatly extended by Professor Lenard of the University of Kiel. He would have undoubtedly reached the final goal if Roentgen had not announced, in December, 1895, that he, experimenting with Lenard vacuum tubes, had discovered the X-rays. This discovery marked the last step in the survey which Goldstein, under the initiative of Helmholtz, had undertaken some fifteen years before Roentgen had entered the field of electrical discharges in high vacua. It was a great triumph for German science. The science of electrical discharges in rarefied gases was started in Germany and in less than forty years it had reached there its highest point. It is a science which may justly be said to have been "made in Germany," just as the science of radiation. It started a new and most remarkable era in physical sciences by extending the meaning of the Faraday-Maxwell electromagnetic theory.

No other discovery within my lifetime had ever aroused the interest of the world as did the discovery of the X-rays. Every physicist dropped his own research problems and rushed headlong into the research of the X-rays. The physicists of the United States had paid only small attention to vacuum-tube discharges. To the best of my knowledge and belief I was at that time the only physicist here who had had any laboratory experience with vacuum-tube research, and I got it by overtime work in the electrical-engineering laboratory of Columbia College. I undertook it because my intercourse with Mueller, the glass-blower of Berlin, directed my attention to this field of research, and particularly because I did not see that with the equipment of that laboratory I could do anything else. I decided, as mentioned above, to leave the field to Professor J. J. Thomson, of Cambridge, and to watch his work. When, therefore, Roentgen's discovery was first announced I was, it seems, better prepared than anybody else in this country to repeat his experiments and succeeded, therefore, sooner than anybody else on this side of the Atlantic. I obtained the first X-ray photograph in America on January 2, 1896, two weeks after the discovery was announced in Germany.

Many interesting stories have been told about the rush to the West during the gold-fever period, caused by the discovery of gold in the far West. The rush into

WILHELM KONRAD RŒNTGEN (1845-1923)

SIR J. J. THOMSON (1856——)

X-ray experimentation was very similar, and I also caught the fever badly. Newspaper reporters and physicians heard of it, and I had to lock myself up in my laboratory, which was in the cellar of President Low's official residence at Columbia College, in order to protect myself from continuous interruptions. The physicians brought all kinds of cripples for the purpose of having their bones photographed or examined by means of the fluorescent screen. The famous surgeon, the late Doctor Bull of New York, sent me a patient with nearly a hundred small shot in his left hand. His name was Prescott Hall Butler, a well-known lawyer of New York, who had met with an accident and received in his hand the full charge of a shotgun. He was in agony; he and I had mutual friends who begged me to make an X-ray photograph of his hand and thus enable Doctor Bull to locate the numerous shot and extract them. The first attempts were unsuccessful, because the patient was too weak and too nervous to stand a photographic exposure of nearly an hour. My good friend, Thomas Edison, had sent me several most excellent fluorescent screens, and by their fluorescence I could see the numerous little shot and so could my patient. The combination of the screen and the eyes was evidently much more sensitive than the photographic plate. I decided to try a combination of Edison's fluorescent screen and the photographic plate. The fluorescent screen was placed on the photographic plate and the patient's hand was placed upon the screen. The X-rays acted upon the screen first and the screen by its fluorescent light acted upon the plate. The combination succeeded, even better than I had expected. A beautiful photograph was obtained with an exposure of a few seconds. The photographic plate showed the numerous shot as if they had been drawn with pen and ink. Doctor Bull operated and extracted every one of them in the course of a short and easy surgical operation.

Prescott Hall Butler was well again. That was the first
X-ray picture obtained by that process during the first
part of February, 1896, and it was also the first surgical
operation performed in America under the guidance of
an X-ray picture. This process of shortening the time
of exposure is now universally used, but nobody gives
me any credit for the discovery, although I described it
in the journal *Electricity*, of February 12, 1896, before
anybody else had even thought of it. Prescott Hall
Butler was much more appreciative and he actually proposed, when other offers to reward me for my efforts were
refused, to establish a fellowship for me at the Century
Club, the fellowship to entitle me to two toddies daily
for the rest of my life. This offer also was refused.

On March 2, 1896, the late Professor Arthur Gordon
Webster, of Clark University, Worcester, Massachusetts,
adressed a letter to the *Worcester Gazette*, from which I
quote:

> Sunday morning I went with Professor Pupin to his laboratory to
> try the effect of a fluorescent screen in front of the plate. I placed
> my hand under the bulb and in five minutes the current was stopped
> . . . The result was the best plate that I had yet seen. . . . One
> who has tried the experiments and seen how long it takes to obtain a
> good result can judge of an improvement. I think that Doctor Pupin
> should enjoy the credit of having actually . . . shortened the time of
> exposure ten and twenty times.

A description of the improvement, which I published in
final form in *Electricity*, of April 15, 1896, ends with the
following sentence:

> My only object in working on the improvement of the Roentgen
> ray photography was for the purpose of widening its scope of applica-
> tion to surgical diagnosis. I think that I have succeeded completely
> and I wish full credit for the work done.

My friends suggested that I apply for a patent on the
procedure and enforce recognition that way, but I was
having one expensive experience in the patent office with

my electrical resonators and did not care to add another.

The question of reflection and refraction of the X-rays had to be answered, and several strange claims were brought forward by investigators. My investigations of this matter, aided by Thomas Edison's most efficient fluorescent screen, resulted in a discovery, which, in a communication to the New York Academy of Sciences, on April 6, 1896, I summed up as follows: "*Every substance when subjected to the action of X-rays becomes a radiator of these rays.*" The communication was published in several scientific journals, like *Science* and *Electricity*, and no statement can claim the discovery of the now well-known secondary X-ray radiation more clearly than the one given above. But of this matter I shall speak a little later.

Looking up some data lately I found that I had finished writing out these communications relating to my X-ray research on April 14, 1896. I also found a reprint of an address delivered before the New York Academy of Sciences in April, 1895, and published in *Science* of December 28, 1895, at the very time when the X-ray fever broke out. It was entitled: "Tendencies of Modern Electrical Research." But the X-ray fever prevented me from reading it when it was published. I saw it three months later, but never again since that time, and I had forgotten that I had ever composed it. I find now that the picture which I had drawn then of the growth of the electromagnetic theory is in every detail the same as that which I have given in this narrative. Both of them are due to the lasting impressions received in Cambridge and in Berlin. Evidently these impressions are just as strong to-day as they were twenty-eight years ago, proving that the tablets of memory have a mysterious process of preserving their records. I remember that on April 14, 1896, I did not go to the laboratory, but stayed at home and reflected, and read my address mentioned above. I took an inventory of what I had done during my six years' activity at Columbia and I closed the books satisfied with the results. My wife, who had helped me, writing out my reports, lectures, and scientific communications, and who knew and watched every bit of the work which I was doing, also was satisfied, and congratulated me. My colleague Crocker, I knew, was satisfied, and so were all my scientific friends, and that was a source of much satisfaction. But nothing makes one as happy as his own honest belief that he has done his best.

XI

THE RISE OF IDEALISM IN AMERICAN SCIENCE

I must make a digression now, to arrange suitable con-
tacts between the preceding parts of my narrative and
its concluding chapters. The main object of my narrative has been to describe the rise of idealism in American
science, and particularly in physical sciences and the
related industries. I witnessed this gradual development; everything I have written so far is an attempt
to qualify as a witness whose testimony has competence
and weight. But there are many other American scientists whose opinions in this matter have more competence and weight than my opinion has. Why, then,
should a scientist who started his career as a Serbian
immigrant speak of the idealism in American science,
when there are so many native-born American scientists who know more about this subject than I do?
Those who have read my narrative so far may answer
this question. I shall only point out now that there are
certain psychological elements in this question which
justify me in the belief that occasionally an immigrant
can see things which escape the attention of the native.
Seeing is believing; let him speak who has the faith,
provided he has a message to deliver.

A foreign-born citizen of the United States has many
occasions to sing praises of the virtues of this country
which the native-born citizen has not. Such occasions
arise whenever the foreign-born citizen revisits his native land and hears opinions about America which are
based upon European prejudice born of ignorance. On

311

these occasions he can, if the spirit moves him, say many
things with much more grace than a native American
could.   The spirit will move him if his naturalization
means that he knows America's traditions and embraces
their precepts with sincere enthusiasm.   Statements
which, coming from a native American, might sound as
boasts and bragging, may and often do sound different
when they are made by a naturalized American citizen.
I have had quite a number of experiences of this kind;
one of them deserves mention here.

Four years ago, while visiting my native land, I was
invited to attend a festive public meeting in a town not
far from my native village.   It was the town of Panchevo,
where in my boyhood days I went to school, and where
from my Slovenian teacher, Kos, I had heard for the first
time of Benjamin Franklin and of his kite.   The earliest
parts of this narrative show that many memories of my
boyhood days had nourished in my heart an affectionate
regard for this historic town.   Panchevo reciprocated,
and hence the invitation.   There was another reason.
In March of 1919, the chairman of the Yugoslav delegation at the Paris peace conference invited me to go to
Paris, expecting that with my knowledge of the English
language and of the Anglo-Saxon mentality I could probably assist the delegation in its work.   I spent seven weeks
in Paris.   The result, I was assured by Premier Pashitch
of Serbia, was very satisfactory; and he invited me to go
to Belgrade as guest of the government, for the purpose
of studying the condition of the war orphans in Serbia.
This study resulted in the organization of the Serbian
Child Welfare Association of America, whose splendid
work is known and appreciated in every part of the Serbian nation.   When Panchevo heard that I was in Belgrade it sent me the invitation.

The literary society of Panchevo, called the Academy,
had arranged a gala public session, and the occasion was

the "Wilson Day," which the town was celebrating. The orator of the day was a young Slovene, a learned lawyer and man of letters. The subject of his oration was: "President Wilson and his fourteen points." He wound up his splendid eulogy of President Wilson by exclaiming: "*President Wilson is an oasis of idealism in the endless desert of materialism.*" The image of my old friend Bilharz, the hermit of Cortlandt Street, suddenly appeared before me, and his favorite phrase "American materialism" rang violently in my ears. I was afraid that the United States of America would be understood to be a part of the endless desert mentioned by the speaker, and the possibility of such an inference I did not like. A most enthusiastic and long-continued applause greeted this oratorical climax, and before the applause was over the chairman, who was the mayor of the town, approached me and asked whether I should like to address a few words to the great assembly of the intellectuals of the town. "I not only like to do it," said I, "but I insist upon it." The chairman looked pleased, because he could not help observing that the orator's concluding figure of speech had stirred me up considerably, and that my response to it might add a few lively notes to the rather monotonous programme of the Academy session.

I repeat here some of the sentiments which I expressed on that occasion:

President Wilson is an idealist, and his idealism commands my deepest respect and admiration. I deny, however, that he represents an "oasis of idealism in an endless desert of materialism," that is, if the United States of America are understood to be a part of this endless desert. I am sure that in this town, liberated only a few months ago from the Austrian yoke, the expression "materialism" cannot refer to the United States of America. Two million American soldiers were fighting on the Western front when, a few months ago, the armistice was signed; several million more were waiting in America for their turn to join the ranks of the allied armies in France. American industries and American savings made a supreme effort to brace up the allied cause, and the war was won. Go to Paris now and watch the proceedings at the peace conference, as I was doing during the last seven weeks, and you will find that America asks for no territories, for no mandates, and for no onerous compensations. It is the only great power there which preaches moderation, and demands unreservedly full justice for the little nations. Yugoslav Dalmatia, Istria, Goricia, and Fiume had been, in a period of stress, bartered away by some of our allies; America is to-day the only fearless champion of your claims to these Yugoslav lands. American men and women hastened to every front, and there, amid many perils and discomforts, they nursed the sick and the wounded. They fed the hungry and clothed the naked and the destitute. This they did even before America had entered the world war. Need I remind you that it was an American mission which, in 1915, saved Serbia from the destructive ravages of typhus, and that several Americans, victims of these very ravages, are now buried in Serbia's soil? To-day you will find Americans even in the countries of our former enemies, in Germany, Austria, and Hungary, doing the work of mercy and of charity. The name of Hoover is just as well known and beloved in Vienna and Budapest as it is in Belgium. A country of materialism cannot display that spirit which America has displayed during this war. Let the idealism of President Wilson remind you of American idealism.

The phrase "American materialism" is an invention of ill-informed Europe; but the European who has lived in the United States, and has had the good fortune to catch the spirit of America, revolts whenever he hears the untutored European mind utter that phrase. Read the history of the United States from its earliest beginnings, when the Pilgrim fathers landed at Plymouth Rock, three hundred years ago, and you will find that idealism runs through it from beginning to end. The Pilgrim fathers themselves were idealists, who undertook the perilous voyage "for the glory of God and the advancement of the Christian faith."

A hundred and fifty years later the Continental Congress of the colonies issued, at Philadelphia, the "Declaration of Colonial Rights," and this declaration, as well as the documents accompanying it and addressed to the people of the United Kingdom and of British America, breathes the spirit of lofty idealism. The same Congress in 1775 issued another declaration, setting forth causes which forced the American colonies to take up arms; and in 1776 it issued the Declaration of Independence, which announced to the world the ideals for the attainment of which the colonists were ready to sacrifice their lives. No other human documents ever stated so clearly and so definitely the "divine right of man" as these documents did. The men who composed these documents were not ordinary men; they were idealists of the highest type. Read the lives of Washington, Hamilton, Franklin, Jay, Jefferson, and of other leaders of the American Revolutionary period, and you will find what a wonderful power idealism has when the destiny of a young nation hangs in the balance. But when the struggle was over, after the victory had been won, the leader of the new nation, immortal Washington, assumed the supreme executive office of the land and retired from it after two terms of service with a spirit of dignity and of humility which has no equal in human history. His Farewell Address to the American people, advocating the practice of idealism by the cultivation of religion, morality, patriotism, good faith, and justice toward all nations, is an echo of the voice of idealism which was the driving power of the American Revolution.

The idealism of the Revolutionary period was the guiding star of the American patriots of the stormy period preceding the Civil War. One of them, Daniel Webster, was a youth of seventeen when Washington died, and he knew personally some of the great leaders of the Revolutionary period, like Jefferson and Adams. He certainly caught by direct contact the idealism of this period. Read his speeches, as I have read them during my apprenticeship days in America, and you will understand what I mean by American idealism, if this war has not shown it to you better than any words of mine can do it. Webster's idealism was in the hearts of men of his generation, who, under the great leadership of Lincoln, one of the greatest among American idealists, conducted the Civil War and preserved the American Union. Lincoln's immortal words: "With malice toward none, with charity for all," will forever remind the world of the idealism which was in the hearts of the American people who fought for the preservation of the American Union. President Wilson is one of the best biographers of George Washington, and he also published a splendid study of the constitutional government of the United States. No profound student of these themes can escape becoming an exalted idealist. His speeches, which during the World War he addressed to the American people and to the whole world, are sermons on American idealism, which have guided the people of the United States from the very beginning of their history; but some of you in Europe never understood it. The world war has made you eager to listen to every word which inspires your anxious hearts with new hopes. President Wilson's words and his acts at the Paris peace conference inspire you with these new hopes, and hence this Wilson Day, an honor to him and a credit to you. In honoring him you are honoring the idealism of the American people, for which act I am most grateful to you.

It was here in Panchevo that I first heard of Benjamin Franklin, nearly fifty years ago; to-day I deliver to you, people of Panchevo, a greeting from Franklin's native land and a message that the cultivation of American idealism is the most powerful arm for the defense of the destiny of your young nation.

Hamilton Fish Armstrong, our military *attaché* in Belgrade at that time, was present at the meeting. He did not understand a word of my address, because it was delivered in Serbian, but he assured me that, judging by appearances, it must have been at least as good as my address in Princeton in the beginning of the World War in 1914; he was then a senior at Princeton College. The Princeton address was a eulogy of Serbian idealism, which I had imported into America when I landed at Castle Garden in 1874; the Panchevo address was a eulogy of American idealism, which I had brought back to Panchevo forty-five years later. I must confess, however, that, twenty-five years earlier, the above address was delivered in substance to Protoyeray Zhivkovich, the poet-priest of Panchevo, when after graduating at Columbia in 1883 I returned for the first time to my native village. On that occasion the poet said, and here I quote from an earlier chapter of my narrative:

Tell your mother that I am happy to bear the whole responsibility for your wandering away to distant America. It is no longer distant; it is now in my heart; you have brought America to us. It was a new world in my terrestrial geography; it is now a new world in my spiritual geography.

I often think of these words now, and I firmly believe that there are many millions of people in Europe to-day who think that America is a new world in their spiritual geography. The people in Panchevo, I am certain, think so. But it needed a world war to eliminate from their minds the old superstition that this is the land of "American materialism." The world pendulum has swung the other way, and I often wonder whether we can live up to the very high reputation which we enjoy in the opinion of a large part of the world, which now knows our virtues but does not know our shortcomings.

A short time after the Panchevo celebration, a number of scientists of the University of Belgrade, members of the Royal Serbian Academy, invited me to an informal conference, and asked me to tell them something about American science and its National Research Council in Washington. I do not think that on that occasion my discourse on this most interesting topic impressed my Serbian friends as strongly as my Panchevo discourse did. For a long time after this conference I thought of many things that I might have said, but did not say. The more I thought about it the more I was dissatisfied. I was informed several months after this conference that one of the Serbian scientists present remarked to a mutual friend that from my Panchevo address on American idealism he had been led to believe that at the Belgrade conference I would say something about idealism in American science. But I said nothing, and he inferred, therefore, that there could not be much idealism in American science, a thing which he had always suspected. Many European scientists suspected that long before he did. That permissible inference of the Serbian scientist hurt me, and it hurt the more because I felt that the omission was unpardonable. But the psychology at the Panchevo celebration was different from that at the conference in Belgrade. In Panchevo a remark was made from which, I was afraid, one might have inferred that this is a country of materialism. Nobody at the Belgrade conference suggested the thought that American science might, perhaps, have a taint of materialism. But, of course, no Serbian scientist could have suggested such a thing when the memory of the service of American science to Serbia during the typhus ravages of 1915 was still fresh in everybody's mind.

A fireplace fed by slow-burning wood must be stirred

up often to maintain a lively flame. Similarly, the flame of a slow mental combustion cannot be maintained without occasional stirring. My mental combustion at the Belgrade conference was certainly slow, and needed a stirring up, similar to that which it received in Panchevo. My early studies of American history and American traditions would have proceeded much more slowly, if it had not been for my old friend Bilharz, who stirred me up with his prejudices against American democracy, and with his everlasting complaints against the imaginary spectre which he called American materialism.

This stirring up is experienced by many American citizens of foreign birth whenever they visit their native land. Every one of these visits speeds up the Americanization process which is going on in them. I firmly believe that the amalgamation of the foreign-born would be speeded up wonderfully if we could make it obligatory that every foreign-born American citizen should revisit his native land at stated intervals of time. Had I not visited my native land so many times since my landing at Castle Garden in 1874, the memory of my early experiences in America, described in the earlier parts of this narrative, would probably have faded away completely long ago. Had I not visited Belgrade and Panchevo in 1919 I should not have been stirred up on the subject of American idealism, and particularly about the American idealism in science. It was in Belgrade and Panchevo where the stimulus was applied which revived the memory of my experiences in Columbia College, in the Universities of Cambridge and Berlin, and in my professorial work at Columbia University, and made me pass in rapid review through all my experiences which have a bearing upon American idealism, and particularly upon the idealism in American science. Ever since, I have been revolving in my mind many of the things relating to American science that I might have mentioned at the Belgrade conference, but did not mention. The painting, "Men of Progress," which I first saw at Cooper Union in 1876, came back to my mind. The men represented in it, like Peter Cooper, McCormick, Goodyear, Morse, and others, did not represent the idealism in science which the Belgrade scientist had in mind; they were practical inventors. They were the scientific idols of the American people, but they were not idealists in science. The time for idealism in American science had not yet arrived. The Union Pacific Railroad had not yet been built when that picture was painted; the Western plains had not yet been compelled to yield their potential treasures of golden grain; and the vast quantities of coal and mineral ore were waiting anxiously to be raised to the surface of the earth to serve in the development of our vast territory between the Atlantic and the Pacific. He who could aid the people in this gigantic development became the idol of the people. The names of inventors, like McCormick, Goodyear, and Morse, were household words with the people of the United States, just as the names of Edison and of Bell are to-day. Joseph Henry, the famous scientist, was also in that historic painting, but he was in the background of it. His expression seemed to indicate that he did not feel quite at home in a group of men who were practical inventors. He was a friend of Lincoln, and his idealism in science was just as exalted as Lincoln's idealism in political philosophy. But in those days an idealist in science attracted little attention among the people of the United States, who were busily engaged in solving their numerous economic problems. Hence Joseph Henry, the idealist in science, was practically unknown. This was the mental attitude which Europe called "American materialism" in science. De Tocqueville, the famous French traveller and keen observer, said this about us in a book which he published over seventy years ago:

It must be confessed that, among the civilized peoples of our age, there are few in which the highest sciences have made so little progress as in the United States. . . . The future will prove whether the passion for profound knowledge, so rare and so fruitful, can be born and developed so readily in democratic societies as in aristocracies. . . . The man of the North . . . does not care for science as a pleasure, and only embraces it with avidity when it leads to useful applications.

To-day this criticism sounds like a national libel, but fifty years ago it was swallowed like a bitter pill which, in the opinion of many patriotic thinkers, we needed if we were to be cured of a malady which threatened to become a national calamity. The greatest leaders of scientific thought in this country pointed to our educational system, in order to prove that de Tocqueville was right and that science was neglected in our schools and colleges. Foremost amongst them were, as I have already pointed out in this narrative, Joseph Henry, President Barnard, of Columbia, President White, of Cornell, Draper, Youmans, and others. They were all idealists in science, and when they invited Tyndall to this country, fifty years ago, they invited the most eloquent apostle of scientific idealism. The great movement for higher scientific research, inaugurated in England by the immortal Maxwell and his supporters, and in this country by the great Joseph Henry and his followers, was a movement for idealism in science, or, as Andrew White called it, "hope for higher endeavor."

When the European speaks of materialism in American science, he is resurrecting notions which de Tocqueville had in his mind when he wrote the lines quoted above. These notions were correct, but wonderful changes have taken place in this country since de Tocqueville wrote his book. If he were living now and published another edition of his famous book, I am sure that he would insert a chapter which would speak of idealism and not of materialism in American science.

What is the mental attitude which I call "idealism in science"? Before answering this question it is well to quote here from an earlier part of my narrative:

The *eternal truth* was, according to my understanding at that time, the sacred background of Tyndall's scientific faith, and the works of the great scientific discoverers, their lives, and their methods of inquiry into physical phenomena were the only sources from which the human mind can draw the light which will illuminate that sacred background. He nourished that faith with a religious devotion, and his appeals in the name of that faith were irresistible. His friends in America and in England, who were glad to have him as their advocate of the cause of scientific research, had the same faith that he had, and they nourished it with the same devotion. I know to-day . . . that this faith was kindled and kept alive . . . by the light of the life and of the wonderful discoveries of Michael Faraday. . . . He was their contemporary, and his achievements, like a great search-light, showed them the true path of scientific progress.

The worship of the eternal truth and the burning desire to seek an ever-broadening revelation of it constitute the mental attitude which I call "idealism in science." Its growth in the British Empire, and particularly at the University of Cambridge, has been most remarkable since the great movement started under the leadership of Maxwell a little over fifty years ago. What progress have we made since Tyndall's visit to this country in 1872? If in my narrative I succeed in answering this question I shall be more than satisfied, and I shall certainly send a translation of it in part to my scientific friends in Belgrade. It will tell them what I ought to have told them four years ago.

I return now to the point in my story where I digressed. The 14th of April, 1896, is recorded in my calendar as a happy day. The 15th started with a balmy spring morning full of glorious sunshine. The suggestion to walk through Central Park to Columbia College to my morning lecture could not be resisted, and I reached the

lecture-room full of the joy of life which fills the heart
of every healthy youth. My students told me later that
the first part of my lecture that morning displayed that
joy. But, near the end of the lecture, I suddenly col-
lapsed. A sudden chill struck me like a bolt from a clear
sky. Five days later my life hung in the balance; there
was a desperate struggle between a stout heart and the
busy poisons of dreaded pneumonia. The heart won
out. But when the crisis had passed, and my physician
thought that I was sufficiently strong to stand the shock
of terrible news, he told me that my wife had died several
days before, a victim of dreaded pneumonia. She had
caught the seed of this merciless disease while nursing
me. My weakened heart stood the shock, but every
one of my nerves seemed to snap in two. For the first
time in my life I recognized the full meaning of will-power;
I recognized it because I knew that the spiritual motor,
the power of which I had always felt, was there no longer.
For the first time since leaving my native Idvor, twenty-
six years before, I had to be steered and looked after by
others. Life never looked so hopeless as it did during
that awful spring of 1896. But I wanted to live, because
I had a little daughter to bring up. That, in fact, was
the only thing that I wanted to live for; everything else
seemed either devoid of interest, or much beyond my
reach. It is an awful thing to lose one's self-reliance.
Aims and aspirations appeared to me like little toy balloons that children play with; our nerves, I thought, are
the strings which keep them afloat within the reach of
our vision. When these strings snap in two, our aims
and aspirations, like toy balloons, disappear rapidly into
thin air.

My physician recommended that during that summer
I should settle down in Norfolk, Connecticut, to give
the bracing climate of this New England town in the
Berkshire hills a chance to rebuild what overwork, under

nervous tension, and pneumonia had undermined and torn down. A New York physician, who knew me through my X-ray work, offered to rent me his summer residence, facing Haystack Mountain, the highest peak in Norfolk, and I accepted it. This mountain is really only a hill, hardly one thousand feet higher than the road at its foot, but as I sat on the piazza in front of that little cottage and looked at the so-called observatory, a square frame structure on the top of this hill, from which people caught the distant view of the Housatonic valley, I wondered whether I should ever be strong enough to climb to its top. I recalled my exploits in Switzerland, thirteen years before, and, utterly discouraged by the comparison, I accepted with calm resignation that I had grown old and decrepit in less time than it takes other people to become middle-aged. Whenever I thought of my past, present, or future, I always managed to draw some gloomy conclusion of that kind, and, so far as my cloudy fancy could see, I felt that I had finished my career in dismal failure. People told me that these were queer notions due to mental depression, from which I would soon recover. But, as time went on and there was no relief, I resented it when people tried to console me with, what I considered, empty promises of a brighter future. There suddenly appeared an angel who promised nothing but gave much.

Another New York physician, the well-known Doctor Frederick Shepard Dennis, also an admirer of my X-ray work, had a summer residence at Norfolk. He was practically a native of this quaint New England town, and believed in its great virtues as a resort for convalescents. He was very anxious that my summer vacation there should put me on my feet again, but he saw that my introspective life on the lonely piazza facing Haystack Mountain blocked every road which might lead to my physical and mental restoration. "Professor," said he

Reginald Rives, one of the social leaders of New York, was the judge at Wissahickon who awarded the prizes to my cobs. We had been in college together, but when he saw me at the horse-show he did not recognize me at first, because, as he informed me later, he did not expect to see a college professor driving high-steppers at a horse-show. He spoke very highly of my cobs, which won from a competitor like millionaire Widener's stable in Philadelphia.

"Pupin," exclaimed Rives, "if you can handle your students as well as you can handle your cobs, you are the greatest professor in America." "I could," said I, "if I had to handle only two students at a time, but not two hundred." Rives repeated this remark to his brother, a trustee of Columbia University, and the trustee saw in it quite a chunk of educational philosophy. The preceptorial system at Princeton reminds one of this philosophy. Will the American colleges ever adopt it?

A famous Boston lover of horses, a Mr. Jordan, saw my cobs at the Wissahickon horse-show and made me a handsome bid for them in cash besides "throwing in" a very handsome Irish hunter which had won a prize in the jumping class. The hunter became my saddle-horse, and served me loyally for fully twelve years. No better saddle-horse ever cantered over the hillsides of Litchfield County than Clipper, the Irish hunter, my trusty friend and companion, particularly during my summer vacations. Thanks to Comet and Princess Rose, and to good old Clipper, and to the bracing climate of Norfolk hills, the joy of life returned again.

My first job after landing at Castle Garden was on a farm, and there I had vowed that as soon as I could afford it I would buy myself a real American farm. A little over twenty years later, in 1897, I bought a farm at Norfolk; this blessed spot, where I regained my health and happiness, became my real American home, and I

nervous tension, and pneumonia had undermined and torn down. A New York physician, who knew me through my X-ray work, offered to rent me his summer residence, facing Haystack Mountain, the highest peak in Norfolk, and I accepted it. This mountain is really only a hill, hardly one thousand feet higher than the road at its foot, but as I sat on the piazza in front of that little cottage and looked at the so-called observatory, a square frame structure on the top of this hill, from which people caught the distant view of the Housatonic valley, I wondered whether I should ever be strong enough to climb to its top. I recalled my exploits in Switzerland, thirteen years before, and, utterly discouraged by the comparison, I accepted with calm resignation that I had grown old and decrepit in less time than it takes other people to become middle-aged. Whenever I thought of my past, present, or future, I always managed to draw some gloomy conclusion of that kind, and, so far as my cloudy fancy could see, I felt that I had finished my career in dismal failure. People told me that these were queer notions due to mental depression, from which I would soon recover. But, as time went on and there was no relief, I resented it when people tried to console me with, what I considered, empty promises of a brighter future. There suddenly appeared an angel who promised nothing but gave much.

Another New York physician, the well-known Doctor Frederick Shepard Dennis, also an admirer of my X-ray work, had a summer residence at Norfolk. He was practically a native of this quaint New England town, and believed in its great virtues as a resort for convalescents. He was very anxious that my summer vacation there should put me on my feet again, but he saw that my introspective life on the lonely piazza facing Haystack Mountain blocked every road which might lead to my physical and mental restoration. "Professor," said he

one day to me, "if you do not stop thinking about your-self you will never get well." "But," said I, "what else is there to think about? I hate to think about that hor-rible green phosphorescence of vacuum tubes, about the X-rays, fluorescent screens, and skeletons of hands and feet and ribs. Those are the things which haunted in-cessantly my burning brain during the pneumonia fever, and I shall never think of them again if I can help it. I should like to think about some other problems which are waiting in my laboratory, but what is the use? I have no hope of living long enough to solve them, or that, if I live, I shall have the necessary brain energy to work out their solution. Besides, whenever I begin to think of something pleasant or interesting my heart suddenly gives a violent thump, and sends a cold shiver through my timid veins. I must think of myself, be-cause I am always on my guard against something that might happen at any moment to cut the last thread of my shaky vitality. It is this everlasting fear that keeps me thinking about myself." The good doctor looked thoughtful, but said nothing; a few days later he drove up in a little yellow runabout, drawn by a pair of cobs of beautiful dark chestnut color, which were a splendid product of his stud farm; they shone like old mahogany. "How do you like them, professor?" asked the doctor, as he scrutinized my admiring gaze. "They are a thing of beauty and a joy forever," said I, and I meant what I said. The next day the cobs, with wagon and harness, were mine; they were only three years old, and, although broken to harness, they were quite raw and needed train-ing. I got them after pledging my word to the doctor that I would train them. My native Banat is like Ken-tucky. Everybody raises horses, and everybody knows by intuition how to handle a horse. I was told by ex-perts that I handled those cobs just right. While train-ing them I really trained my own nerves. They needed

it more than the cobs did. "Horse sense" has meant to me ever since a sense which enables man to train a horse, and that means to give up your whole heart and soul to the horse. The trainer must never think of himself, but always of his beloved animal. He must be patient and persistent, kind and affectionate, forgiving mistakes and showing full appreciation for even the smallest honest effort. Only by the exercise of these virtues can he succeed in developing in the horse the habit of being a splendid horse. Doctor Dennis was a great lover of horses, and he knew all that, and thought, as he told me later, that it was the best medicine for me.

My cobs acquired the best of habits, and at the end of a year they were two beautifully balanced animals, carrying their proud heads on high, and stepping up in perfect unison. They seemed, when in full action, to be anxious to strike their foreheads with their knees. To sit behind those animals, and watch their swaggering motion around the horse-show ring, gave a thrill never to be forgotten. The New York horse-show in Madison Square Garden, in the autumn of 1897, and the Philadelphia horse-show at Wissahickon, in the spring of 1898, established the great reputation of Comet and Princess Rose, the cobs that I had been training during eighteen months. They won many prizes, but none of them was as welcome as the prize of my restored health. I got well without knowing that I was getting well; the only improvement that I was watching and thinking about was the improvement of my beautiful cobs, but, nevertheless, my laboratory assistant Cushman noticed in the early spring of 1897 that I had already begun to speak much more encouragingly about some of my old laboratory problems; he noticed it, and he was happy again. The X-ray problems were not among them; I never recovered from the feeling of horror which the thought of them gave me during my sickness in April, 1896.

Reginald Rives, one of the social leaders of New York, was the judge at Wissahickon who awarded the prizes to my cobs. We had been in college together, but when he saw me at the horse-show he did not recognize me at first, because, as he informed me later, he did not expect to see a college professor driving high-steppers at a horse-show. He spoke very highly of my cobs, which won from a competitor like millionaire Widener's stable in Philadelphia.

"Pupin," exclaimed Rives, "if you can handle your students as well as you can handle your cobs, you are the greatest professor in America." "I could," said I, "if I had to handle only two students at a time, but not two hundred." Rives repeated this remark to his brother, a trustee of Columbia University, and the trustee saw in it quite a chunk of educational philosophy. The preceptorial system at Princeton reminds one of this philosophy. Will the American colleges ever adopt it?

A famous Boston lover of horses, a Mr. Jordan, saw my cobs at the Wissahickon horse-show and made me a handsome bid for them in cash besides "throwing in" a very handsome Irish hunter which had won a prize in the jumping class. The hunter became my saddle-horse, and served me loyally for fully twelve years. No better saddle-horse ever cantered over the hillsides of Litchfield County than Clipper, the Irish hunter, my trusty friend and companion, particularly during my summer vacations. Thanks to Comet and Princess Rose, and to good old Clipper, and to the bracing climate of Norfolk hills, the joy of life returned again.

My first job after landing at Castle Garden was on a farm, and there I had vowed that as soon as I could afford it I would buy myself a real American farm. A little over twenty years later, in 1897, I bought a farm at Norfolk; this blessed spot, where I regained my health and happiness, became my real American home, and I

have never had a desire to seek a better haven of happiness in any other place, either here or in Europe.

The native of Norfolk is a typical Connecticut Yankee.
Neither the wealth nor the social position of a new summer visitor can faze him. His dignity and self-respect
forbid him to kowtow to any city swell. You will get
his respectful attention if you deserve it; but you must
earn it by your acts at Norfolk. You cannot command
it by the power of anything you bring with you from the
city to your summer vacation. While you are in Norfolk in summer, you are a summer boarder, an outsider,
with traditions back of you which no native of Norfolk
knows anything about. The force of all this was once so
strongly impressed upon me that I never forgot it.

Norfolk, like every New England town, has its annual
town meetings, when the accounts of the town for the
closing current year are carefully analyzed, appropria-
tions are made for the coming year, and the selectmen
and other administrative officers are elected. After I
had become a landowner in Norfolk, I attended these
town meetings regularly, and took part in their discussions, and there for the first time I became acquainted,
by personal contact, with the fundamental elements of
Anglo-Saxon civilization. At one of those town meetings I urged the improvement of the public highways,
using the argument that better roads would attract more
summer residents from the great cities and, I was certain, would advance the prosperity of the town. My
arguments were received with respectful silence, and no
sooner had I finished my speech than a Mr. Nettleton,
the oldest voter in the township, got up and, turning
his black goggles toward me, addressed me somewhat as
follows:

"Our roads are just as good as they ever were; our
ancestors taught us how to take care of them, and they
are good enough for us. You say that if we improve them

we would get more summer visitors, who, with their wealth, would increase the prosperity of our town. We don't care for that kind of prosperity; it brings vanity and false pride into our New England homes, which you city people carry around with you." Then, pointing his trembling finger at me, the old man exclaimed: "You, particularly, are guilty of this offense; you were the first who showed our simple people here how to swagger about this town on a horse with a rabbit tail."

He referred to the almost universal custom at that time of docking a horse's tail; the tails of my famous cobs as well as of my saddle-horse Clipper had been docked. After this speech, I suspended my propaganda for more up-to-date roads. Two years later, another incident occurred which is worth relating here. Mr. Carter, a Norfolk hunter of much local fame, had a fine pointer dog. He went to Europe one summer and left his dog in charge of a friend. But the dog ran away, and chased through all the woods of Norfolk, looking for his master. One day he came to my house; he was hungry, thirsty, tired out, and perfectly unhappy, having failed to find his master. I petted him, gave him fresh water to drink and some food to eat, and, while he was feasting, spoke to him and paid him many compliments on account of his affectionate attachment to his master. After his hearty meal he fell asleep near my feet on the piazza, and when he woke up he looked at me and seemed to be a much happier dog. From that moment on he followed me everywhere, running after my horse when I went out riding. One day I was cantering slowly along the road passing old Nettleton's house. I saw the old man standing near the road, apparently waiting for somebody. When I was quite near him he beckoned me to stop, which I did, and he addressed me:

"Professor, I was very severe with you two years ago at that town meeting. But I did not know you; now I do. That dog there would not stay with anybody in this

PUPIN'S RESIDENCE AT NORFOLK, CONN., WITH ADJOINING FARM BUILDINGS
AND THE 500-TON SILO

town, but he stays with you, and he follows you just as he followed his master. You are good to him, and the dog knows it. I have great confidence in a dog's judgment, and I know now that you are a good man, just as good as any of the folks in this here New England town." Then, stretching out his bony hand to me, he said: "Shake, forgive and forget, and let us be good friends. I shall never oppose you again at our annual town meetings. What's good for you is good enough for me and for our little town."

No offer of friendship was ever more welcome to me, and there never was a friendship of which I was more proud. Before many days had passed, the natives of Norfolk, from the illustrious Eldridge family, the angels of the town, down to the most humble day-laborer, felt the same toward me as old Nettleton did; that is, I always thought so, and I have never had any reason to think otherwise. No resolution moved by me at the annual town meetings ever failed to pass, but I always moved slowly, and not until I was quite sure that the motion was in the right direction. I would sooner have risked losing the good opinion of the trustees of Columbia University than that of the good people of Norfolk, my American Idvor. During my summer vacations in Norfolk, I have always felt just as much at home, and as happy and contented, as I did in my native Idvor when, during my student days in Europe, I spent my summer vacations there. Whenever I returned to my laboratory from my summer vacation in the bracing atmosphere of Norfolk, I have always felt that no problem there could resist the force of my stored-up nervous energy. That feeling early encouraged me in the belief that I had completely recovered from the breakdown of the spring of 1896, and this belief gave wings to every new effort.

When the news of the discovery of the Roentgen rays reached me in December of 1895, I was busy with the research of a problem which I had taken up in 1894, while making a foot tour in Switzerland. This is the problem which I took up again after the recovery from the breakdown of 1896. I must confess here that I never returned to X-ray research, because for a long time after my illness even the sight of an X-ray tube made me almost hysterical.

During the first half of the summer of 1894, Mrs. Pupin and I were staying at a little hotel on Lake Wannensee in Switzerland; I was preparing my lectures on the mathematical theory of sound. Lord Rayleigh's treatise called my attention to the classical problem which ten years before I first saw in La Grange's famous treatise. I had bought it second-hand in Paris, and had studied it in my mother's garden at Idvor. The problem was a hypothetical one relating to an imaginary and not to a real physical case. It may be stated as follows:

A string without weight is stretched like a violin string between two fixed points; at equidistant intervals along this string are attached equal weights, say bird-shot. The problem is, how will this string, loaded with weights, vibrate when disturbed by an impulse? La Grange found a beautiful solution for this historic problem, and the solution marks the beginning of an epoch in the history of mathematical physics. This solution enabled him to analyze mathematically the vibrations of a violin string, one of the famous mathematical problems of the eighteenth century. I made a bold attempt to find a solution for a more general and less hypothetical form of this problem. I supposed that the string itself had weight, and that it, as well as the little weights attached to it, moved through a viscous medium. I felt intuitively what the solution should be, and considered it of much scientific importance. I finally found the most general mathematical solution of this generalized problem, and the beauty of it was that it could be stated in a very simple language. I shall

second reaction is against the elastic compression of the receiving element. It is called the elastic reaction, and was discovered by Hook, a contemporary of Newton, two hundred years ago. The third is a frictional reaction, the knowledge of which is very old. There are, therefore, three forms of energy generated in the reacting element of every vibrating body by the work of the acting element. The first reaction results in energy of motion of the mass of the reacting element; the second one results in the energy of its elastic compression; and the third one generates heat. The first and the second are energies of sound vibration and are transmitted again to the contiguous elements, but the third is not a vibratory sound energy and is not transmitted as such; it remains as heat and represents the reduction of sound energy transmitted from any one part to the contiguous parts. It is obvious that this reduction will be, relatively, the smaller the greater the first two reactions are in comparison with the frictional reaction. Heavy, incompressible bodies, like water, metals, or hard solid ground, have incomparably greater kinetic and elastic reactions than air, hence they transmit sound much better than air does. This physical principle did splendid service during the World War in submarine and subterranean detection by sound. The herdsman's assistants in Idvor, when I was a boy, profited much from it in their signalling through the ground. I am not aware that Vaschy and Heaviside had a clear knowledge of it. If I am correct, then it is quite remarkable that Serb peasants should have been cognizant of a physical principle which was probably unknown to English and French savants, like Vaschy and Heaviside.

Passing now by analogy from motion of matter to motion of electricity, we can, speaking figuratively, state that vibratory motion of electricity will be transmitted from one end of a conducting wire to the other the more

experience no serious difficulty in working it out. Vaschy, a Frenchman, and Heaviside, an Englishman, were the first to work it out; they did it in the chronological order just indicated, Vaschy leading Heaviside by about two years. They both observed that just as in cable and land-line telegraphy so also in telephony the reduction of the transmitted electrical force was the smaller the larger the so-called inductance of the transmitting wire. Many people believe that this observation was an important discovery; I never thought so, because I believed that Thomson's and Kirchhoff's work made that observation obvious. But, however that may be, the observation was made by Vaschy two years before it was made by Heaviside, and neither one nor the other saw in it a special case of a general physical principle, which the Allies appreciated much during the World War in their struggles against the submarines. I shall describe it briefly:

Sound is transmitted through water or through a solid much more efficiently than it is through air. I knew that, when, as herdsman's assistant in Idvor, I learned the art of signalling through the ground. Now why should water or hard and heavy ground transmit sound better than air does? Idvor's herdsman did not tell me that, but, having gained the knowledge of the fact very early, I was prepared to seize upon the dynamical explanation as soon as I needed it; and I felt the need of it in Switzerland in the summer of 1894.

Transmission of sound means transmission of vibratory motion from one element of a substance to the contiguous elements. The element which transmits its vibratory energy acts and the elements which receive it react. Each element is capable of exerting three reacting forces. One is against the change of velocity of its motion, that is, against change of momentum. This reaction is called the kinetic reaction, and, as I have pointed out before, it was discovered by Galileo three hundred years ago. The

bia College, and that too in spite of the heavenly beauty
of the views which on my walks met me on every turn
of the winding roads which lead up to the wonderful
passes of Switzerland. I was most anxious to submit
my theory to an experimental test. When our tour in
Switzerland was finished I had every detail of the proposed experimental tests worked out in my head, and
yet my good wife never accused me of being absent-
minded. In less than a year from that time I had finished
my first rough test, and was preparing for a more elaborate investigation when the discovery of the X-ray was
announced, at the very end of 1895, and I, like everybody else, dropped everything and eagerly sought information about this wonderful discovery. It was the
work I dropped then which I took up again after my
recovery from the breakdown of 1896.

Now what is the invention which occurred to me first
on my walk to the Furka pass in Switzerland in the summer of 1894? A bit of scientific history is connected
with it, which I shall tell here briefly:

A vibrating motion of electricity at one end of a long
wire is propagated along the wire in much the same way
as the vibratory motion of a rope or string is propagated
from one of its terminals to the other. This propagation
of electrical motion from one end of a long conducting
wire to the other was first investigated by Professor William Thomson, the late Lord Kelvin, of the University
of Glasgow, in 1855, when the first Atlantic cable was
projected. He worked out the problem for electrical
signalling over a submarine cable, and three years later
Kirchhoff, who was one of my teachers in Berlin, worked
it out for telegraphic signalling over land-lines stretched
over poles. When telephony was invented in 1876, there
was, of course, a demand for a mathematical theory of
telephonic transmission over long conducting wires. He
who understood Thomson's and Kirchhoff's work could

state it later. The solution was exactly what I had expected it to be, and it thrilled me more than any work that I had ever done. I always believed that my training in ground-signalling which the herdsman of Idvor had taught me some twenty years before was responsible for this intuitive guess. Early impressions, particularly those relating to novel scientific facts, are very intense.

I was much encouraged by the thought that I was able to add very substantially to the solution of a historic problem first solved by famous La Grange. In order to communicate some of my joy to Mrs. Pupin, I told her that I was ready to give up mathematical reading for the rest of that summer, and we started on a drive through Switzerland. That is, she drove, while I walked a good part of the time, particularly when the carriage was moving along the zigzag roads going up to a pass, which happens often in Switzerland drives. Making short cuts, I met her every now and then on the up-grade parts of the steep and winding roads, and rode with her on the down-grade. During these walks, being alone, I pondered a great deal about my solution of the generalized La Grangian problem. One day, while climbing up to the Furka pass, it occurred to me that since the motion of electricity through a wire experiences reacting forces similar to those in the motion of the material elements in a stretched string, my generalized solution should be applicable to the motion of electricity, and I was immediately aware that I had made a very important invention. I tried to convince Mrs. Pupin of it, but she said: "I will believe what you say and will gladly congratulate you if you will promise that you will not be absent-minded during the rest of our trip." I promised, but it was very difficult to live up to the promise. I never told her how often I longed to be back in my modest laboratory in the musty cellar under President Low's office at Colum-

efficiently the heavier and the less compressible that electricity is, or, dropping now our figurative mode of speech, we can say that, other things being equal, the higher the kinetic and the elastic reaction of the moving electricity the more efficiently will the energy of its vibratory motion be transmitted over the wire. But that means that the inductance of the wire should be made as large and its capacity as small as possible. That much was perfectly obvious in Thomson's and Kirchhoff's work, some twenty years before Vaschy and Heaviside took up the mathematical theory of telephonic transmission. These two celebrated mathematicians, however, deserve much credit for their enthusiastic backing of inductance among the sceptical telephone engineers, who, at that time, knew little of the mathematical theory and of the general principle of transmission of vibratory motions.

A coil of wire wound around an iron core is the first picture in our mind when we hear inductance mentioned. Hence, if inductance increases the efficiency of transmission in a telephone transmission-line, and you cannot introduce it into the line in large amounts in any other way, then one would certainly suggest putting a lot of coils into the telephone-line and examining the results of this haphazard guess. Vaschy tried this guess, and failed. The late Mr. Pickernell, chief engineer of the long-distance department of the American Telephone and Telegraph Company, also tried it, and he also failed. It was obvious that, as Heaviside expressed it, experiment gave no encouragement with regard to inductance introduced in this way. I tried it and found that experiment offered very much encouragement to inductance introduced this way; I succeeded, because I did not guess; I was guided by the mathematical solution of the generalized La Grangian problem. What does this solution say when applied to electrical motions in a wire? It says this: Place your inductance coils into your telephone-line at such distances

tute of Electrical Engineers there was hidden an invention for which telephone engineers had been eagerly waiting ever since the birth of the telephone art. This created an interference in the Patent Office which annoyed me, but not nearly so much as I had been annoyed there before. About a year from the date of my application for patent, the American Telephone and Telegraph Company acquired my American patent rights, treating me most generously. It gave me what I asked; my friends thought that I had not asked enough, but to a native of Idvor a dollar looks much bigger than to a native of New York who may be a next-door neighbor to some Morgan or Rockefeller. Besides, the opinion of the highest telephone authority in the world that my solution of the extended La Grangian problem had a very important technical value was much more gratifying to me than all the money in the world.

In Europe, and particularly in England, the invention came as a surprise; they did not expect an American to make an invention which required so much mathematical analysis of electrical motions, to which the American physicist had contributed very little, whereas Vaschy and Heaviside had written volumes about it. But these writers had paid too little attention to classical writers like La Grange, Thomson, and Kirchhoff. The construction of the inductance-coil required almost as much mathematical analysis as the dynamical theory of the invention, and the method of testing it also was new to the telephone engineers. The coil is now known all over the world as the Pupin coil, and many people think that the coil itself is the invention.

When it became known that I had studied at the Universities of Cambridge and of Berlin, my English and German friends claimed the credit of the invention for the scientific training which I had received at their universities. I think the French had a better claim, because it was La Grange who helped me more than any other mathematical reading. As a matter of fact, the engineers of the American Telephone and Telegraph Company and the herdsmen of Idvor deserve most of the credit. The first formulated the problem the solution of which led to the invention, and the second taught me the art of signalling through the ground which guided me to the physical principle which underlies the invention.

A vice-president of the American Telephone and Telegraph Company, who is a very high authority in telephony, informed me recently that one way to describe, roughly, the value of the invention is as follows: If during the past twenty-two years his company had been compelled to extend its network of conductors so as to give, without employing my invention, the same service which it is giving to-day, it would have had to spend at least one hundred million dollars more than it has actually expended. But after quoting him I wish to call attention to a fact which the public often overlooks. I ask, where are those one hundred million dollars which the invention has saved? I know that not even a microscopic part of them is in the pockets of the inventor. I have figured out also, with the same accuracy with which I once figured out the invention, that those hundred million dollars are not in the pockets of the telephone company. They must be, therefore, in the pockets of the American public. The invention made it possible to give the telephone service, which is now being given, at a lower rate than would have been possible if one hundred million dollars more had been spent. Every good invention benefits the public immeasurably more than it benefits the inventor or the corporation which exploits the invention. I certainly consider myself a public benefactor, and the National Institute of Social Sciences called me so when it gave me a gold medal almost as big as the full moon. But this gift would have made me much

more happy if the institute had at the same time given
another gold medal to the American Telephone and
Telegraph Company.

Some fifteen years ago, when Frederick P. Fish, the
famous patent attorney, was the president of the American Telephone and Telegraph Company, I asked him
in the course of a conversation whether he would like to
sell me back my invention. "Yes," said he, "but only
if you will buy the whole telephone company with it.
Our whole plant has been adjusted to the invention, and
when one goes the other also must go. The invention has
enabled us to detect many defects in our transmission
system, and if it had done nothing else than that it would
have been worth at least ten times what we paid you. It
is the greatest faultfinder that we ever struck, and it is
the only form of faultfinder for which we have any use."
A progressive industrial organization courts the criticism
of an accurate and friendly faultfinder. It leads to research and development, and that supplies the vital
energy to every industry. Twenty-five years ago the
American Telephone and Telegraph Company had a small
laboratory in Boston, where it did all its scientific research
and development. But, presently, faultfinders like my
inventions moved into the peaceful and drowsy precincts
of that tiny laboratory, and stirred up the engineers and
the board of directors. I am very happy whenever I
think that, possibly, my inventions have contributed
some to this healthful stirring up. What was the result?
To-day the American Telephone and Telegraph Company
and the affiliated Western Electric Company employ
about three thousand persons at an expenditure of some
nine million dollars annually in their research and development work. The scientific research work at our
universities looks very modest in comparison with operations of this kind. Young men of the highest academic
training and splendid talents are busy day and night ex-

ploring the hidden treasures on the boundary-lines between the various sciences and the science and art of
telephony, and their discoveries, I am sure, are the best
investment of this great industrial organization.   For
instance, their development of the many details in my
invention have been wonderful, and give testimony of
the highest kind to the excellence of their scientific research.   It is not so much the occasional inventor who
nurses a great art like telephony and makes it grow beyond all our expectations, as it is the intelligence of a
well-organized and liberally supported research laboratory.
When I think of that I am perfectly convinced that very
few of the great advances in the telephone art would have
happened under government ownership.   That explains
why telephony is practically dead in most European countries.   What little life it has in Europe is due to the
American research in the above-mentioned laboratories.

The General Electric Company, The Westinghouse
Company, the Eastman Kodak Company, and many
other industrial corporations in this country are supporting similar research and development laboratories, where
scientific men of the highest training are busily exploring
what Helmholtz called the rich territories near the boundary-lines of the various sciences and of the science forming the foundation of their respective industries.   This
reminds me of what I saw on a much smaller scale in
Germany, nearly forty years ago, when I was a student
there.   We copied Germany's good example, but are
leading now, and the pace is so swift that Europeans are
dropping behind us very rapidly.   The spirit of scientific
research has moved into our universities, and from the
universities it has moved into our industrial organizations.   Industrial research is making bigger and bigger
demands upon the universities for highly trained scientific
research men; the demand is larger than the supply, and
because the industries can pay much higher salaries than

the universities can much difficulty has been experienced in inducing bright and promising young scientists to pursue the academic career of a teacher. The quality of the scientific teacher in the university is temporarily deteriorating, that of the industrial research scientist is steadily rising; on the whole, however, the country is a gainer. The university man in the industries will transplant there the scientific idealism of the university. The captains of our leading industries already admit, as will be pointed out below, that the cultivation of scientific idealism is the best policy for our American industries. Listen to the papers which are read by their research men and you will see that the industries actually practise the new gospel of scientific idealism which they are preaching.

But I must not depart too far from the main thread of my story. When it became known that the American Telephone and Telegraph Company had acquired the rights to my *high inductance wave conductors*, all kinds of legends were told about the invention and the fabulous price paid for it. Newspapers love legends, because the public loves them. The public is a child which loves to listen to fairy-tales. The only good that this publicity did was to help me sell my inventions relating to electrical tuning and rectification in wireless telegraphy. These lay idle for quite a number of years, and waited for further developments in the wireless art before they could be employed to advantage. Electrical tuning and electrical rectification are fundamental operations in the radio art to-day, but the wireless telegraphy of the early days is a distant and poor relation of our present radio art. The world had to wait quite some time for new discoveries which gave birth to the epoch-making inventions of new men, like Lee De Forest and Major E. H. Armstrong. It had to wait also for the great industrial research laboratories before electrical tuning and rectification could come into their own. In the early days of

wireless telegraphy I suggested several novel developments which might give a fair chance to tuning and
rectification, but I attracted scarcely any attention.
The legends just mentioned made people a little more
attentive.

One morning a man stepped suddenly into my office
at Columbia, and introduced himself as Mr. Green, or-
ganizer and promoter of the Marconi Company of America. He was full of action and looked like business.
"Are your wireless inventions for sale?" asked Mr.
Green, without much preliminary talk. "They are," I
answered, and I felt that my heart was quivering on account of the unexpected blow which this laconic question
had given it. "How much?" asked Mr. Green. I gave
him the first figure that came into my head, and he, not
a bit daunted, asked whether I would take one-half in
cash and one-half in stock. I asked him twenty-four
hours to decide. "All right," said he, and promised to
call again the next day at the same hour. I should have
been perfectly satisfied to accept the cash offer and
close the deal even without the stock, but I was afraid
that any over-anxiety on my part might scare him away.
The next day he called and the deal was closed, he making a certain cash payment immediately and I agreeing
to furnish certain documents before the final payment
was made. I was fairly well acquainted with trading
transactions in my native land; my father often took me
to market-places where he bought and sold cattle and
horses. I remember well the never-ending bartering
which very often ended in a fizzle. The nearer you get
to Constantinople the worse becomes the custom of this
Oriental method of trading. Mr. Green had none of that
Orientalism, and his utter indifference to the figures involved in the deal astonished me. He also took it for
granted that I could and would perform all the fine things
which I promised to perform; that was very flattering to

would be guided entirely by the decision of the Berlin experts. Vienna did not seem to have a mind of its own, and all its thinking apparently was done for it by the experts in Berlin. I was quite elated by the idea that the Berlin experts who did the thinking for the Austrian Empire had been most happy to spend a whole month with me in daily conferences, eager to learn all they could from me. I could not help exclaiming: "Oh, what a fortunate thing it was that in my early youth I ran away from this moribund Empire, and landed in a country of opportunities, where every individual thinks through his own head and carries his load on his own back." Germany, at that time, was so vigorous that she did not hesitate to do all the thinking and hustling for Austria as well as for Turkey, and did not realize that she was carrying around two corpses which could not be revived by even the combined vitality of all the young and vigorous nations, like the United States of America and United Germany.

Before returning to the United States I visited my sisters in Banat. One of them was living in Idvor. On a Sunday in August during that visit I was dining in her garden. There was a high fence around it, and not far from it the boys and the girls of Idvor were dancing kolo on the village green and the older people were looking on. Presently somebody knocked on the garden-gate and my brother-in-law opened it. There stood a rider, holding with one hand his horse, which was covered with foam; in the other hand he held a telegram which he had brought in haste from the telegraph station in another village, about five miles away from Idvor. My native village had neither a telegraph nor a telephone line, although I, its son, aspired to connect telephonically every person in the United States to every other. The telegram in the rider's hand was for me, sent by my attorney, telling me that, on the day before, my final papers had been delivered to the Marconi Company and that the check for the final payments was in his hands. "Good news," I said to myself, and gave the rider a tip of ten florins to reward him for his haste, evidenced by the white foam on his horse. The bagpiper and the kolo-dancers stopped when they saw a ten-florin note in the rider's hand and heard him brag that he had delivered to me a telegram from America. The wondering crowd assembled at the garden-gate, and the older peasants who had gone to school with me in my boyhood days asked me if the telegram really had come from America. When I said yes, and that it had been sent on that very morning they looked at each other and winked, as if signalling to each other to be on guard lest I fool them with an American yarn. Then the oldest one among them addressed me as follows: "Did you not tell us that between here and America there are four empires, each bigger than Austria, and then the great ocean, which one cannot cross in less than a week even in the fastest of ships?" "I certainly did say that, and I repeat it now," said I. He added: "How can a telegram cross all that distance in less than a day?" "It could do it in less than a minute if man's clumsiness did not delay it. It could travel from here to Vienna in less than a second," said I, and carefully watched his expression. The old man seemed undecided; he did not know whether to take offense at my attempt to work off a silly yarn on him, or to proceed with his cross-examination, and finally decided in favor of the latter course. "Who invented all that?" asked he impatiently. "An American did it," said I boastfully. "These Americans must be very clever people," said he and waited eagerly for my reply. "Yes, indeed, they are very clever people," said I. "Much more clever than anybody in this village?" was his next question, and when I assured him that the Americans were much more clever than anybody in Idvor, he fired at me the following shot: "Then how in the name of St. Michael do you manage to make a living there?"

This incident in my native Idvor did me a lot of good. The experts in Berlin and the high officers in Vienna had been most polite and complimentary, and all their well-meant adulation coming on the top of the newspaper legends about my inventions might have turned my head and made me imagine that I was a "wizard." Many an inventor and scientist has been ruined by being persuaded that he is a "wizard." I have always believed that when a successful inventor is exposed to dangers of that kind he should, somewhat like that king of antiquity, hire somebody to whisper as often as possible into his ear: "You are an ordinary mortal." Whenever I see now the Elliot Cresson Gold Medal of the Franklin Institute, the gold medal of the National Institute of Social Sciences, the Edison Medal of the American Institute of Electrical Engineers, the Hebert prize of the French Academy, and several other evidences of recognition in my possession, I always think of that professor who blamed his hard luck for his failure to infer from the loaded strings which hung daily over his head what I had inferred from La Grange's imaginary string. It was, I know, a lucky day when on the 14th of July, 1884, I found that second-hand bookshop in the Quartier Latin in Paris and picked up there a copy of La Grange's treatise. Without it, I might have remained as ignorant of the remarkable properties of a loaded string as that professor was. My answer to the peasant's question, "How in the name of St. Michael do you manage to make a living there?" is this: "The humble herdsman of Idvor and the famous La Grange of Paris told me how to do it."

XII

THE NATIONAL RESEARCH COUNCIL

THE mathematical problems in the theory of electrical transmission, and the research of the behavior of materials employed in the construction of inductance-coils kept me busy, and made me forget that I was missing the splendid opportunities offered by New Physics, which I always represented symbolically by the picture of a vacuum-tube, because its origin dates from Roentgen's discovery. My complete recovery from the shock of 1896 did not reconcile me to the vacuum-tube, until several years had wiped out the memory which my mind had associated with it. By that time I had dropped too far behind the men who were leading in the procession of the revelations which New Physics had disclosed to man.

No sooner had Perrin, a French physicist, demonstrated that the cathode rays were negative electricity moving from the negative electrode of a vacuum-tube to the positive electrode than Professor John Joseph Thomson, of the University of Cambridge, proved that this negative electricity is concentrated in small corpuscles, called electrons to-day, which move with great velocities, and that the ratio of the electrical charge to the mass of each electron is experimentally determinable, and is, under ordinary conditions, a definite and invariable quantity. This learned man, when a youth of only twenty-five, had predicted in 1881, fourteen years before Roentgen's discovery, that the cathode rays were small negatively charged bodies, moving with great velocities. Assuming them to be spherical, he calculated, by the Faraday-

Maxwell electromagnetic theory, the ratio of their charge to their mass. He showed theoretically that their mass consisted of two parts, one of which is the ordinary gravitational or material mass, and the other a new mass which is proportional to the electrical energy in the electron, and that this mass also depended upon the velocity of the motion in a definite way. He devised and employed an experimental method to determine this ratio. The most remarkable feature of this interrelation between the electromagnetic mass and the velocity of motion was the fact that when the velocity approached the velocity of light the mass approached an infinitely large value. But no such extremes of velocity of motion of the electrons in a vacuum-tube were found at that time.

Becquerel, the French physicist, discovered, soon after Roentgen's discovery, that certain substances associated with the element uranium emitted electrons, both negative and positive, without being in a vacuum-tube and submitted to the action of a great electrical force. Madame Curie isolated the most active of these substances and called it *radium*. The action of electron emission discovered by Becquerel was called radioactivity. Three distinct things, it was found, were emitted by radium: negative electrons, the so-called beta rays, some of which were moving with enormous velocities; positive electrons, the so-called alpha rays, moving with smaller velocities; and, finally, an emission which had the same physical properties as the X-rays. The beta rays, some of which move with a velocity nearly equal to the velocity of light, enabled the physicists to determine experimentally, employing J. J. Thomson's method, the relation between the mass of the electron and its velocity, and lo and behold, it was found that, in all probability, the negative electron contained no other mass except the mass due to its electromagnetic energy. In other words, a negative electron is concentrated electricity and nothing else.

Similar experiments with positive electrons led to similar conclusions. Another most remarkable result was the revelation of the great difference between the masses, and, therefore, between the electrical energies residing in the negative and in the positive electron. The mass of a positive electron was found to be very nearly equal to the mass of a hydrogen atom, and the mass of a negative electron was found to be only about one two-thousandth part of the mass of the positive electron, and this meant that if the electrons are of spherical shape then the diameter of the positive electron is only one two-thousandth part of the diameter of the negative electron, since the energies and therefore the masses are inversely proportional to the diameters. In other words, there is in the positive electron a much bigger concentration of electricity than in the negative and, therefore, much more work was used up to produce that concentration. Experimental data and calculation gave for the diameter of a negative electron one ten-thousandth part of the diameter of the smallest atom, that is, of the hydrogen atom, and therefore the diameter of the positive electron should be only one twenty-millionth part of the diameter of a hydrogen atom. A most bewildering revelation!

The remarkable results of these historic experiments forced, one may say, upon the physicist the electromagnetic theory of matter, the theory, namely, that the ultimate components in the structure of matter are positive and negative electrons. This theory was vaguely foreshadowed by Faraday in his poetic visions suggested by his researches on electrolysis. Needless to say, the physicists in the United States were thrilled by these revelations, and by the new views disclosed by them, perhaps even more than by the discoveries of the X-rays and of radioactivity. The first visible effect of this thrill was the organization in 1899 of the American Physical Society, a quarter of a century after Tyndall's visit to this country. Just think of it, the great United States had no physical society prior to that time!

It is an interesting fact that two of the most important American organizations in abstract science were started at Columbia College. The first was the American Mathematical Society. In 1888, two young instructors at Columbia College, Fiske and Jacoby, started a mathematical club. To-day the first is a professor of mathematics, and the second is a professor of astronomy at Columbia University. I joined them in 1889, as soon as I had returned to Columbia. We transformed the mathematical club into the New York Mathematical Society, and elected for president the famous Columbia don, the late Howard Van Amringe, for many years senior professor of mathematics at Columbia College. Doctor Fiske was its secretary; no young and struggling scientific organization ever had a better secretary. The society prospered, and in 1894 it was transformed into the American Mathematical Society, counting among its members most of the distinguished mathematicians of the land. I am certainly very proud that I am one of its charter members.

In 1899 several Columbia physicists, including myself, and their friends from Johns Hopkins, Harvard, Yale, Princeton, Cornell, Clark, and other places, met at Columbia and organized the American Physical Society. The late Professor Rowland, of Johns Hopkins, was elected its president, and one of its most distinguished members was Professor Ernest Rutherford, of McGill University, Montreal. He is now Sir Ernest Rutherford, the Cavendish professor of physics at the University of Cambridge, occupying the professorial chair once occupied by Maxwell, then by Rayleigh, and then by Thomson, now Sir John Joseph Thomson, master of Trinity College, Cambridge. Their names I have mentioned often in the course of this narrative. It was most unfortunate for the progress of American physics that because of his failing health Rowland's wonderful influence in the society was of short duration. He died in April, 1901, while still a young man. Rutherford's wonderful discoveries in radioactivity were reported regularly by himself at the meetings of the society, and I often thought that these reports alone, even without the many other good things which came along, amply justified the existence of the society. When I compare the American Physical Society of twenty years ago with the American Physical Society of to-day I can scarcely believe that so much progress has been possible in so short a time. I recognize, however, that this remarkable growth is due not only to the energy of youth of this country but also to the energy of youth of New Physics, which I call Electron Physics.

In October, 1899, Rowland delivered his presidential address before the society at whose head he stood. I can see now how happy he looked on that memorable occasion. Inspired by the latest revelations in Electron Physics, he prophesied what new revelations the physicists should expect in the approaching future. After describing physics as "a science above all sciences, which deals with the foundation of the universe, with the constitution of matter from which everything in the universe is made, and with the ether of space by which alone the various portions of matter forming the universe affect each other . . ." he stated frankly that the physicists of America "form an aristocracy, not of wealth, not of pedigree, but of intellect and ideals. . . . Let us cultivate the idea of the dignity of our pursuit so that this feeling may sustain us in the midst of a world which gives its highest praise, not to the investigator in the pure ethereal physics which our society is formed to cultivate, but to the one who uses it for satisfying the physical rather than the intellectual needs of mankind." He then

pleaded that we "recognize the eras when great thoughts
have been introduced into our subject and honor the great
men who introduced them and proved them correct."
Then, enumerating the great problems of the physical
universe, he asked: "What is matter; what is gravitation;
what is ether and radiation; what is electricity and magnetism; how are these connected together, and what is
their relation to heat?" Now, these are the very questions which Electron Physics has been trying to answer
since that time; and this is the idealism which the American physicist has had before him ever since the days of
Rowland.

Electromagnetic theory of matter was the first answer
to Rowland's question: What is matter? But how about
the answer to his second question: What is gravitation?
If matter contains nothing but electrons, if they are really
the most fundamental building stones of matter, then
electricity as concentrated and stored up in the electrons
can exert in addition to the well-known electrical force
also a gravitational force. A somewhat novel idea, but
. . . why not, and why so? Einstein gives the best answer to this.

To Rowland's question: What is Ether? Electron Physics gave a puzzling answer, but the puzzle has led us
into a side path of surpassing beauty. Our famous
physicists, Michelson and Morley, are a combination of
two names better known in the world of physical science
to-day than Castor and Pollux were known when Zeus,
descending from the heights of Mount Olympus, sought
the companionship of mortal men. The fame of the
twins, Michelson and Morley, not, however, of Michelson alone, rests upon an experimental demonstration,
the importance of which was not until recently fully appreciated, the demonstration, namely, that there is no
ether drift; that is to say, so far as man can tell, there is
no relative motion between the earth moving through

space and the ether which is supposed to fill all inter-
stellar space. On the other hand, the hypothesis that the
ether moves with the moving earth leads to insurmount-
able difficulties. This was, indeed, a most embarrassing
situation! Since Michelson originally, and, later, Michelson and Morley, employed the radiation of light in their
attempts to detect the ether drift, it became necessary
to re-examine the electromagnetic theory of propagation of light for the case that light, as in the Michelson
and Morley experiment, proceeds from a source which
together with the observer is moving through space.
The famous Professor Lorentz, of Leyden, Holland, whom
I have the honor of knowing personally, made the first
successful extension of this theory, and explained satisfactorily Michelson and Morley's result. But the extension was obtained by what was acknowledged to be a
clever notion, and not by an unavoidable physical fact.
The same extension of the theory was obtained by Einstein, but it was founded upon a broad physical principle
which Lorentz's extension lacked. Lorentz preferred Einstein's deduction of his extension, called the Lorentz
transformation. The physical principle just referred to
is now popularly known as the Special Relativity Theory,
which Einstein extended later into the General Relativity Theory. Einstein's theory explains very simply
the Michelson-Morley experiment, but how does it answer Rowland's question: What is Ether? Also very
simply by saying that ether is superfluous in our analysis of physical phenomena. Faraday expressed a similar
view nearly eighty years ago. That, however, which is
essential in this narrative in connection with Einstein's
relativity theory is the great fact that by it a general
demonstration is furnished that all forms of electrical
energy are a mass which has *inertial as well as gravitational* activity. In the electromagnetic theory of matter
this demonstration plays a most important part. One of

the schemes of this theory is so simple and so beautiful, and appeals so strongly even to an imagination not scientifically trained, that I must tell here very briefly some of its most striking features.

All atoms are built up from a single atom, the atom of hydrogen, which consists of a positive electron or proton, the nucleus, and a single negative electron revolving around it like a satellite around the central planet. A heavier atom, say an atom of oxygen, consists of sixteen atoms of hydrogen, the positive nuclei of which form the positive nucleus or central portion of the oxygen atom. Some of the negative electrons are distributed among the positive electrons of the central nucleus, serving to cement them together, and the other negative electrons are revolving like satellites around the central nucleus. The number of these satellites is the atomic number of the atom, and it is this number, and not the atomic weight, which determines the chemical characteristics of the atoms. This is only a mere glance into the structure of Electron Physics, made here for the purpose of pointing out some of the never-dreamt-of possibilities that Electron Physics holds in view. For instance, four atoms of hydrogen combining into an atom of helium give off a certain amount of energy. We say the atoms of hydrogen degrade into the heavier atom of helium and, thereby, a certain amount of energy is liberated. A helium atom weighs less than four atoms of hydrogen, because of the diminished energy per atom of hydrogen, the decrement of the weight being proportional to the decrement of energy. This is demanded by Einstein's theory, which is really an extension of the theory first proposed by Sir John Joseph Thomson, and it is a remarkable fact that these weight relations satisfy the prophecy of the theory. The amount of energy obtained by the degradation of the lighter into heavier atoms is enormous. But we do not know how to produce the process of this degradation. The question arises: Do not the young stars, the very hot stars, which always consist of gases of small atomic weight, obtain a supply of radiant energy from the degradation of atoms of small into atoms of high atomic weight, and, if this is so, then why shall we not some day learn this great secret from the stars? The language of the stars has many deep secrets to tell; it mystifies me just as much to-day as it did on the pasturelands of my native village fifty years ago.

Many other most startling contemplations may be connected with the new views opened up by Electron Physics, all of them illustrating the beauty, the wealth, and the power of a new science which represents the marriage of two great sciences, physics and chemistry.

Industrial science is very much impressed by new discoveries which, as Rowland expressed it, "deal with the foundation of the universe," but which in spite of their revolutionary character are easily understood by the practical man. Electron Physics abounds in discoveries of that kind, and it seems that they have rushed upon us like a cloud-burst. Things have been done that formerly seemed impossible. Take, for an illustration, a thing which is so familiar to all, the complete transformation of wireless telegraphy into the new art which is called Radio. A vacuum-tube with a hot filament fills up with negative electrons, which are thrown off by the hot filament. The filament may be said to be radioactive. A current can be established by applying an electromotive force which drives these negative electrons from the space surrounding the hot filament to a positive electrode. Here we have a new type of Crookes's tube, operated by a small electrical tension, and not by that of a powerful induction-coil, which is necessary when the negative electrode is cold. This current is called the thermionic current, and its value can be varied in any way we please by a second electrical force which acts through a third electrode, called

most of the present associations in abstract science, that is in mathematics, physics, chemistry, and biology were organized. Even the youngest among the leading engineering societies, that is, the American Institute of Electrical Engineers, was organized in the early eighties, whereas the American Physical Society was organized nearly twenty years later, in 1899.

The organization of these technical societies did not wait for the arrival of the American university. But, nevertheless, when the American university arrived, and with it the research laboratories in the fundamental sciences, it improved the quality of the American engineer, and of the American engineering societies, just as it improved the scientific standards of the American industrial organizations. The National Academy of Sciences deserves here a special consideration. It is an association of workers in *abstract science*, principally, but, contrary to what I have just said, it is, like the American Philosophical Society, founded by Franklin, older than any of our national engineering societies. Its early birth was due to the conditions created by the Civil War. Joseph Henry, I imagine, suggested to President Lincoln that a mobilization of the scientific resources of the North would improve greatly its military strength, and thus the National Academy of Sciences was chartered by Congress during the Civil War, in 1863, and was approved by President Lincoln. It was a creation of the Civil War, and is in many respects an institution which forms a part of the Federal Government. I shall describe now how the National Academy of Sciences, itself a creation of the Federal Government during the Civil War, gave birth during the World War to another national scientific institution which is the climax of the great scientific movement started fifty years ago. I have watched this movement almost from its very beginning up to the present time; yes, I have been a part of it during its most active period, and I believe that I understand its full meaning.

The four leading engineering societies, mentioned above, were in quite a flourishing condition at the beginning of this century; flourishing not only with regard to the number, but also with regard to the quality of their membership, and their progress was speeding on with remarkable rapidity. For instance, the papers read before the American Institute of Electrical Engineers in 1900, and the discussions which followed them, were immeasurably superior to those read in 1890, when I first became a member of this Institute, because the quality of its membership was also immeasurably superior. The great American industries paid much more respectful attention to these engineering societies than when I first came to Columbia College in 1889. The greatest among the American captains of industry of those days, the late Andrew Carnegie, held them in so high an esteem that he presented a magnificent gift to them which led to the formation of the United Engineering Society. This happened in 1904, and marks one of the great events in the history of American technical science.

It is of considerable historical interest to observe here that Carnegie's magnificent gift to these national engineering societies is closely connected with a very modest move made by the American Institute of Electrical Engineers, nearly thirty years ago. The late Doctor Schuyler Skaats Wheeler, at one time president of the American Institute of Electrical Engineers, had purchased the famous electrical library of the late Latimer Clark, of London, and had presented it to the Institute. But the Institute had no building of its own, and, therefore, no place for housing permanently this unique library. Several of the members of the Institute, including myself, were looking around anxiously for some practical scheme which would provide the Institute with a home of its

small training in technical sciences. What he knew about engineering and manufacturing he had obtained by practical experience. Ambrose Swasey is a splendid illustration of a disciplined intellect trained by the training of his hand. I have always believed that the most striking difference between the American and the European is due to the fact that the American in his early youth receives a much better manual training than the European does, and that this accounts for the American directness of thought, judgment, and action. I never saw a better illustration of this theory than Mr. Ambrose Swasey. He began his career as a machinist, and when a little over thirty years of age he and a friend of his, Mr. Warner, another young machinist, started a manufacturing plant of their own, making fine machine-tools and astronomical instruments of precision. The shops of Warner and Swasey became famous all over the world for their wonderful workmanship.

The American manufacturer has achieved great things in mass production. This was Mr. Carnegie's strong point; but Mr. Swasey did not belong to that type of American manufacturer. His aim was few products but each one of them as perfect as careful manipulation, personal attention guided by superior intelligence, and inventive ingenuity, could make it. Most of the telescope mountings of the great astronomical observatories in this country were made in Mr. Swasey's Cleveland shops. His shop experience made him an engineer of a very high order, so high indeed, that the American Society of Mechanical Engineers elected him president, and, later, honorary member. The charter of the United Engineering Society speaks of "advancing the engineering arts and sciences in all their branches," but there was no other visible instrumentality for doing that work than the free engineering library. Ambrose Swasey proposed to correct this deficiency when, in 1914, he offered to the

United Engineering Society a gift of two hundred thousand dollars as a nucleus for an endowment the income of which was to be used for "the furtherance of research in science and engineering, or for the advancement in any other manner of the profession of engineering and the good of mankind." These words, dictated by an American captain of industry, bear witness to the fact that there is much idealism in American industry. The United Engineering Society accepted Mr. Swasey's gift, and established the Engineering Foundation, which was managed by its own board, the Foundation Board, nominated by the four founder societies. Its members acted as trustees of Mr. Swasey's gift and of any other gift that might be given to the Engineering Foundation to serve a purpose similar to that of Mr. Swasey's gift. This Foundation became an instrumentality of the United Engineering Society for the stimulation, direction, and support of scientific research. It became, furthermore, the liaison agency between the engineers on the one hand and the technologists and scientists on the other hand, in activities concerned with research in all branches of mathematical, physical, and biological sciences. In other words, one of the great captains of American industry, Andrew Carnegie, was instrumental in bringing the great national engineering societies together into the United Engineering Society, and another great captain of American industry, Ambrose Swasey, invented and by his generosity constructed an instrumentality, the Engineering Foundation, which he put into the hands of the United Engineering Society for the purpose of enabling it to do the work which its charter demands, "advancing the engineering arts and sciences in all their branches." I never think of these two generous acts on the part of Mr. Carnegie and of Mr. Swasey, without being reminded that these two great organizers of American industry were guided by the same motives of idealism which had guided the great

the National Research Council during its formative period. The Board of the Foundation accepted enthusiastically this suggestion, recommended by Mr. Dunn and myself, and from September 1916 to September 1917 the administrative organization as well as the total income of the Foundation was devoted to the organizing work of the National Research Council. I am very proud that during a part of that period I was the chairman of the Engineering Foundation, succeeding Mr. Dunn, and had splendid opportunities to aid Professor Hale and his committees in the historic work of organizing the National Research Council. Mr. Swasey was very happy in this national work of the Foundation, and he added to its income for that year a sum of five thousand dollars as additional aid for its great undertaking. At the expiration of that year, the National Research Council did not need any further financial assistance from the Engineering Foundation, but the co-operation started in 1916 between the two national bodies continued and produced splendid results; so much so that in 1918, during my term of office as chairman of the Foundation, Mr. Swasey added one hundred thousand dollars to his original gift, and in 1920 two hundred thousand dollars more, and the Engineering Foundation became the guiding and controlling factor in the activities of the engineering division of the National Research Council. Mr. Swasey always hoped that others would follow his example and by their generous contribution increase the income of the Engineering Foundation to what it should be. This institution, as the directing instrument of the engineering division of the National Research Council, could, with an adequate annual income, say one hundred thousand dollars or more, do a world of good in the research of our great national engineering problems. I trust that Mr. Swasey's hopes will not meet with disappointment, because his hopes are based upon his accurate estimate of what the engineering profession needs. An estimate supported by the judgment and vision of a Swasey, and by his generous financial efforts, should receive the most respectful attention and warmest sympathy of our public-spirited men.

It goes without saying that during the World War the National Research Council was organized mainly with a view to aiding the government in the pursuit of the war, and for that purpose it was closely associated with the government's scientific bureaus, and with the technical department of the Army and Navy. This arrangement is referred to, and receives the highest official sanction, in the executive order issued by President Wilson, which I quote now in full:

EXECUTIVE ORDER ISSUED BY THE PRESIDENT OF THE UNITED STATES

The National Research Council was organized in 1916 at the request of the President by the National Academy of Sciences, under its Congressional charter, as a measure of national preparedness. The work accomplished by the Council in organizing research and in securing co-operation of military and civilian agencies in the solution of military problems demonstrates its capacity for larger service. The National Academy of Sciences is therefore requested to perpetuate the National Research Council, the duties of which shall be as follows:

1. In general, to stimulate research in the mathematical, physical, and biological sciences, and in the application of these sciences to engineering, agriculture, medicine, and other useful arts, with the object of increasing knowledge, of strengthening the national defense, and of contributing in other ways to the public welfare.

2. To survey the larger possibilities of science, to formulate comprehensive projects of research, and to develop effective means of utilizing the scientific and technical resources of the country for dealing with these projects.

3. To promote co-operation in research, at home and abroad, in order to secure concentration of effort, minimize duplication, and stimulate progress; but in all co-operative undertakings to give encouragement to individual initiative, as fundamentally important to the advancement of science.

cal simplicity of its design and its snowy marble make it appear at a distance like a Grecian temple. It will always invite the visitor to the nation's capital to its peaceful precincts, whence one can get the impressive view of the beautiful monument to great Lincoln and of the Arlington heights on the distant bank of the Potomac River. When Lincoln and those buried on these sacred heights died, the National Academy of Sciences was born. The lives of these dead heroes of sixty years ago, as well as the life of the institution born then and living to-day, will always remind us that national defense is a stern reality and the most sacred of our patriotic duties. National defense is and always should be the uppermost idea in the history of the National Research Council, but national defense in its broadest sense, that is, defense by powder and sword and scientific invention when a brutal enemy attacks us, and by the stored-up accomplishments of scientifically trained intellects and disciplined spirits whenever this nation engages in peaceful competitions with other nations.

The rapid rise of the Council into public favor is due principally to its wise programme and to the standing of the men and of the scientific organizations engaged in the carrying out of that programme, the fundamental feature of which is "to promote scientific research and the application and dissemination of scientific knowledge for the benefit of our national strength and well-being." This expression, often heard within the ranks of the National Research Council, always reminds me of the following words in Washington's Farewell Address:

Promote, then, as an object of primary importance, institutions fo the general diffusion of knowledge. In proportion as the structur of a government gives force to public opinion, it is essential that publi opinion should be enlightened.

In no branch of human activity does public opinio need enlightenment so much as it does in the fundamen

DR. GEORGE ELLERY HALE
Honorary Chairman of the National Research Council

THE NATIONAL RESEARCH COUNCIL BUILDING, WASHINGTON, D. C.
From a preliminary sketch by the architect, Bertram G. Goodhue

als of science, and in their relation to technical arts. One weak point in every democracy, particularly when poorly understood and practised, is the belief among those who control political patronage that any man can do any job as well as any other man. The scientific man believes that a man must be trained for the job; hence his profound respect for the expert. Nothing in his opinion will advance our national strength and well-being so much as the ability of enlightened public opinion to differentiate between the expert and the clumsy product of political patronage. A motto of the Allies in the World War was: make the world safe for democracy. But those who are to-day associated in the National Research Council believe that it is even more important to "make democracy safe for the world" by the dissemination of scientific knowledge for the benefit of national strength and well-being. Many of us believe that this is the most important part of the national defense, to which the Council will always be pledged.

The National Research Council is not an organization which operates scientific laboratories; it confines its attention to the stimulation of co-operation between scientific workers, where such co-operation is necessary. This is not the place to discuss in detail all the aims and aspirations of the National Research Council and of the instrumentalities which it has created in order to reach these aims. A survey, even a brief one, of the work of the divisions belonging to the two groups of the National Research Council will give some idea of these aims. There are, however, two great aims which should be mentioned here, which have been well expressed by Doctor Vernon Kellogg, Permanent Secretary of the Council and chairman of its division on Educational Relations. He describes one of them as follows: "It [the National Research Council] will try constantly to encourage the interest of universities and colleges in research and in the

training of research workers, so that the inspiration and
fitting of American youth for scientific work may never
fall so low as to threaten to interrupt the constantly
needed output of well-trained and devoted scientific tal-
ent in the land." The other principal aim he describes
in the following significant words: "Still another [assis-
tance to science] is the stimulation of larger industrial
organizations, which may be in the situation to maintain
their own independent laboratories, to see the advantage
of contributing to the support of pure science in the universities and research institutes, for the sake of increasing the scientific knowledge and scientific personnel upon
which future progress in applied science absolutely de-
pends."

The appeal of the National Research Council to the
American universities and colleges in behalf of scientific
research will not be like a voice in the wilderness.   There
never was so much enthusiasm for scientific research in
the American colleges and universities as there is to-day.
This enthusiasm will continually increase as time goes on,
because many of the scientific workers in these institutions are gradually catching that enthusiasm during their
term of office as members of the divisions of the National
Research Council.   Before very long most of these workers will have served as such members, because the election
to membership is for a short term only, so that every
scientist in the land who wishes to serve will get a chance
to serve, and in this manner will become familiar with the
aims and aspirations of the National Research Council.
This rotational term of membership in the divisions of
the Council is a splendid method of carrying on the educational propaganda, particularly among the younger
scientists of the United States.   Before very long the scientists associated by service in the Council will be like
the soldiers of a great army of volunteers, each one of
them believing in and ready to struggle for the same

ideals, and all of them controlled by the same *esprit de corps*, which the world will soon recognize as the *esprit de corps* of American science.

With regard to the Council's second principal aim, described so well by Doctor Kellogg, I am happy to make the following comment: A distinguished lawyer, chairman of the board of directors of a large industrial corporation, which maintains a splendid industrial research laboratory, said in my presence recently that he thought every successful and prosperous industrial organization should set aside a goodly portion of its profits from new developments, made possible by scientific research, and turn it over to the universities, to enable them to pay better salaries to their professors and instructors in science and to increase their research facilities. He confessed frankly that the training in scientific research in the universities is the fountainhead from which success is derived in industrial research and development, and that without industrial research American industries will not gain and hold the leading position in the world to which they may rightfully aspire. What a splendid thing it is to hear a lawyer express an opinion which is in perfect harmony with the opinion of every scientific man in the United States! It has been this mental attitude on the part of the American philanthropists and public-spirited captains of industry like Carnegie, Rockefeller, Swasey, Eastman, and others which has helped us to accomplish wonders in scientific advancement during the last twenty-five years. It has been men of this type who have built research laboratories in the American universities and endowed them generously.

Of the many physical laboratories which have arisen in American universities through private munificence since the time when, fifty years ago, Joseph Henry, Barnard, Draper, Andrew White, and other American scientists started the great movement for higher research in sci-

Their zeal, their devotion, their faith, furnish one of those very protests which are most needed against that low tone of political ideas which in its lower strata is political corruption. Their life gives that very example of a high spirit, aim, and work, which the time so greatly needs.

The aims and aspirations and the life of American scientists have not changed since Andrew White spoke these memorable words fifty years ago. A life guided by aims and aspirations such as he describes is a life of saints and not of ordinary materialistic clay. Such a life cannot be attained without unceasing nursing of the spirit and unrelenting suppression of the flesh. Men of Andrew White's clearness of vision will certainly tell you not only that the disciplined army of American scientists mobilized under the flag of the National Research Council will not interfere with the spiritual development of our national life, but that, on the contrary, nothing else will advance that spiritual development so rapidly and so irresistibly. The intellectual and spiritual discipline which, according to White, our nation needs, is certainly one of the ideals of these men of science.

I shall mention now two other ideals. Just watch on some summer morning how the early rays of the sun arouse the slumbering rose from its blissful dreams, and remember that the rose responds because its body and soul are tuned to the melodies which the glorious sunlight is pouring into its enchanted ear. Remember also that what I have just described is not merely a flowery figure of speech, but that it is a concise description of a beautiful physical relationship, which science has discovered in the life of the rose. I proceed a step further, and ask: Have you ever feasted your joyful eye upon the beauties of the landscape when on a golden May day you behold the blossoming fruit-trees cover as far as your vision can reach the velvety green turf of the numerous orchards of some blessed countryside? What does each of these fruit-trees with its countless blossoms suggest to your imagination? "The honey-hearted fruit of the mellow summer season," many of you will say. Yes, the blossom and the fruit are so far as the untutored mind can see the beginning and the end of the short chain of apparently commonplace events which make up the annually returning life activity of the humble fruit-tree. Who cares what happens between so beautiful a beginning and so satisfactory an end? The scientist cares; his trained eye detects here an enchanting tale. Every one of those fruit-trees on the golden May day appears to him like a bride arrayed in the gayest of wedding raiment, waiting for the approaching bridegroom. Its countless blossoms invite with longing lips the life-giving kiss of the heavenly groom, the glorious sun. The balmy breath of this golden bridegroom fills the air, kissing the lips of every flower in the gay and festive orchards, and in the juicy pastures and meadows. A heavenly thrill fills the hearts of these enamoured blossoms, when, with sighs of delicious perfume, they, like blushing brides, respond to the tender caresses of the heavenly bridegroom! Yes, there will be honey-hearted fruit in the mellow summer season; the busy bee knows it when it sucks its honey from the joyful bosoms of the blessed brides; it knows that this honey is the first message to you that the marriage between the heavenly bridegroom, the golden sun, and the terrestrial brides, the countless blossoms, will be blessed with many a heavenly offspring, the honey-hearted fruit of the mellow summer season.

This is, I admit, somewhat unusual language for a scientist to use. It is, according to the opinion of many, unsuited to the description of what people call the cold facts of science. They call them so, but is their language justified? The physical facts of science are not cold, unless your soul and your heart are cold. There is white heat somewhere in every physical fact when we decipher out the life of its own heart, in order to beget new life. Oh, what a beautiful vista that opens to our imagination, and what new beauties are disclosed by science in the meaning of the words in Genesis: "He breathed into his nostrils the breath of life, and man became a living soul." The light of the stars is a part of the life-giving breath of God. I never look now upon the starlit vault of the heaven without feeling this divine breath and its quickening action upon my soul. But here I must stop. I feel the heavy hand of the fundamentalist pulling me down, and the icy chill of his disapproving voice reminds me that his theology will not permit an interpretation of the words of Genesis which cannot be understood by people whose knowledge of science is about the same as that of the Assyrians and Chaldeans of several thousand years ago.

I have taken some pains here to point to some beauties in one particular department of physical science. Such beauties abound in every other department of science, and they are in no respect inferior to those which form the subject of the fine arts, like music, painting, sculpture, and poetry. To cultivate the beautiful in science, is, according to my view, the second ideal of the many loyal workers associated in the National Research Council. Will that kind of science interfere with the spiritual development of our national life?

The third ideal may be described as follows: All changeable things are subject to the play of evolution, and are mortal, from the tiny flower in the field to the awe-inspiring cloud figure in the heavens which is called the nebula of Orion. But the laws which the stars and the planets obey in their paths through the heavens never change nor grow old; they are immutable, they are immortal. The elements of the microcosm, the electrons in the atom, are as far as we know immutable and immortal, because man knows no natural process by which

ie electrons and the laws which they obey can ever be
ianged. They are not the product of any natural proc-
s of evolution known to man. To discover the im-
.utable laws which this substantia, this immutable foun-
ition of the universe, obeys is the highest aim of scien-
fic research. ⌈The existence of these eternally unchange-
)le things brings us face to face with a power which is
ie eternally immovable background of all physical
nenomena. We feel intuitively that science will never
enetrate the mysteries beyond it, but our faith encourages
; in the belief that there behind the impenetrable veil of
iis eternal background is the throne of a divine power,
ie soul of the physical world, the activity of which we
)ntemplate in our research of physical phenomena.⌋ I
n sure that many loyal members of the National Re-
;arch Council believe that scientific research will bring
; closer to this divinity than any theology invented by
ian ever did. The cultivation of this belief is certainly
ne of the ideals of American science, represented by the
ien who are associated in the National Research Council.
n the face of this ideal, there certainly cannot be any
)nflict between science and religion.

I firmly believe that in the National Research Council
e have an organization which represents the mobilized
cientific intellect of the United States, which in the pur-
uit of its lofty ideals will some day succeed in creating in
ur democracy a profound respect for the services of the
ighly trained intellect. A democracy which believes that
;s destiny should be intrusted to the leadership of men
f training, discipline, and lofty aspirations and knows
ow to secure the services of such men is a democracy
vhich is safe for the world. Such a democracy, I believe,
vas the vision of the scientific men who, fifty years ago,
tarted the great movement for higher endeavor. Such
, democracy will lead some day to what I call ideal
lemocracy, that is, a state organism in which each human

THE WHITE HOUSE
WASHINGTON

October 14, 1922.

My dear Doctor Pupin:

    I accept with regret your resignation as a member of the National Advisory Committee for Aeronautics. In doing so I want to express to you the thanks of the Government and people of the United States of your services as a member of the National Advisory Committee for Aeronautics since its organization in 1915.

    I take this occasion to record recognition and appreciation of the fact that, as Chairman of the Subcommittee on Aircraft Communications, during the World War you undertook to develop a reliable means of communication between aircraft in flight, and that, by virtue of experiments conducted and directed in your own laboratory, you were successful in contributing in an important respect to the development of one of the great marvels of our age, the radio telephone.

    I regret that you cannot continue to devote your talents to the scientific study of the problems of flight as a member of the National Advisory Committee for Aeronautics.

        Most sincerely yours,

                Warren Harding

Dr. Michael I. Pupin,
Columbia University,
New York City.

with his physical and mental faculties more highly developed?—or the superman as represented by what I call ideal democracy? Carty, guided by his life experience and by the opinion of some biologists and philosophers, favors the latter view. There certainly is something in the evolutionary progress of the world which favors the view that the coordinating instrumentalities which guide the activities of every organism, and which are very powerful in man, may enable us some day to find a way of coordinating the non-coordinated activities of the many millions of individuals of a great community like these United States, and thus of creating an ideal democracy. I see in the organization of the National Research Council the first step in that direction.

Ideal democracy, if attainable at all, will certainly be attainable in our country, whose traditions are gradually eliminating racial hatreds and suspicions and making them unknown human passions on this blessed continent. If I have ever contributed anything substantial to the progress of this splendid movement, whether as an immigrant or as an inventor, it has been most amply rewarded by the generous spirit of the letter on the opposite page, written by a man whom I had the honor of knowing personally and who to me always represented the ideal type of a genuine American.

These few concluding lines I wrote on the day when this good American breathed his last. His memory will always encourage us in the belief that our blessed country is destined to become the first ideal democracy of the world.

INDEX

389